Woman's Day Bazaar Best Sellers

Bazaar

Woman's Day Best

Sellers

edited by Julie Houston

Sedgewood Press

For CBS Inc.
    Editorial Director: *Dina von Zweck*
    Editor: *Julie Houston*
    Project Coordinator: *Lisa LeFever*

For Sedgewood™ Press
    Editorial Director, Sedgewood™ Press: *Jane Ross*
    Project Director: *Virginia Colton*
    Managing Editor: *Gale Kremer*
    Designer: *Bentwood Studio/Jos. Trautwein*
    Production Manager: *Bill Rose*

Distributed in the Trade by Van Nostrand Reinhold.
ISBN 0-442-28100-5
Library of Congress Catalog Number 82-51035.
Manufactured in the United States of America.

Contents

Bazaar Planner's Handbook

JUST AS RURAL AMERICAN FOLK ART originated as an outlet for self-expression — in tools handcrafted by amateurs for the routine activities of life, in whimsies, toys and decorations concocted to brighten the day — so native creativity gave rise to the grassroots fund-raising event we call a bazaar.

Originally, bazaars were held in rural areas where people emerged from their geographical isolation to socialize and work together raising money for a common cause, usually religious or political. The goods they donated for sale were the same ingenious originals they made, out of necessity, for their own households.

Today, bazaars have spread to urban areas as well, where they are organized by block associations, homeowners' groups, tenant committees and other city interest groups. These city dwellers share the same sense of community as their rural cousins, and they bring, in that sharing, a special vitality to their neighborhoods.

That fund-raising — for a school, a church, a political party — should spring from the joint effort of a community, is truly an American phenomenon. Bazaar crafters pool skills and materials readily at hand and, applying imagination and ingenuity, transform lowly but practical household goods into something pleasurable to the eye. With boundless energy and a free and generous spirit, they work side by side to stitch colorful garments, decorative needlework and more — not for any personal gain but to give financial aid to a good cause.

What turns up at a successful bazaar is a vast array of artfully made goods—a happy blend of delightful, practical handcrafts that reflect the interests and skills of a particular group and region at a particular time. As fund-raising activity has risen to an all-time high, bazaar crafts have developed ever-greater precision: the crafting process sharpened, the crafts themselves more keenly attuned to the decorative tastes of the day. In addition, handmade pieces are sought after today with an unprecedented intensity. Many of the eager seekers are collectors of

Americana who browse bazaar aisles looking for fresh design finds from the spontaneously expressive hand of the amateur. But there is also a vast and growing number of ordinary folk who know that, while the quality of household goods has diminished at the retail level, it has gotten steadily better at local bazaars. There workmanship is back where it began—in the hands of the people.

Though the communal effort is most visible in the busy aisles of a well-organized bazaar, it is the behind-the-scenes bustle that sets bazaars apart from other forms of craft expression. Pieces are ingeniously worked in multiples, with volunteer crafters on their own improvised assembly line; together they turn out a maximum number of articles, quickly, economically, yet as high in quality as if they had been custom-made. The projects in this book have been chosen to represent the best of this unique method of crafting, with an unusually diverse range of items that can be made in quantity to appeal to, and capitalize on, a crowd.

Participating in a bazaar may bring an individual no material profit, but the personal rewards are many, and unquestionably more important: old friendships renewed and new ones made; the excitement of pooling efforts, ideas and skills; the special pride to be taken in shared success; the experience, in the best American tradition, of working with others toward a common goal.

Making yours the best bazaar ever

What makes a bazaar a huge, resounding success? Ask anyone who has either planned one or purchased at one and the answer will be the same: The success of a bazaar depends primarily on the quantity and quality of the handmade goods it offers for sale, and the proud and enthusiastic spirit with which these crafts are displayed. To sell at a bazaar, your "merchandise" has to sparkle with sales appeal, and be tagged at the right price to reap profits.

The purpose of this book is to supply the means for running the most outstanding, most profitable bazaar ever, stocked with the biggest and brightest collection possible of items made by hand. The projects are diverse, but they have a single aim: Everything has been chosen with great care for its bazaar-selling potential, to attract a constant flow of customers and keep the cash registers humming all day.

Unlike other crafts, which need only serve some personal purpose, items handmade for a bazaar must meet certain requirements if they are to generate profits. They must be:

- *instantly recognizable for what they are;*
- *competitive with their retail counterparts;*
- *easy to execute; and*
- *adaptable to the "assembly line" process.*

"Instantly recognizable" simply means that passersby must know at a glance what any item is. Clean, uncomplicated designs are what sell at bazaars today, meticulously interpreted in crisp fabrics, colorful yarns and attractive materials that will appeal to all tastes and blend with most decorating schemes.

To be good competition, the item for sale must more than equal, it must *surpass* comparable merchandise in a store. That is, it must be higher in quality and lower in price than rival pieces that are produced commercially. People are attracted to bazaars in ever-growing numbers because they realize that the potential for quality is high in handmade goods. And as demand for bazaar crafts has increased, their taste level has taken an upward turn. Gone are the days of dowdy potholders, dreary aprons and recycled whats-its. The times, and the customers, call for up-to-the-minute materials and clear-cut, timely designs—and they will get them when you use this book, as a glance through its pages will confirm. Although many of the bazaar projects are made with scraps, they have anything but a recycled look. Small amounts of fabric or yarn must be transformed into treasures if they are to sell. Quite often, you will save money buying *new* material in quantity, and you will ultimately sell more goods because of the greater potential for working in multiples and for coordinating displays.

Easy execution is indispensable if both skilled and unskilled hands are to take part and to turn out uniformly high-quality, saleable results, without waste or worry. It goes without saying that the more hands at work, the merrier the making, and the more you will have to offer for sale. Booth planners should familiarize themselves with the abilities of volunteers and see to it that projects are geared to the individual and combined capacities of the group.

Finally, consider adaptability to the assembly line approach. Group work is the key to working miracles—producing fine crafts fast, in quantity, and for a minimum of money. Nothing does more to help this along than crafts that can be completed in clear, divisible stages. That way, the various steps to a finished project can be spread out among several people. Some will be making patterns; some cutting fabric or other materials; some gluing, sewing or clamping; some covering boxes, tying ribbon, filling sachets, and so on.

The success of a group operation isn't guaranteed, of course. It depends on the individuals working well together and making good use of their time. Because their time is donated and usually isn't figured into the selling price of their projects, they must make it their business, if their efforts are to show a profit, to find every possible shortcut and save every conceivable penny. Fortunately, bazaar crafters tend to be an ingenious lot, and to work as hard and conscientiously at a joint enterprise as they would at a business of their own.

The projects offered here meet the basic requirements, with some noteworthy exceptions. These are the one-of-a-kind crafts that call for an expert crafter or demand an extra time commitment. In this group are the quilts, afghans and other strikingly handsome needlework that always draws such a crowd, especially as the focal point of the crafts booth or as a prize for a raffle. For your convenience (and to help you enlist highly skilled volunteers), we have brought together a group of such crafts on pages 143 to 149. Shawls, another fabulous focal point, are featured on pages 42 to 45.

Some bazaar fundamentals

Before you set to work on the early stages of your next bazaar, it will be useful to review some basic information, given on the next few pages. Of course every bazaar is different, but at least a few of the pointers on planning and crafting are bound to apply to your circumstances and your group.

The general planning meeting This should be scheduled well in advance of the bazaar date, preferably at the close of the preceding one. This timing permits procedures to be evaluated, and modifications considered, while ideas about what might be done differently are still fresh in everyone's mind. Items that sold particularly well can be earmarked at this time for inclusion in the next bazaar.

It is usual, at the first planning meeting, to elect committee chairmen for booths, publicity, etc.; to discuss a theme, if there will be one; to formulate a budget, based on the previous year's figures, for each booth, display or necessary procedure— crafts, needlework, food, games, publicity, advertising, etc. At this first session, also, the overall objective of the fair is set, with the goal expressed in dollar amounts or in fair attendance, whichever seems most practical.

The crafts committee Ideally, the chairperson of the crafts committee should also be skilled at needlework and home sewing, so that judgments about projects and materials needed can be made knowledgeably and volunteers can be guided in techniques or assigned diplomatically to tasks that suit their skills.

It often helps to have two people share the job of chairing the crafts committee, particularly if the group is large and the contemplated crafts are diverse.

The best way to put together a group of crafts volunteers is to solicit them actively, writing a letter first and then following it up with a telephone call. Willing as they may be to help, people like to be asked; very few will volunteer on their own. When you talk to potential helpers, give examples of the kinds of tasks you will need done: knitting, crocheting, piecework, pressing, stitching, decorating with trims, etc. Ask specifically what each individual really prefers to do, and then sign them up for it. Much more is accomplished when a group sets willingly to work, with no grumbling about the tasks assigned.

Planning the crafts booths Make the booths look professional by approaching the bazaar as a business, setting the same high standards as you would if you were breaking ground for your own shop or boutique.

Consider how much money you need or want to make from the needlework and crafts you sell. If a grand total has been set for the entire bazaar, what proportion of profit is expected from the crafts booths? Alternatively, you can base profit objectives on the crafts budget. Do you want to make your expenses back, plus double that amount in profit? Triple? If the crafts budget is low,

launch an all-out campaign for donated materials. Collect recyclables and scraps of all kinds from individuals, new or used goods, perhaps seconds or mill-ends, from local retailers (and be sure that they, in turn, are given prominent credit at the bazaar for their donations).

How much space is allotted to the crafts displays? Five tables? Three booths? Space is a major factor in determining what it is possible and advisable to sell. To use your space well and show crafts to advantage, it is essential to visualize your booth displays in the space they will have.

To make the most of limited space, you'll need to establish a purpose for each booth or display. This book can help with that—the projects are clearly organized by function. If there are special interests in your area—gourmet cooking, home entertaining, gardening, canning, etc.—plan a representative range of practical, saleable items that cater to these interests. If your area draws seasonal visitors, be sure to play up regional features in a way that will appeal to them. Does everyone in the community work? Concentrate on household accessories that will help busy citizens to get their chores done fast. Which would go over better in your community, sophisticated designs and fabrics or an older-fashioned homespun look? You'll be smart to consider these questions at the planning stage.

Once general display ideas have been established, try to tie each one to a theme or motif. If the bazaar has a general theme, link your projects to that. If it does not, create your own unifying theme for each booth. When you give them a context, the individual pieces really appear to belong. Think about the theme before making any material purchases, since it is color and fabric that create the mood. If, for example, the bazaar's general theme is "Good Old Days" nostalgia, you might want to stress lacy Victorian designs, hearts and flowers, and old-fashioned fancies in all the displays. For individual booths, what could be more endearingly old-fashioned than "A Calico Christmas"? Or, at "The Country Fair," as country-fresh as kitchen and dining accessories made

up in eyelet, gingham or bandanna prints? A simple, distinctive motif can be as effective as a theme, or a striking complement to it. Hearts, snowflakes, stars are all lovely possibilities, and only a few of the many you might choose. If you decide on such a motif, repeat it over and over again, in appliquéd, stencilled, painted or sewn renditions.

Whatever the chosen theme or motif, make this unifying element your springboard for selecting specific projects. Along with display impact, coordinated colors, motifs and designs permit substantial savings in time and money. Also working with similar materials assures coherent, predictable results. This steers your displays away from the flea-market look, important to avoid for the sake of sales. Customers will be more receptive to buying if they feel they're getting a bargain on items they associate with high-quality boutiques or specialty stores rather than so-called "buys" in a bargain basement. Look at the composite photographs in each major section of the book to see what coordinated colors and materials do to enhance eye appeal. You can be sure they will do the same for sales.

To plan specific projects, first assess the skills of your craft volunteers. Are there many needleworkers? More people interested in sewing than in knitting, or vice versa? Any special expertise in the group—woodworking, decoupage, stencilling, etc.? These specialized skills might best be applied to the costlier one-of-a-kind projects, and be planned by the individuals who will do them. Discuss them first, however, to be sure valuable time is not wasted on individual pieces that might better be spent on group activities. Most of the projects in this book require little or no skill to execute. You'll find a great many easy crochet and knitting ideas because, along with sewn items, these rank highest in bazaar sales.

When you are planning the range of pieces to be crafted, make sure that low-priced items (in the $1 range) are well represented; these are guaranteed to keep traffic flowing and sales activity high while customers consider the higher-priced goods.

As soon as projects have been chosen, and you've decided how many there will be of each and who will produce them, canvass the market for the best buy in the materials you will need. If a sensational bargain turns up, it is worth revising your projected plans to take advantage of it. And don't overlook the cost-cutting possibilities of donated materials and recyclables as you plan what bazaar items to make.

Pricing your goods Pricing goes hand in hand with project planning. Everything in this book is aimed at attracting profits—that is, to offer an appealing quality look at a price far lower than people would expect to pay. Remember that it isn't charity that attracts customers—it's the anticipation of getting great things at a bargain. So you must price accordingly.

There are several ways to go about pricing. At some bazaars, prices are set by figuring the cost of materials, then estimating profits according to what the item would cost if the minimum hourly wage were paid for the crafting. At others, the cost of materials is used as a base, and a percentage of overhead added on. (This overhead, or operating cost, is determined by the fair's treasurer, who tallies up expenditures for advertising, promotion, printing, etc., and passes a portion of this amount on to each booth.) With the cost figure in hand, the market value for the same item is then considered. Market value comparisons are always useful. Check the pricing of comparable items in mail order catalogs, department stores and specialty shops in your area, and use that as a guide to price. Whatever considerations you decide should go into your pricing, be sure not to *overprice*. Bazaar customers expect, and should get, a bargain.

One big advantage of an early start on organizing is that samples can be made up and evaluated for their potential as multiple projects—in terms of material costs; the time it takes to cut, sew and assemble or decorate; and the optimum price to charge. The more you can make of one item, the lower the unit price you can offer your customer. Some items might easily be priced and sold at three times what it cost to make them; on others, the asking price might be double.

Working together effectively Time is usually donated for bazaar work, and does not figure in the final costing of a piece. But that does not mean that it is "free." A commitment to work for the bazaar is going to cut into the valuable time, and add to the work load, of every individual who makes it.

You can accomplish more, with less disruption to individual lives, by making bazaar work part of everyone's routine. At the first meeting of the crafts committee, set up and stick to a regular schedule of work sessions where the people involved can meet and work together, on multiple projects and on individual ones. Usually, the long winter months or summer "dog days" are perfect for weekly or biweekly crafts sessions. Working together, rather than in isolation, helps keep quality standards high, particularly when the work is done under the guidance of one or more skilled supervisors.

Once craft items are completed, "prop" construction and arrangements for booth displays should begin. One of the most effective ways of displaying goods is to show them in use and in combination. Thus, for instance, potpourri sachets (page 110) might be hung on covered coathangers (page 109); a dining table might be set with place mats (page 104), candleholders (page 105) and flowers (page 104). Desk accessories could be arranged to show the attractive organizing job such conveniences can do. You might display sewing notions in an actual "sewing nook." Such "in action" displays are an effortless way to turn passersby into customers because the items literally sell themselves. But of course there are many other approaches. For example, though it is true that *most* bazaar goods make wonderful gifts, it is nice to set aside a display just for gift-giving, perhaps for a special, upcoming occasion. Christmas is a natural, of course, but it could also be Mother's or Father's Day, Easter, baby or bridal showers, etc. The point is that a carefully thought-out special display has an extra appeal that makes fairgoers more interested in looking and more receptive to buying.

At the bazaar Tag everything individually before you set anything out, or list prices together on a board that is easily visible at the booth.

Hold back "refills" for your display, especially pieces that are made in quantity, so that the booth will look well-stocked and inviting all day.

If the budget permits, package bazaar crafts for customers in brown bags (the kind you get in supermarkets) decorated for the occasion. Buy a supply at wholesale prices in several sizes, and decorate them by hand. It's easy: Cut out flat erasers in geometric shapes and use ink pads in two or three colors to rubber-stamp the designs. Or you could buy rubber stamps with designs already cut—they are not costly.

How to use this book

This book can be your all-purpose reference all the way from the planning stage of your booths to the moment that the last item is sold. The parts of the book are arranged in such a way that any one of them could be viewed as a display or booth, with a wide and representative range of projects. For some general tips about planning and making bazaar projects, see page 157. The lists that follow, though only a sampling of what the book includes, suggest a most practical way to approach project selection: by similar techniques or similar materials.

Finds for
favorite people

Starting at top left: **1.** Knitted two-tone hats, page 21. **2.** Matching knitted mittens, page 28. **3.** Granny-square crocheted slippers, page 34. **4.** Twist-edge crochet hat, page 21. **5.** Knitted turtleneck collars, page 31. **6.** Crocheted flower pins (on turtlenecks), page 51. **7.** Hair ornaments (clips, bobby pins and combs with crocheted flowers or satin-ribbon posies, plus a row of painted barrettes), page 51. **8.** Calico checkbook holder, page 57. **9.** Crocheted bow ties, page 50. **10.** Wooden-key chains, page 57. **11.** Calico conveniences (makeup kit, tissue holder, eyeglass case), page 57. **12.** Pomponed elf slippers to knit or crochet, page 40. **13.** Fireside slippers to crochet (ruffles for her, plain cuff edging for him), page 35.

Cold-weather warmups are real discoveries, the kind of handmade hats, scarves, mittens and such you rarely see in shops, and *never* at these prices.

Snug styles in slippers is a family group: fancy footwork for the whole crowd, from infants on up. Cozy, of course, but amusing in the bargain, as you'll see.

Shawl & stole spectacular almost says it all about these ultra-feminine wraps—except that these prizes can be sold for precious little, which means lots of sales.

Accessory originals is a bit like a boutique: ideas by the dozen to give a lift to wardrobes and spirits. Bags, belts and ties . . . hair ornaments . . . conveniences to tuck into purse or pocket!

cold-weather warmups

Crocheted and knitted designs to rival any boutique: Hats and hoods … scarves and mufflers … mittens and leg-warmers! Plus projects ideal for advance ordering—a his-or-hers turtleneck sweater and a crocheted coat for a favorite canine.

Rib-knit Ski Hoods

Great for quantity knitting—and yarn scraps are ideal for stripes. Both adult and child's versions.

CHILD'S SKI HOOD

SIZE Medium.

MATERIALS Coats & Clark's Red Heart Fabulend (acrylic and wool knitting-worsted-weight yarn), 1 (3½-ounce) skein Mexicana No. 950 (ombre) and 1 skein devil red No. 903 (yarn will make 2 hoods); 1 pair No. 8 knitting needles (or English needles No. 5) **or the size that will give you the correct gauge;** tapestry needle.

GAUGE 5 sts = 1" when stretched.

Starting at lower edge with ombre, cast on 88 sts. Work even in ribbing of k 2, p 2, working 2 rows ombre, 2 rows red for 8", ending with 2 rows ombre.

Face opening Next row (right side): With red, rib across 1st 26 sts, bind off next 36 sts, rib to end of row. **Following row:** Rib to opening, cast on 36 sts, rib to end of row (88 sts). Starting with ombre, continue in stripe and rib pattern for 3" more. Break off ombre. With red only, continue to rib for 2", ending with a wrong-side row. Entire piece should measure 13" from beg.

To shape crown Change to stockinette st. **1st row:** * K 2 tog, k 4. Repeat from * across, ending k 2 tog, k 2. **2nd and 4th rows:** P across. **3rd row:** * K 2, k 2 tog. Repeat from * across, ending k 2, k 3 tog. **5th row:** K 2 tog across. Cut yarn, leaving an 18" end. Thread end in tapestry needle and draw through remaining sts. Pull up tight and sew to secure. Sew back seam.

ADULT'S SKI HOOD

SIZE Medium.

MATERIALS Coats & Clark's Red Heart 4-ply Wintuk (acrylic knitting-worsted-weight yarn), 3 (1-ounce) skeins emerald green No. 676, 1 skein each skipper blue No. 848 and jockey red No. 902; 1 pair No. 8 knitting needles (or English needles No. 5) **or the size that will give you the correct gauge;** tapestry needle.

GAUGE 5 sts = 1″ when stretched.

Starting at lower edge with green, cast on 92 sts. Work even in ribbing of k 2, p 2 in the following colors: * 8 rows green, 4 rows blue, 8 rows green, 4 rows red. Repeat from * once more, then, with green, work 3 rows. Piece should measure 8″ from beg.

Face opening Next row (wrong side): With green, rib across 1st 26 sts, bind off next 40 sts, rib to end of row. **Following row:** Rib to opening, cast on 40 sts, rib to end of row (92 sts).

Continuing in stripe and rib pattern, work 3 more rows green, 4 rows blue, 8 rows green, 4 rows red, 8 rows green, 4 rows blue, 4 rows green. Last row is a wrong-side row. Piece should measure 14½″ from beg.

To shape crown Change to stockinette st. **1st row:** * K 2 tog, k 4. Repeat from * across, ending k 2 tog. **2nd and 4th rows:** P across. **3rd row:** * K 2, k2 tog. Repeat from * across. **5th row:** K 2 tog across, k last st. Cut yarn, leaving 20″ end. Thread end in tapestry needle and draw through remaining sts. Pull up tight and sew to secure. Sew back seam.

Two-tone Knitted Hats

(Project **1** in group photograph, page **18**)

Worked sideways in vertical rows to hug any head size.

SIZE Adult.

MATERIALS Bucilla Win-Knit (acrylic knitting-worsted-weight yarn), 2 ounces light beige No. 404 (main color, MC) and 1 ounce light rust No. 501 or blue frost No. 410 (contrasting color, CC) make 1; 1 pair size 8 knitting needles (or English needles size 5) **or the size that will give you the correct gauge;** tapestry needle.

GAUGE 4 stockinette sts = 1″.

HAT Starting along side of hat with MC, cast on 23 sts. * Starting with a k row (right side), work 5 rows in stockinette st. Break off. Join CC. Starting with k row (wrong side), work 5 rows in stockinette st. Break off. Join MC. Repeat from * (10 rows) until there are 13 stripes each MC and CC. Do not work last row on last stripe. **Last row:** Bind off 4 sts (lp on right needle is 5th st), * drop next st off left needle, then (sl lp from right needle onto left needle and k it) twice; bind off next 5 sts. Repeat from * across. Break off.

With fingers, push dropped sts all the way down to cast-on edge. This forms openwork.

CUFF With right side of hat facing you, using MC, pick up and k 3 sts across each 5-row stripe (78 sts). Work in ribbing of k 1, p 1 for 3″. Bind off loosely in ribbing.

FINISHING Sew hat and cuff seams. Gather top edge tightly. Turn cuff in half to right side.

Twist-edge Crochet Hat

(Project **4** in group photograph, page **18**)

Easy-fitting hat works up fast in single-crochet rounds.

SIZE Adult.

MATERIALS Lion Brand La Difference (acrylic knitting-worsted-weight yarn), 2 ounces per hat; aluminum crochet hook size I (or international size 5:50 mm) **or the size that will give you the correct gauge.**

GAUGE 7 sc = 2″; 7 rnds = 2″.

HAT Starting at top, ch 4. Join with sl st to form ring. **1st rnd:** Work 2 sc in each st around (8 sc). Do not join rnds, but mark beg and end of rnds. **2nd rnd:** (Sc in next sc, 2 sc in next sc) 4 times (12 sc). **3rd rnd:** 2 sc in each sc around (24 sc). **4th rnd:** Sc around, increasing 6 sc evenly spaced (30 sc). **5th rnd:** Sc in each sc around. Repeat 4th and 5th rnds twice more (42 sc). Repeat 4th rnd 5 times (72 sc). Work 5 rnds sc even. **21st rnd:** Sl st in each sc around. Hat should measure about 6″ from beg. Break off.

FINISHING Braid Cut thirty 40″ lengths yarn. Tie tog at one end, divide into 3 equal groups and braid; tie other end. Sew around edge of hat, lapping ends neatly.

Fringed Muffler and Cap

SIZE Muffler measures 78″ x 10″, not including fringe. Cap in one size that fits all.

MATERIALS Unger Cozy (acrylic-wool bulky yarn), 9 (1¾-ounce) balls rust No. 30 for muffler, 3 balls rust for cap, 2 balls gold No. 40 for muffler, 1 ball gold for cap; Unger Foliage (acrylic-wool bulky tweed yarn), 2 (1⁷⁄₁₀-ounce) balls rust tweed No. 73 for muffler, 1 ball for cap; 1 pair No. 13 knitting needles (or English needles No. 00) **or the size that will give you the correct gauge.**

GAUGE 5 sts = 2″.

NOTE For multicolor sections, use 1 strand each rust, gold and tweed held tog. **For rust sections,** use 2 strands rust held tog. **When working multicolor and rust in same row,** carry yarn not in use loosely across wrong side of work.

MUFFLER

Border Starting at 1 end with multicolor (see note above), loosely cast on 29 sts. **1st row (wrong side):** P 1, * k 1, p 1. Repeat from * across. **2nd row (right side):** K 1, * p 1, k 1. Repeat from * across. Repeat last 2 rows 4 times more, then repeat 1st row once again.

Rib pattern 12th row (right side): With multicolor, k 1 (bring to back of work), attach rust (see note above) and p 1 (bring to back of work), k 1 multi, * p 1 rust, k 1 multi. Repeat from * across. **13th row (wrong side):** P 1 multi (hold yarn in front), * k 1 rust (hold yarn in front), p 1 multi (hold yarn in front). Repeat from * across. Repeat last two rows once more. **16th row (right side):** K 1 multi, * with rust p 1, k 1, p 1, with multi k 1. Repeat from * across. **17th row:** P 1 multi, * with rust k 1, p 1, k 1, with multi p 1. Repeat from * across. Repeat last 2 rows 3 times more. Break off multi.

Main section With 2 strands rust, repeat 1st and 2nd rows of border pattern for 46″, ending on wrong side.

Rib pattern Attach multi and repeat 16th and 17th rows 4 times, then repeat 12th and 13th rows twice.

Border Repeat 1st and 2nd rows 5 times, then 1st row once more. Bind off loosely in pattern.

Fringe Cut thirty 30″ strands each rust, gold and tweed. Hold one strand of each color tog and fold in half to form lp. With right side of muffler facing you, pull lp from front to back through last row of a k st; draw cut ends through lp and pull tight to form knot. Make 15 fringe knots at each end of muffler, one in each k st.

CAP

Border With multi, loosely cast on 60 sts. **1st row (wrong side):** * K 1, p 1. Repeat from * across. Repeat last row until piece measures 2¼″.

Rib pattern 6th row (right side): (See rib pattern for muffler.) With multi k 1, attach rust and p 1. * K 1 multi, p 1 rust. Repeat from * across. **7th row:** * K 1 rust, p 1 multi. Repeat from * across. Repeat 6th row once more. **9th row:** * With rust k 1, p 1, k 1, with multi p 1. Repeat from * across. **10th row:** *K 1 multi, with rust p 1, k 1, p 1. Repeat from * across. Repeat 9th row once. Break off multi.

Crown 11th through 16th rows: * With rust, k 1, p 1. Repeat from * across. Shape top as follows: **17th row (wrong side):** * K 2 tog, k 1, p 1. Repeat from * across (45 sts). **18th row:** * K 2 tog, p 1. Repeat from * across (30 sts). Break off 1 strand rust. **19th row:** With remaining strand, k 2 tog across. Break off, leaving 12″ strand. Draw strand through remaining 15 sts on needle and draw sts tog. Tie off on wrong side of work. Sew seam.

Rolled-brim Crochet Hat and Muff

MATERIALS Bernat Willowspun (nylon/wool nubby yarn), 4 (50-gram) balls ashes-of-roses No. 5239;

Bernat Berella "4" (acrylic knitting-worsted-weight yarn), 1 (4-ounce) ball China rose No. 8923; aluminum crochet hook size J (or international hook size 6:00 mm) **or the size that will give you the correct gauge.**

GAUGE 3 sts = 1″.

HAT

Starting at top with Willowspun, ch 2. **1st rnd:** Work 6 sc in 2nd ch from hook. Mark beg of rnds but do not join rnds. **2nd rnd:** Work 2 sc in each sc around (12 sc). **3rd rnd:** (Hdc in next sc, 2 hdc in next sc) 6 times (18 sts). **4th rnd:** Hdc in each hdc around and inc 6 hdc evenly spaced. Repeat 4th rnd 8 times more (66 hdc). Work even on 66 hdc until piece measures 7½″ from beg; sl st in next st. Break off Willowspun; join Berella "4". **1st rnd:** Ch 3 (counts as 1 dc), dc in each st around (66 dc); join with sl st in top of ch-3. Repeat last rnd 3 times more. Break off. Roll up brim.

MUFF

Cuffs (make 2) Cuffs are worked vertically. With Berella "4", ch 12. **1st row:** Dc in 4th ch from hook and in each ch across (10 dc, counting turning ch as 1 dc); ch 3, turn. **2nd row:** Working in back lp only of each st, skip first dc (directly below ch-3), dc in each dc across, dc in top of turning ch; ch 3, turn. Repeat 2nd row until piece measures 8″ (to fit loosely around wrist). Break off. Sew cuffs to form rings.

Body With Willowspun, ch 24; join with sl st to form ring. **1st rnd:** Ch 2 (counts as 1 hdc), hdc in each ch around and inc 10 sts as evenly spaced as possible (34 hdc); join with sl st in top of ch 2. **2nd rnd:** Repeat 1st rnd (44 hdc). Work 2 rnds even. Mark last rnd.

To make doubled center of body: Outer layer: 1st rnd: Ch 2, working in front lp only of each st, hdc in each st around; join. Work even in hdc until piece measures 7″ from marked rnd. Break off. **Inner layer: 1st rnd:** Sl st in any skipped lp on marked rnd, ch 2, hdc in each skipped lp around; join. Work even in hdc until piece measures 7″ from marked rnd.

To join layers 1st rnd: Holding last rnd of both layers tog and working through both thicknesses, sl st in next st, ch 2, hdc in each st around; join. **2nd rnd:** Work even. **3rd rnd:** Ch 2, hdc in each st around and dec 10 sts as evenly spaced as possible (to dec 1 hdc, * yo, insert hook in next st, yo and draw lp through. Repeat from * once more; yo and draw through all 5 lps on hook); join. **4th rnd:** Repeat 3rd rnd. Break off.

FINISHING Sew cuff to each end of muff, easing fullness.

Neck string With Willowspun, make 24″ chain. Join each end to muff as shown.

Rolled-brim Knit Hat and Scarf

Knitters will love this stockinette-style hat. Scarf is garter stitch with bramblestitch ends.

MATERIALS Lion Brand Molaine (brushed acrylic sport-weight yarn), 2 (40-gram) balls queens blue No. 108; 1 pair size 11 knitting needles (or English needles size 1) **or the size that will give you the correct gauge.**

GAUGE 3 sts = 1″.

HAT

Starting at lower edge, cast on 60 sts. Work even in stockinette st for 7″, ending with a wrong-side row.

To shape top 1st row: (K 1, k 2 tog) 20 times. P l row. **3rd row:** (K 2 tog) 20 times. P 1 row. **5th row:** (K 2 tog) 10 times. Break off. Thread end in tapestry needle, draw through remaining sts, pull up tight and secure. Sew back seam. Roll up brim.

SCARF

Starting at one end, cast on 27 sts. **1st row:** (right side): P across. **2nd row:** P 3 tog. * (k, p and k) in next st, p 3 tog. Repeat from * across (25 sts). **3rd row:** P across. **4th row:** (K, p and k) in first st, * p 3 tog, (k, p and k) in next st. Repeat from * across (27 sts). Repeat these 4 rows for bramble-st pattern until piece measures 10″, ending with a 4th pattern row.

Next row K 1, (k 2 tog) 13 times (14 sts). Work even in garter st for 28″, ending with a right-side row. **Following row:** K 1, (k and p in next st) 13 times (27 sts). Work even in bramble st for 10″, ending with a 4th pattern row. Bind off.

Cuffed Crochet Hats

Two yarn weights give these a tweedy look; chain loops make Persian-lamb look-alikes of cuffs.

SIZE One size stretches to fit all adult head sizes.

MATERIALS Bucilla Win-Knit (acrylic knitting-worsted-weight yarn), 4-ounce Twin-Paks, and Bucilla fingering yarn (acrylic), 1-ounce skeins. **For woman's hat,** 2 Twin-Paks Win-Knit light beige No. 404 and 2 skeins fingering yarn natural heather No. 130; **for man's hat,** 2 Twin-Paks Win-Knit cloud gray No. 504 and 2 skeins fingering yarn gray heather No. 136; aluminum crochet hook size K (or international hook size 7:00 mm) **or the size that will give you the correct gauge.**

GAUGE 3 sts = 1″.

NOTE Hat is worked in vertical rows. Curly stitch on cuff is crocheted afterward.

CROWN Using 1 strand each Win-Knit and fingering yarn held together, ch 36 to measure about 12″. **1st row:** Sc in 2nd ch from hook and in each ch across (35 sc); ch 1, turn. **2nd row:** Working in back lp of each st, sc in each sc across; ch 1,

turn. Repeat 2nd row 58 times more. Pattern forms "ridges" and "valleys." Break off.

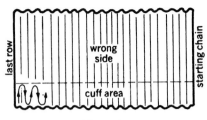

Diagram 1

CUFF Start at end of row (see cuff area of Diagram 1) and work back and forth in direction of arrow on ridges and valleys as follows: * Working along ridge of row, sl st in 1st st, (ch 4, sl st in next st) 10 times; ch 4. Turn piece around with same side facing you and work into sts along valley of next row as follows: Sl st in next st, (ch 4, sl st in next st) 10 times; ch 4, turn with same side facing you. Repeat from * across hat.

Sew beg and end of hat to form tube. With right sides together, following Diagram 2 for shape, sew across upper edge, then sew curved shape. Turn right side out. Fold up cuff and sew in place.

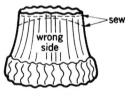

Diagram 2

Tasseled Stocking Cap and Leg-warmers

Girlish charm in bright red and soft gray. Worked in easy rib knit—no heel to turn!

MATERIALS Knitting-worsted-weight yarn, 1 ounce gray (color A) and 2 ounces red (B) for cap, 2 ounces gray and 3 ounces red for leg-warmers; 1 pair each sizes 6 and 9 knitting needles (or sizes 7 and 4 English needles) **or the size that will give you the correct gauge.**

GAUGE On larger needles in rib pattern: 6 sts = 1″; 13 rows = 2″.

CAP

Starting at lower edge with smaller needles and color A, cast on 96 sts. K 1, p 1 in ribbing for 3½″. Break off A; join B. With larger needles, k across (right side). **Next row:** (K 3, p 1) 24 times. **Following row:** (K

1, p 3) 24 times. Repeat last 2 rows for 4″, ending with a right-side row.

To shape top **1st row:** (K 2 tog, k 1, p 1) across (72 sts). **2nd row:** (K 1, p 2) across. **3rd row:** (K 2, p 1) across. **4th through 12th rows:** Repeat 2nd and 3rd rows 4 times, then repeat 2nd row once more. **13th row:** (K 2 tog, p 1) across (48 sts). **14th row:** (K 1, p 1) across. **15th through 24th rows:** Repeat 14th row. **25th row:** (K 1, p 2 tog, p 1) across (36 sts). **26th row:** (K 2 tog, p 1) across (24 sts). **27th row:** (K 1, p 1) across. Repeat last row for 5½″. Break off, leaving 24″ end for sewing.

FINISHING Thread end through sts on needle, pull up tight and sew center back seam. Make 4″ tassel (see page 160), leaving two 12″ lengths of yarn on tassel. Using 12″ lengths held tog, crochet 2″ chain. Sew end to top of hat.

LEG-WARMERS

Starting at upper edge with smaller needles and A, cast on 60 sts. K 1, p 1 in ribbing for 4½″. Break off A; join B. With larger needles, k across (right side). **Next row:** (K 3, p 1) across. **Following row:** (K 1, p 3) across. Repeat last 2 rows for 4″, ending with a right-side row.

To shape (K 2 tog, k 1, p 1) 15 times (45 sts). **Next row:** (K 1, p 2) 15 times. **Following row:** (K 2, p 1) 15 times. Repeat last two rows for 6¾″. Bind off.

FINISHING Sew inner leg seam. **Instep strap:** With right side facing you, using smaller needles and B, pick up and k 9 sts along lower edge of leg-warmer exactly opposite inner leg seam. Work in stockinette st for 6″. Bind off. Sew other end of strap to lower edge of leg-warmer, centering strap over seam.

Extra-long Leg-warmers

A hot young item, knitted in warm stripes.

SIZE One size fits all.

MATERIALS Coats and Clark's 4 Ply (knitting-worsted-weight yarn), 1 (4-ounce) skein each purple (color A), lavender (B), shocking pink (C), light pink (D), red (E) and orange (F); 1 pair No. 10½ knitting needles (or English needles No. 2) **or the size that will give you the correct gauge;** round elastic for tops of leg-warmers; tapestry needle; aluminum crochet hook size H or J (optional).

GAUGE 9 rib sts (not stretched) = 2 ″.

Starting at top edge with color A, cast on 68 sts. Working in ribbing of k 1, p 1 throughout, work 2 rows each A, B, C and D; 1 row E; 2 rows each F, E, D, C, B and A; 6 rows B. With C, work 4″. With F, work 6 rows.

Shape leg as follows: Working with F, dec 1 st at beg and end of every other row 3 times (62 sts); work 1 more row F. Working with C, dec 1 st at beg and end of every other row 3 times (56 sts).

Work even with C until piece measures 20″ from beg, or 6″ less than desired length. Starting with B, work stripes as for 1st 12 stripes. Bind off. Sew seam.

With A, work sl st with crochet hook or embroider chain stitch (see stitch diagram, page 159) over seam. Run elastic through top edge. Make other leg-warmer in same manner.

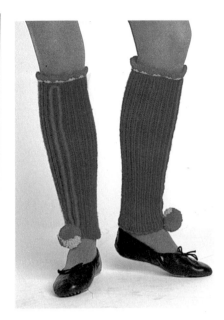

Below-the-knee Leg-warmers

Rib knit tubes with crochet trim. Snappy stripes lead to pert pompons.

SIZE Fits young adult.

MATERIALS Knitting-worsted-weight yarn, 5 ounces blue (color A), 1 ounce each orange (B) and red (C); 1 set (4) size 6 knitting needles (or English needles size 7) **or the size that will give you the correct gauge;** aluminum crochet hook size E (or international hook size 3:50 mm).

GAUGE 13 sts = 2″; 6 rows = 1″.

LEG-WARMERS (make both the same) Starting at bottom with 2 needles and color A, cast on 50 sts *loosely.* Work double-knitting hem as follows: **1st row:** K 1, yarn forward and sl 1 as if to p, * yarn back and k 1, yarn forward and sl 1 as if to p. Repeat from * across. Repeat last row for 1″. Divide st on 3 needles and work in rnds as follows:

1st rnd: Form work into ring and k first st to join ends of ring, p 1, * k 1, p 1. Repeat from * around (sew ends of double-knitting hem later). **2nd rnd:** * K 1, p 1. Repeat from * around. Repeat last rnd until piece measures 14½″ or desired length. Bind off in ribbing. Seam ends of double-knitting hem.

TRIM Shell-stitch border 1st rnd: With right side facing you, with B and crochet hook, work sc in back lp of each bound-off st; sl st in first sc. Break off. **2nd rnd:** With C, sl st in any sc, ch 3, work 4 dc in same sc (first shell made); * skip next sc, sc in next sc, skip next sc, work shell of 5 dc in next sc. Repeat from * around (13 shells), sc in last sc; join to ch-3. Break off.

Stripes Holding leg-warmer upside down, start at hem on opposite side from seam and work up to shell border as follows: Hold color C against wrong side of ribbing; working along a p row, insert hook through first p st, catch lp of C and draw through to right side, * insert hook through next p st, draw up another C lp, drawing it through lp on hook (ch st made). Repeat from * the length of p-rib row to bound-off edge, work 3 ch sts parallel to edge, then turn piece around and work in same manner along next p-rib row to hem edge. Fasten on wrong side and break off.

Pompon With C and small amount of B, make 2″-diameter pompons (see page 160) and sew on at position shown in photograph.

Striped Knitted Mittens

Dazzling mix of ombre and solids appeals to kids of all ages.

ADULT'S STRIPED MITTENS

SIZES Woman's medium [man's large].

MATERIALS Knitting-worsted-weight yarn, **for woman's only:** 2 ounces each hot pink (color P), turquoise (T) and yellow (Y), 1 ounce green (G); **for man's only:** 2 ounces each red (color R) and royal blue (B) and 1 ounce white (W); if using leftover yarn, you will need a total of 3 ounces assorted colors for each pair. **For both:** 1 pair No. 7 knitting needles (or English needles No. 6) **or the size that will give you the correct gauge;** stitch holders; tapestry needle.

GAUGE 9 sts = 2″.

NOTE Carry yarns not in use loosely

along side edge, attaching and breaking off colors as necessary.

FIRST MITTEN Cuff Starting at edge with color P [R], cast on 34 [38] sts. Work in ribbing of k 1, p 1 for 3" [3½"].

Hand and thumb Change to stockinette st and, using Y [B], work next 4 rows as follows: P 1 row, k 1 row, p 1 row. **4th row (right side):** K 16 [18] sts, put marker on needle, k in front and back of each of next 2 sts (2-st inc), put marker on needle, k to end of row. (Always slip markers on each row.)

Using P [W], work next 4 rows as follows: P 1 row. **6th row:** K to 1st marker, inc 1 st in next st, k 2, inc 1 st in next st, k to end of row. P next row. **8th row:** K to 1st marker, inc 1 st in next st, k 4, inc 1 st in next st, k to end of row (40 [44] sts).

9th through 15th rows Inc 1 st in 1st and last thumb sts between markers every k row, working in the following color sequence: 4 rows with Y [B], 1 row with G [W] and 2 rows with Y [B].

For woman's size only With Y, work even on 46 sts for 2 more rows.

For man's size only With B, continuing to inc as before, work 2 more rows (52 sts).

For both sizes 18th through 21st rows Starting with k row with T [R], work even on 46 [52] sts for next 4 rows.

To divide for thumb With Y [B], k across 17 [19] sts and place on holder; drop Y [B] but do not break off; with T [R], k 12 [14] thumb sts. Place the last 17 [19] sts on another holder.

Thumb Working on thumb sts only with T [R], work even for 1¼" [1½"], ending with a p row. **Next row:** K 2 tog across. Break off, leaving long end; with tapestry needle, draw remaining sts tightly together, then sew thumb seam.

Hand Place sts from 1st holder on needle, pick up Y [B] and k across sts from 2nd holder. Starting with

p row with Y [B], work even on 34 [38] sts for 3 more rows. Continue to work even in the following color sequence: 1 row with G [W], 4 rows with Y [B], 4 rows with P [W], 4 rows with Y [B], 1 row with G [W], 4 rows with Y [B], 4 rows with P [W], then work 0 [2] rows with B. Mitten should measure 10" [10½"] from cast-on row.

To shape tip Use Y [B] to complete mitten. **1st row:** * K 2, k 2 tog. Repeat from * across, ending k 2. P 1 row. **3rd row:** * K 1, k 2 tog. Repeat from * across, ending k 2. P 1 row. **5th row:** K 2 tog across. Finish as for thumb, then sew side seam.

SECOND MITTEN Mittens are interchangeable. **For woman's size only:** Work as for 1st mitten, using color T for P and color P for T.

For man's size: Make same as 1st mitten.

CHILD'S STRIPED MITTENS

SIZE Will fit 6- to 8-year-old child.

MATERIALS Knitting-worsted-weight yarn, 1 ounce each emerald green (color G) and green/orange/rust/ white ombré (O); 1 pair No. 7 knitting needles (or English needles No. 6) **or the size that will give you the correct gauge;** stitch holders; tapestry needle.

GAUGE 9 sts = 2"; 13 rows = 2".

MITTEN Cuff Starting at edge with G, cast on 28 sts. Work in ribbing of k 1, p 1 for 2½". Break off G; attach O.

Hand and thumb Change to stockinette st and, starting with p row, work even for 5 rows. **6th row (right side):** K 13 sts, put marker on needle, k in front and back of each of next 2 sts (2-st inc), put marker on needle, k to end of row. (Always slip markers on each row.) P 1 row. **8th row:** K to 1st marker, inc 1 st in next st, k 2, inc 1 st in next st, k to end of row. P 1 row.

Inc 1 st in 1st and last thumb sts between markers every k row until

there are 38 sts on needle, ending with p row.

To divide for thumb With O, k 14 sts and place on holder, drop O but do not break off; with G, k across 10 thumb sts; place last 14 sts on another holder.

Thumb Working on thumb sts only with G, work even for 1", ending with p row. **Next row:** K 2 tog across. Break off, leaving long end; with tapestry needle draw remaining sts tightly together, then sew thumb seam.

Hand Place sts from 1st holder on needle, pick up O and k across sts from 2nd holder. Starting with p row, continue to work even on 28 sts until mitten measures 7½" from cast-on row.

To shape tip 1st row: * K 2, k 2 tog. Repeat from * across. P 1 row. **3rd row:** * K 1, k 2 tog. Repeat from * across. P 1 row. **5th row:** K 2 tog across. Finish as for thumb, then sew side seam.

Make other mitten in same manner; they are interchangeable.

Two-tone Knitted Mittens

(Project **2** in group photograph, page **18**)

As basic as can be. Cuffs add contrast but no extra time. Directions explain easy hand length adjustment.

SIZE Adult, length adjustable.

MATERIALS Bucilla Win-Knit (acrylic knitting-worsted-weight yarn), 1 ounce light rust No. 510 or blue frost No. 401 (main color, MC) and ½ ounce light beige No. 404 (contrasting color, CC) make 1 pair; 1 pair size 8 knitting needles (or English needles size 5) **or the size that will give you the correct gauge;** tapestry needle.

GAUGE 4 sts = 1″.

CUFF Cast on 32 sts with CC. Work in ribbing of k 1, p 1 for 3″. Break off. Join MC.

To shape thumb Work in stockinette st for 8 rows. Work shaping as follows: **1st row (right side);** K 15, place marker on needle, inc in each of next 2 sts, place marker, k to end. **2nd row:** P across, slipping markers. **3rd row:** K to marker, sl marker, inc in next st, k to st before next marker, inc in next st, sl marker, k to end. Repeat 2nd and 3rd rows 3 times more (42 sts), ending with p row.

Thumb K 16 and place on holder, k next 10 st for thumb, place remaining sts on another holder. Work on thumb sts only for 1¼″, ending with p row. **Next row:** (K 2 tog) 5 times. Break off, leaving 8″ end. Thread end in tapestry needle, draw through sts, pull up and sew thumb seam.

Hand Place sts from first holder on right needle, join MC at base of thumb, place sts from 2nd holder on left needle and k across them. Work on 32 sts until entire mitten, from beg of cuff, measures 8½″ (or 1″ less than desired length), ending with p row.

To shape tip 1st row: (K 2, k 2 tog) across row. **2nd row:** P across. Repeat last 2 rows once more, then repeat 1st row again. Break off, leaving 12″ end. Thread in tapestry needle, draw through sts, pull up and sew side seam (sew cuff with CC).

Crocheted Scarf

SIZE 6½″ x 50″.

MATERIALS Plymouth Indiecita (3-ply Peruvian alpaca fleece sport-weight yarn), 2 (50-gram, about 1¾-ounce) balls light Oxford gray No. 401 and 1 ball each black No. 360 and cream No. 201; aluminum crochet hook size F (or international hook size 4:00 mm) **or size that will give the correct gauge.**

GAUGE 5 sts average 1″.

NOTE When not in use, carry gray yarn loosely along side edge. **To change color at end of row:** Work last st with old color, join new and work ch sts required, turn.

FIRST HALF Starting at lower edge, with black, ch 35 to measure about 6¾″. **1st row (right side):** Dc in 4th ch from hook and in next 2 ch, * ch 1, skip ch, dc in 3 ch. Repeat from * across, ending ch 1, skip ch, dc in last 4 ch; break off, join cream and ch 1, turn. **2nd row:** Sc in first dc, * ch 1, skip dc, sc in next dc, ch 1, skip dc; working over black ch-1 of last row, work dc in skipped ch st of starting ch. Repeat from * across, ending ch 1, skip dc, sc in next dc, ch 1, skip dc, sc in turning ch. Break off; join black and ch 2, turn. **3rd row:** Skip first sc (turning ch 2 always counts as 1 st), working over ch-1 of last row, work dc in black dc of first row (directly below ch-1 of 2nd row), dc in next cream sc; working over ch-1, work dc in black dc below next ch-1, * ch 1, skip cream dc of last row, dc in black dc below ch-1, dc in next sc, dc in black dc below ch-1. Repeat from * across, ending with dc in turning ch. Break off; join gray and ch 1, turn (border completed). Work in pattern st as follows:

4th row: Sc in first dc, * ch 1, skip dc, sc in next dc, ch 1, skip dc; working over black ch-1 of last row, work dc in cream dc 2 rows below. Repeat from * across, ending ch 1, skip dc, sc in next dc, ch 1, skip dc, sc in turning ch; ch 2, turn. **5th row:** Skip first sc, working over ch-1 of last row, work dc in black dc 2 rows below, * ch 1, skip sc; working over ch, work dc in black dc 2 rows below, dc in next dc of last row; working over ch, work dc in black dc 2 .rows below. Repeat from * across to last 3 sts, ch 1, skip sc, work dc in black dc 2 rows below, dc in last sc; ch 1, turn. **6th row:** Sc in first 2 dc; * working over ch, work dc in gray sc 2 rows below, sc in dc, ch 1, skip dc, sc in next dc. Repeat from * across, ending with dc in sc 2 rows below, sc in dc, sc in turning ch; ch 2, turn. **7th row:** Skip first sc, dc in 3 sts, * ch 1, skip next st, dc in 3 sts. Repeat from * across, ending dc in last sc; drop gray, join cream and ch 1, turn. **8th row:** Sc in first dc, * ch 1, skip dc, sc in next dc, ch 1, skip dc; working over ch, work 1 dc in gray ch-1 st 2 rows below. Repeat from * across, ending ch 1, skip dc, sc in next dc, ch 1, skip dc, sc in turning ch; break off cream, join black and ch 2, turn. **9th row:** Skip first sc, working over ch-1 of last row, work dc in next dc 2 rows below, dc in sc of last row; * working over next ch, work dc in dc 2 rows below, ch 1, skip dc; working over next ch, work dc in dc 2 rows below, dc in sc of last row. Repeat from * across to last 2 sts, work dc in next dc 2 rows below, dc in last sc. Break off black; pick up gray and ch 1, turn.

Repeat 4th through 9th rows for pattern st until piece measures about 25″ from beg, ending with 5th row. **Last row:** With gray, sc in first 2 dc; working over ch, work dc in gray sc 2 rows below, sc in 3 dc. Repeat from * across, ending by working over ch, then work dc 2 rows below, sc in dc, sc in turning ch; break off.

SECOND HALF Work as for first half.

FINISHING Right sides facing, sew last rows of pieces tog with gray.

Twin Turtlenecks and Vest

Ideal offerings for custom orders. Sweaters are knitted in a diagonal pattern, repeated in panels of woman's vest.

SIZES Sweaters: Woman's and man's sizes 32″ [34″–36″–38″–40″–42″–44″]. **Vest:** Woman's sizes 33″ [35″–37″–39″]. Sweater measures 16″ [17″–18″–19″–20″–21″–22″] across back at underarms. Vest measures 16½″ [17½″–18½″–19½″] across back at underarms.

MATERIALS For sweaters: Bucilla Win-Knit (acrylic knitting-worsted-weight yarn), 4 [4–5–5–5–6–6] (4-ounce) Twin-Paks parchment No. 453; Bucilla Melody (mohair/acrylic yarn), 8 [8–10–10–11–11–12] (1-ounce) balls champagne No. 4; 1 pair each size 7 and size 9 knitting needles (or English needles size 6 and size 4) **or the size that will give you the correct gauge. For vest:** Bucilla Win-Knit, 3 (4-ounce) Twin-

Paks parchment No. 453; Bucilla Melody, 5 [5–6–6] (1-ounce) balls champagne No. 4; 1 pair size 7 knitting needles (or English needles size 6) **or the size that will give you the correct gauge.**

GAUGE On size 7 needles: 4 sts = 1″; 6 rows = 1″.

TURTLENECKS

NOTE Work with 1 strand each Win-Knit and Melody held tog throughout.

BACK Starting at lower edge with smaller needles, cast on 64 [68–72–76–80–84–88] sts. Work in k 1, p 1 ribbing for 1½″. Change to larger needles.

To establish pattern 1st row (right side): * P 1, k 3. Repeat from * across. **2nd row:** P 2, * k 1, p 3. Repeat from * to last 2 sts, k 1, p 1. **3rd row:** K 2, * p 1, k 3. Repeat from * to last 2 sts, p 1, k 1. **4th row:** * K 1, p 3. Repeat from * across. Repeat 1st through 4th rows for pattern st.

Work even in pattern st until piece measures 12″ (12½″–12½″–13″–13½″–14–14½″] or desired length to underarms.

To shape armholes Bind off 3 [4–4–5–5–6–6] sts at beg of next 2 rows. Dec 1 st at beg and end of every other row 2 [2–3–3–4–4–5] times, then work even on 54 (56–58–60–62–64–66] sts until armholes measure 7″ [7½″–8″–8″–8½″–9″–9½″].

To shape shoulders Bind off 6 [6–7–8–8–9–9] sts at beg of next 2 rows. Bind off 6 [7–7–7–8–8–9] sts at beg of following 2 rows. Place remaining 30 sts on holder for back neck.

FRONT Work same as back until armholes measure 5″ [5½″–6″ –6″–6½″–7″–7½″].

To shape neck Work across first 20 [22–24–26–28–30–32] sts; place center 14 sts on holder for front

continued on p. 30

continued from p. 29

neck; attach another 2 balls (for double strand) of yarn and work across remaining 20 [22–24–26–28–30–32] sts. Working on both sides at once, dec 1 st at each neck edge every row 8 times. Work even on 12 [13–14–15–16–17–18] sts of each side until armholes measure same length as back.

To shape shoulders Work as for back shoulders.

SLEEVES Starting at lower edge with smaller needles, cast on 32 [34–36–38–40–42–44] sts. Work in k 1, p 1 ribbing for 1½". Change to larger needles. Working in pattern st as for back, inc 1 st at beg and end of row every 1" 10 times, then work even on 52 [54–56–58–60–62–64] sts until sleeve measures 17" [17½"–17½"–18"–18"–18½"–18½"] or desired length to underarm.

To shape cap Bind off 3 sts at beg of next 2 rows. Dec 1 st at beg and end of every other row 15 [16–17–18–19–20–21] times. Bind off 2 sts at beg of next 5 rows. Bind off.

FINISHING Sew left shoulder seam. **Neckband:** With smaller needles, k 30 sts from back holder, pick up and k 10 sts along left front neck edge, k 14 sts from front holder, pick up and k 10 sts along right front neck edge (64 sts). Work in k 1, p 1 ribbing for 6½". Bind off loosely in ribbing. Sew all sweater seams.

VEST

NOTE Work with 1 strand each Win-Knit and Melody held tog throughout.

BACK Starting at lower edge, cast on 67 [71–75–79] sts. Work in garter st for 8 rows.

To establish pattern 1st row (right side): K 5 (border sts), place marker on needle, k 9 [10–11–12], place marker, k 1, p 1, (k 3, p 1) twice; place marker, k 9 [10–11–12], place marker, p 1, place marker, k 9 [10–11–12], place marker, (p 1, k 3) twice; p 1, k 1, place marker, k 9 [10–11–12], place marker, k 5 (border sts). **2nd row:** Slipping markers, k 5, p 9 [10–11–12], p 2, (k 1, p 3) twice; p 9 [10–11–12], k 1, p 9 [10–11–12], (p 3, k 1) twice; p 2, p 9 [10–11–12], k 5. **3rd row:** Slipping markers, k 5, k 9 [10–11–12], (k 3, p 1) twice; k 2, k 9 [10–11–12], p 1, k 9 [10–11–12], k 2, (p 1, k 3) twice; k 9 [10–11–12], k 5. **4th row:** Slipping markers, k 5, p 9 [10–11–12], (k 1, p 3) twice; k 1, p 1, p 9 [10–11–12], k 1 p 9 [10–11–12], p 1, k 1, (p 3, k 1) twice; p 9 [10–11–12], k 5.

Repeating last 4 rows for pattern, work even until piece measures 6" from beg; then, working 5 border sts at each end of row in stockinette st, work even until piece measures 14" [14½"–14½"–15"] or 1" less than desired length to underarms, ending with a wrong-size row.

To work armhole border and shape armholes Work 10 [10–11–12] sts at each end of row in garter st and remainder in pattern as established for 8 rows. Bind off 5 [5–6–7] sts at beg of next 2 rows. Work even with 5 sts in garter st at each end of row until armholes measure 7" [7½"–7½"–8"]. Bind off. Mark off center 21 sts.

LEFT FRONT Starting at lower edge, cast on 33 [35–37–39] sts. Work 8 rows in garter st.

To establish pattern 1st row (right side): K 5 (border sts), place marker on needle, k 9 [10–11–12], place marker, k 1, p 1 (k 3, p 1) twice; place marker, k 9 [10–11–12]. **2nd row:** Slipping markers, p 9 [10–11–12], (p 3, k 1) twice; p 2, p 9 [10–11–12], k 5. **3rd row:** Slipping markers, k 5, k 9 [10–11–12], (k 3, p 1) twice; k 2, k 9 [10–11–12]. **4th row:** Slipping markers, p 9 [10–11–12], p 1, k 1, (p 3, k 1) twice; p 9 [10–11–12], k 5. Repeating last

4 rows for pattern, work even until piece measures 6" from beg; then, working 5 border sts at side edge in stockinette st, work even until piece measures same as back to within 1" of underarm, ending at side edge.

To work armhole border and shape armhole Work first 10 [10–11–12] sts at side edge in garter st and remainder in pattern for 8 rows. Bind off 5 [5–6–7] sts at beg of next row. Working 5 sts at arm edge in garter st from now on, at same time, dec 1 st at neck edge on next row, then repeat this dec every 4th row 9 times more. Work even on 18 [20–21–22] sts until armhole measures same as back. Bind off.

RIGHT FRONT Starting at lower edge, cast on 33 [35–37–39] sts. Work 8 rows in garter st.

To establish pattern 1st row (right side): K 9 [10–11–12], place marker on needle, (p 1, k 3) twice; p 1, k 1, place marker, k 9 [10–11–12], place marker, k 5 (border sts). **2nd row:** Slipping markers, k 5, p 9 [10–11–12], p 2, (k 1, p 3) twice; p 9 [10–11–12]. **3rd row:** Slipping markers, k 9 [10–11–12], k 2, (p 1, k 3) twice; k 9 [10–11–12], k 5. **4th row:** Slipping markers, k 5, p 9 [10–11–12], (k 1, p 3) twice; k 1, p 1, p 9 [10–11–12].

Repeating last 4 rows for pattern, complete as for left front, reversing shaping.

FRONT AND NECK BORDERS (make 2) Cast on 98 [102–106–110] sts. Work even in garter st for 6 rows. Bind off.

FINISHING Sew shoulders and side seams, leaving 6" of garter st open at lower edge for slits. Sew ends of borders together. Placing seam at center back neck, sew borders in place.

Knitted Turtleneck Collars

(Project **5** in group photograph, page **18**)

So handy, so versatile, such a snap to knit—stitch is simple rib.

SIZE 5″ deep, folded as shown.

MATERIALS Bucilla Win-Knit (acrylic knitting-worsted-weight yarn), 1 (4-ounce) skein light rust No. 501 or blue frost No. 401 makes 2 collars; 1 pair size 8 knitting needles (or English needles size 5) **or the size that will give you the correct gauge.**

GAUGE 6 rib sts = 1″, without stretching.

Cast on 104 sts. Work in ribbing of k 1, p 1 for 7″. Bind off loosely in ribbing. Sew ends tog to form tube and fold as shown.

Dog Coat in Crochet

SIZES 12″ [14″–16″] from neck to tail.

MATERIALS Bucilla Winsom (light knitting-worsted-weight acrylic yarn), 2 (2-ounce) skeins each brick (red) No. 332, royal blue No. 292 and emerald No. 297; aluminum crochet hook size J (or international size 6:00 mm) **or the size that will give you the correct gauge:** three ¾″-diameter red buttons.

GAUGE 7 sts = 2″.

NOTE Work with 2 strands yarn in colors specified held together throughout.

BODY Starting at tail with red, ch 39 [42–45] to measure about 11″ [12″–13″]. **1st row (wrong side):** Sc in 2nd ch from hook and in each ch across (38 [41–44] sc); ch 3, turn. **2nd row:** Skip 1st 2 sc, dc in each of next 2 sc, work long dc as follows: Yo, insert hook from front to back in last skipped sc, yo and draw up long lp (crosses in front of 2 dc just made), (yo and draw through 2 lps on hook) twice to complete long dc (dc cross made); * skip next sc, dc in each of next 2 sc, long dc in last skipped sc (another dc cross made). Repeat from * across, ending with dc in last sc (12 [13–14] dc crosses made). Break off red; attach blue and green, ch 1, turn. **3rd row:** Sc in each dc across, sc in top of turning ch; ch 3, turn. **4th row:** Repeat 2nd row. Break off blue and green; attach red, ch 1, turn. **5th row:** Sc in each dc across; sc in top of turning ch; ch 3, turn. Repeat 2nd through 5th rows for pattern until piece measures 12″ [14″–16″], ending with a 2nd pattern row in red.

To shape neck: Left shoulder: Next row (wrong side), Keeping in established pattern, sc in 1st 11 sts; ch 3, turn. Work in pattern on these 11 sts for about 5″, ending with a 4th pattern row in blue and green. Break off. **Right shoulder: Next row (wrong side):** Skip center 15 [18–21] sts for back neck, sc in each of remaining 11 sts; ch 3, turn. Complete as for left shoulder.

Border 1st rnd: With right side facing you and using red, work sc evenly around edge of piece, working 3 sc in each corner. **2nd rnd:** Ch 3, work dc-cross pattern as evenly spaced as possible; join with sl st to ch-3. Break off.

Collar Mark center 17 [20–23] sts on neck edge. **1st row (wrong side):** With blue and green, sc in each marked center st; ch 3, turn. **2nd row:** Work as for 4th row on body (5 [6–7] dc crosses). Break off.

Belt Mark center 9 sts on left side of border. **1st row:** With blue and green, sc in each marked st; ch 1, turn. Work even in sc for 4″, or 1½″ less than desired length (end of belt will overlap coat edge to button). **To shape end: 1st row:** Draw up lp in each of 1st 2 sc, yo and draw through all 3 lps on hook (1 sc dec), sc in each sc to last 2 sc, dec 1 sc; ch 1, turn. **2nd row:** Repeat 1st row (5 dc). **3rd row:** Dec 1 sc, ch 1, skip next sc for buttonhole, dec 1 sc; ch 1, turn. **4th row:** Dec 1 sc, sc in ch-1 sp, dec 1 sc. Break off.

FINISHING With right side facing you and using red, sc evenly along outer edge of body, collar and belt, working 3 sc at each corner; join. Break off.

Sew 2 buttons along front edge of left shoulder: one in center of row, the other at neck edge. Button through spaces between dc crosses. Sew 3rd button on right edge of body.

snug styles in slippers

Cozy comfort for tired feet, cold feet, feet that just want to relax. Knitting as well as crochet, sizes for everyone, styles to suit all ages and tastes. How can you possibly miss?

The Granny

Crocheted granny squares, 3 per foot, produce all these variations. Trims make the difference.

GENERAL DIRECTIONS

MATERIALS Knitting-worsted-weight yarn, amounts and colors given with individual directions; aluminum crochet hook size G (or international size 4:50 mm) **or the size that will give you the correct gauge.**

GAUGE 7 dc = 2″; 2 rnds = 1″.

BASIC SQUARE Work in back lp only of each st. Starting at center, ch 4. Join with sl st to form ring. Mark beg of rnds. **1st rnd:** Ch 3, work 4 dc over ring, (ch 2, work 5 dc over ring) 3 times; ch 2, join with sl st to top of ch-3 (20 dc, counting ch-3 as 1st dc). **2nd rnd:** Ch 3, dc in each dc to 1st ch-2, work (2 dc, ch 2 and 2 dc) over ch-2 (corner worked); * dc in each dc to next ch-2, work corner as before. Repeat from * twice more; join (36 dc). **3rd rnd:** Ch 3, * dc in each dc to ch-2 of next corner, work corner. Repeat from

* 3 times more; dc in each remaining dc to ch-3; join (16 dc added). Repeat 3rd rnd until square is size specified. (**NOTE** On some sizes directions require sc rnd to be added as follows: **Sc rnd:** Ch 1, sc in each dc around, working (2 sc, ch 2 and 2 sc) over each corner ch-2; join to 1st sc. Break off.)

FINISHING (NOTE On squares, use side with ridges as right side of work.)

Instep joining With right sides together, match a corner of sole square to a corner of a small (instep) square at X (see Diagram 1). Fold side corners of sole to meet at Y and join to instep around 4 sides of instep by working sc through outer lps only of matching sts.

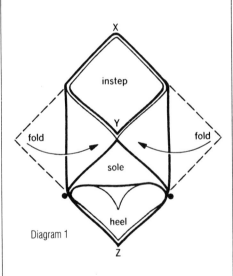

Diagram 1

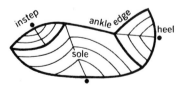

Diagram 2

Heel joining Match free corner (Z) of sole and a corner of other small (heel) square. Join from left dot to Z to right dot. Slipper should look like Diagram 2 (dots mark centers of squares; heavy lines indicate joinings of instep and heel to sole).

To make pompons Follow general pompon instructions on page 160.

WOMAN'S GRANNY

See General Directions for Granny, above.

SIZES 7 [8–9].

MATERIALS 2 ounces orange (color A), 2 [2–3] ounces each red-orange (B) and gold (C), 3 ounces green (D) and 3 [3–4] ounces turquoise (E).

SOLE SQUARE Follow Basic Square for 5 [6–6] rnds, working 1 [2–2] rnds with color A and 1 rnd each of B, C, D and E. For sizes 7 and 9 only, work additional sc rnd with E. Break off.

SMALL SQUARE (make 2 for each slipper) Follow Basic Square for 3 rnds, working 1 rnd each of D, A and B. For size 9 only, work additional sc rnd with B. Break off.

FINISHING Join squares with C. **Leg:** Attach C to free corner of heel square (back of heel). **1st rnd:** With C, ch 3, work 5 dc in same place as ch-3 was worked (1st shell made); work in back lp of sts around opening (ankle edge) as follows: * Skip ¾″ along ankle edge, sc next st, skip ¾″ along edge, work 6 dc in next st (another shell made). Repeat from * around, making 9 shells in all and ending with sc; join to top of ch-3. Break off C; attach D. **2nd rnd:** With D, work 1st shell in same place, * sc in top of next shell, work 6-dc shell in next sc. Repeat from * around, ending with sc in top of last shell; join to ch-3. Break off. Repeat 2nd rnd for pattern and work 1 rnd each of E, B, A, C and D 3 times, then 1 rnd each of E, B, A and C. Break off.

Ties (make 3 for each slipper) With a strand each of D and E held together, crochet 24″ chain. Weave a tie between sts at base of 1st, 3rd and 5th (top of leg) color-C rnds. With D and E, make six 1¾″-diameter pompons for each slipper; attach one to each tie end.

MAN'S GRANNY

See General Directions for Granny, above.

SIZES 9 [10–11].

MATERIALS 3 [3–4] ounces teal blue (color A), small amounts red (B) and rust (C).

SOLE SQUARE With color A, follow Basic Square for 6 [7–7] rnds. For sizes 9 and 11 only, work additional sc rnd. Break off.

SMALL SQUARE (make 2 for each slipper) With A, follow Basic Square for 3 rnds. For size 11 only, work additional sc rnd. Break off.

FINISHING Join squres. **Ankle trim:** Attach B to free corner of heel square (back of heel). **1st rnd:** With right side of work facing you, work sc in back lp of each st around ankle opening. Do not break off. Drop B; attach C. **2nd rnd:** Work sc in back lp of each sc around. Break off C; pick up B and repeat last rnd. Break off.

CHILD'S GRANNY

See General Directions for Granny, above.

SIZES Small (fits 6½″ foot) [medium (7½″ foot)–large (8½″ foot)].

MATERIALS 2 [2–3] ounces turquoise (color A), 1 ounce each white (B), baby blue (C) and golden orange (D).

SOLE SQUARE With color A, follow Basic Square for 4[5–5]rnds. For

continued on p. 34

continued from p. 33

small and large sizes only, work additional sc rnd. Break off.

SMALL SQUARE (make 2 for each slipper) With A, follow Basic Square for 2 rnds. For large size only, work additional sc rnd. Break off.

FINISHING Join squares. **Cuff:** Working 1 rnd each of B, C and D, work as for leg for Woman's Granny for 3 rnds, working 6 [7–8] shells on each rnd. Break off.

Ties (make 1 for each slipper) With double strand of C, crochet 20″ chain. Weave tie between sts at base of cuff. With B and D, make two 1¾″-diameter pompons for each slipper; attach to tie ends.

INFANT'S GRANNY

See General Directions for Granny, above.

SIZE Fits foot about 4″ long.

MATERIALS 1 ounce each baby green (color A) and white (B).

SOLE SQUARE With color A, follow Basic Square for 2 rnds. Work additional sc rnd. Break off.

SMALL SQUARE (make 2 for each slipper) With B, follow Basic Square for 1st rnd only. Break off.

FINISHING Join squares with A. **Cuff:** With A, work as for leg for Woman's Granny for 2 rnds, working 5 shells on each rnd. Break off.

Ties (make 1 for each slipper) With double strand of B, crochet 18″ chain. Weave tie between sts at base of cuff. With B, make two 1¼″-diameter pompons for each slipper; sew one to center of each instep square.

Granny-square Crocheted Slippers

(Project **3** in group photograph, page **18**)

SIZE Will stretch to fit woman's size 8.

MATERIALS Bucilla Win-Knit (acrylic knitting-worsted-weight yarn), 3 ounces tan No. 453 (main color, MC), 1 ounce dusty rose No. 514 (contrasting color, CC); aluminum crochet hook size H (or international size 5:00 mm) **or the size that will give you the correct gauge.**

GAUGE 4 dc = 1″.

Each slipper is composed of one large and 3 small granny squares.

LARGE SQUARE Starting at center with MC, ch 6. Join with sl st to form ring. **1st rnd:** Ch 3, 2 dc in ring, (ch 1, 3 dc in ring) 3 times; ch 1; join with sl st to top of ch-3. **2nd rnd:** Ch 3, dc in each of next 2 dc, * in ch-1 sp work (2 dc, ch 1 and 2 dc) for corner group; dc in each of next 3 dc. Repeat from * twice more;

work corner group; join. **3rd rnd:** Ch 3, dc in next 4 dc, (work corner group in sp, dc in next 7 dc) 3 times; work corner group, dc in next 2 dc (11 dc between corner groups); join.

Continue in this manner, working 4 more dc between corner groups on each rnd until 6 rnds in all have been worked (23 dc between corner groups). Piece should measure 6″ square. Break off. Make another large square.

SMALL SQUARE Work as for large square through 3rd rnd. Break off. Make 5 more small squares (total of 6 needed for pair of slippers).

FINISHING Work flower on 4 of the 6 small squares as follows: With CC sl st around post of any dc on first rnd, * ch 6, sl st around post of next dc on 1st rnd. Repeat from * around. Ch 6; join. Break off.

JOINING Following Diagram 1, place a small flower square on a large square, wrong sides facing. Starting at top dot with CC, join edges with sc in direction of arrows to bottom dot, working through back lp of each sc on small square and through both lps of large square. Now fold in corner A (see Diagram

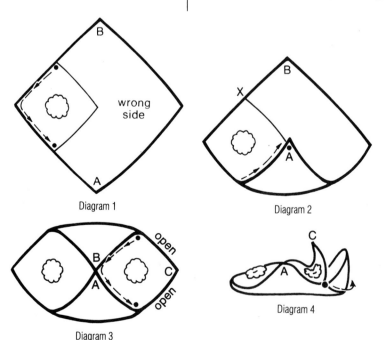

Diagram 1

Diagram 2

Diagram 3

Diagram 4

2) and continue to join to dot. Fold in corner B and join to X (toe formed). Large square forms sole and sides of slipper.

Place 2nd small flower square as shown in Diagram 3 and join to large square along 2 edges in direction of arrows between dots. Fold point C forward for instep.

For heel, pin a plain small square on back of slipper as shown in Diagram 4 and join from dot around 2 edges of square in direction of arrow. Finish with rnd of sc in CC around opening.

Fireside Slippers

(Project **13** in group photograph, page **18**)

A couple of classics, with a ruffle edge for hers, a cuff edging his.

SIZES Hers stretch to size 8, his to size 10.

MATERIALS Knitting-worsted-weight yarn, 6 ounces lilac (main color, MC) and 2 ounces cream (contrasting color, CC) per pair of her slippers, 7 ounces rust (MC) and 1 ounce cream (CC) per pair of his slippers; aluminum crochet hook size 1 (or international size 5:50 mm) **or the size that will give you the correct gauge.**

GAUGE 3 sc = 1″; 3 rnds = 1″.

NOTE Use yarn double throughout, unless otherwise specified. Changes in directions for his size are in brackets.

SOLE Starting at center of sole with MC, ch 16 [21]. **1st rnd:** 2 sc in 2nd ch from hook (inc made), sc in next 13 [18] ch, 4 sc in next ch (working around end of ch). Turn work around and work 13 [18] sc along opposite edge of ch, make inc in last ch (34 [44] sc). Do not join, but mark beg of each rnd. **2nd rnd:** Working in each sc around, make inc in next sc, sc in next sc, inc in next sc, work 10 [18] sc, inc in each of next 2 sc (mark this end for heel), work 10 [18] sc, make inc, sc, make inc (40 [50] sc). **3rd rnd:** Sc around, increasing 6 sc around toe and 4 sc around heel, spacing incs so that sole lies flat (50 [60] sc). **4th rnd:** Inc 4 sc around toe and 2 sc around heel (56 [66] sc). **5th rnd:** Repeat last rnd (62 [72] sc). Sole is completed. Do not break off, but ch 1 and turn work with wrong side facing you. **6th rnd:** Mark this rnd. Sc in each sc around; join. Break off.

TOP Turn work with right side facing you. Mark center st at toe and heel. **1st rnd:** Starting at center heel with MC, sc in each sc to 2 sts before toe marker, draw up lp in each of next 2 sts, yo and draw through all 3 lps on hook (1 sc dec); sc in marked st (transfer marker to new st), dec 1 sc, sc in each sc to end. **2nd rnd:** Sc in each sc to within 4 sts of marked st, dec 2 sc, sc in marked st, dec 2 sc, sc in each sc to end. Repeat last 2 rnds 2 [4] times more. (**NOTE** If center marked st tends to move off center after a few rnds, adjust by transferring marker to new center st and continue to dec each side of new st as before.) Repeat 1st rnd 4 [1] times (36 [40] sc). Break off.

FINISHING With single strand CC, work sc around marked rnd separating sole from top, adding 2 or 3 sc around toe if rnd cups; join. Break off.

Ruffle (on hers) 1st row: Using single strand CC and starting at front ankle, work 3 dc in each sc around top of slipper; ch 3, turn. **2nd row:** Dc in each dc across. Break off. **3rd row:** Using single strand MC, with right side facing you, sc in each dc across. Break off.

Cuff (on his) 1st row: Using single strand CC and starting at front ankle, work dc in each sc around top of slipper; ch 3, turn. **2nd row:** Dc in each dc across. Break off.

Tie With CC double, crochet 28″ chain. Weave through 1st row of ruffle or through 2nd row below cuff. Knot ends and tie in bow. Fold cuff down.

The Moccasin

Designed for cushioned comfort: pliable crochet on sturdy bottoms made with latex-foam insoles and suede fabric.

GENERAL DIRECTIONS

MATERIALS Knitting-worsted-weight yarn, amounts and colors given with individual directions; aluminum crochet hook size G (or international size 4:50 mm) **or the size that will give you the correct gauge;** tapestry needle; 2 pairs of desired size of Dr. Scholl's Air-Pillo® Insoles (or similar quality insoles) for each pair of slippers; ¼ yard cotton-suede fabric for soles.

GAUGE 4 sc = 1″; 7 rows = 2″.

SOLES For child's insole, cut adult size to fit. Make sole pattern by tracing around insole on paper, adding ¼″ all around for seam allowance. Following pattern, cut out 2 right and 2 left soles. With wrong sides of 2 matching soles facing, sandwich 2 insoles between and pin sole edges together. With yarn in tapestry needle and working through both fabric layers, sew a row of blanket st (see stitch diagram, page 159) all around edges, working about 4 sts per inch and being careful not to catch insole in sts. Repeat for other slipper.

INSTEP For woman's moccasin, ch 7; for man's, ch 8; for child's, ch 6.

1st row: Sc in 2nd ch from hook and in each remaining ch (6 sc for woman's moccasin, 7 sc for man's, 5 sc for child's); ch 1, turn. **(NOTE** On wrong-side rows, sc in front lp only of each st; on right-side rows, sc in back lp only. Ridges are formed on right side of work.) **2nd row (wrong side):** Sc in each sc, working 2 sc in last sc (inc made); ch 1, turn. See individual directions to complete instep.

MOCCASIN BODY Sc in back lp of each st throughout. **To dec 1 sc:** Draw up lp in each of next 2 sc, yo and draw through all 3 lps on hook.

WOMAN'S MOCCASIN

See General Directions for Moccasin, above.

SIZES 7 [8–9].

MATERIALS 2 ounces each avocado (color A), orange (B) and gold (C).

SOLE Assemble sole. There should be about 84 [88–92] blanket sts around.

INSTEP Instep is worked in 3 rows each (colors A, B, C) twice (18 rows in all). Follow Instep instructions under General Directions, then repeat 2nd row 7 times more. Work even on 14 sts to complete 18 instep rows.

FOOT (NOTE Right side faces you throughout as you work. Always sc in back lp of each st to form ridge on right side.) Attach B to center heel edge. **1st rnd:** Ch 1, work sc in lp of each blanket st around sole. Do not join but work around and around. Mark beg of rnds. **2nd rnd:** Work sc in each sc around. Repeat last rnd 3 times more, working 1 rnd B and 2 rnds C. Do not break off at end of last rnd.

To join instep Pin instep to last rnd of foot, stretching instep to fit front half. **Next rnd:** Work sc in each st of last rnd, joining edge of instep around front end of moccasin. Break off C; attach A.

LEG See Note under Foot, immediately above. **1st rnd:** With A, work 55 [57–59] sc around ankle. **2nd rnd:** Work sc around, decreasing evenly to 52 [54–56] sc. Work 1 rnd even. With B, * work 3 rnds, decreasing 2 sc on 2nd rnd. Repeat from * once each with C, A and B (44 [46–48] sc). Work even for 3 rnds C, 3 A, 3 B, 3 C, 1 A.

CUFF With A, ch 1, turn. With inside of leg facing you, work sc in back lp of each sc around, working 2 more rnds A, 3 B and 3 C. Break off.

MAN'S MOCCASIN

See General Directions for Moccasin, above.

SIZES 9 [10–11].

MATERIALS 1 ounce each brown (color A), rust (B) and beige (C).

SOLE Assemble sole. There should be about 90 [94–98] blanket sts around.

INSTEP Instep is worked in 3 rows each (colors A, B, C) twice (18 rows in all). Follow Instep instructions under General Directions, then repeat 2nd row 9 times more. Work even on 17 sts to complete 18 instep rows.

FOOT Work as Foot for Woman's Moccasin.

To join instep With C, join instep as for Woman's Moccasin.

ANKLE BAND See Note under Foot for Woman's Moccasin. **1st rnd:** With A, work 61 [63–65] sc around ankle. **2nd rnd:** Sc around, decreasing to fit if necessary. **3rd rnd:** Sc in each sc around. Break off.

CHILD'S MOCCASIN

See General Directions for Moccasin, above.

SIZES Small (fits 6½″ foot) [medium (7½″ foot)–large (8½″ foot)].

MATERIALS 1 ounce each purple (color A), white (B), red-orange (C) and lime green (D).

SOLE Assemble sole. There should be about 68 [74–80] blanket sts around.

INSTEP Instep is worked in 3 rows each B, C, B and D for small size, and 3 rows each A, B, C, B and D for medium and large sizes (12 [15–15] rows in all). Follow Instep instructions under General Directions, then repeat 2nd row 5 [7–7] times more. Work even on 11 [13–13] sts to complete 12 [15–15] instep rows.

FOOT With D, work as for Foot for Woman's Moccasin through 2nd rnd. Do not break off.

To join instep With D, join instep as for Woman's Moccasin. Break off D; attach B.

LEG 1st rnd: With B, work 46 [51–55] sc around ankle. **2nd rnd:** Work sc around, decreasing evenly to 44 [48–52] sc. Work 1 rnd even. With A, * work 3 rnds, decreasing 2 sc on 2nd rnd. With B, repeat from * once more (40 [44–48] sc). With C, work 2 rnds even. Do not break off.

CUFF With C, ch 1, turn. With inside of leg facing you, work 6 rnds even, working in back lp of each st. Break off.

The Bootie

Simplicity itself: knitted flat in a simple seed stitch pattern, then joined at the heel and given ribby toes.

GENERAL DIRECTIONS

MATERIALS Knitting-worsted-weight yarn, amounts and colors given with individual directions; 1 pair No. 8 knitting needles (or English needles No. 5) **or the size that will give you the correct gauge;** aluminum crochet hook size J (or international size 6:00 mm); large-eyed yarn needle.

GAUGE 3 sts = 1″; 6 rows = 1″.

SEED STITCH Work with 2 strands yarn held together throughout. Cast on even number of sts (see individual directions). **1st row:** * K 1, p 1. Repeat from * across. **2nd row:** * P 1, k 1. Repeat from * across. Repeat these 2 rows for seed st.

TOE K 1 row (right-side row). Work in k 2, p 2 ribbing for specified number of inches. Break off, leaving 12″ end. Thread end in yarn needle and draw through all sts; draw sts tog tightly to form toe. Fasten and break off.

WOMAN'S BOOTIE

See General Directions for Bootie, above.

SIZES 7 [8–9].

MATERIALS 3 [3–4] ounces white (color A), 2 ounces turquoise (B), 1 ounce each pink (C) and light blue (D).

BOOTIE BODY Starting at back seam with double strand of A, cast on 57 sts. Work striped pattern as follows: **1st row (right side):** K 1, * p 1, k 1. Repeat from * across. Break off A; attach B. **2nd row:** P across. **3rd through 5th rows:** P 1, * k 1, p 1. Repeat from * across. Break off B; attach A. **6th Row:** P across. **7th through 9th rows:** Repeat 1st row. Break off A; attach C. Repeat 2nd through 9th rows for pattern until piece measures 4½″ [4½″–5″] from beg, working colors as follows: * 4 rows each of C, A, D, A, B, A. Repeat from * for stripe sequence.

To shape cuff Continuing in st and

continued on p. 38

continued from p. 37

color pattern, bind off 14 sts at beg of next 2 rows. Work even on 29 sts until piece measures 8″ [8½″–9″] from beg, ending with a wrong-side row and decreasing 1 st at end of row (28 sts).

TOE Follow General Directions for Bootie toe, working ribbing for 2″.

FINISHING Fold piece in half with gathered toe at one end. Sew top seam from toe to cuff; sew back seam.

   Ties (make 1 for each bootie) With double strand of B, crochet 24″ chain. Weave tie between sts around cuff at ankle; tie in bow.

MAN'S BOOTIE

See General Directions for Bootie, above.

SIZES 9 [10–11].

MATERIALS 3 [3–4] ounces each green (color A) and white (B), 2 ounces red (C).

BOOTIE BODY Starting at back seam with 1 strand each of A and B held together, cast on 42 sts. Work in seed st for 5½″ [5¾″–6″].

   To shape cuff Keeping in pattern, bind off 5 sts at beg of next 2 rows. Work even on 32 sts until piece measures 8½″ [9″–9½″] from beg. Break off A and B; attach double strand of C.

TOE Follow General Directions for Bootie toe, working ribbing for 2″.

FINISHING Fold piece in half with gathered toe at one end. Sew top seam from toe to cuff; sew back seam.

   Cuff trim Fold down cuff. Attach double strand of C to center front at beg of cuff. With right side facing you, work sc evenly all around cuff edge, working 3 sc at each corner. With same side facing you, work 2nd row of sc in back lp only of each st. Break off.

CHILD'S BOOTIE

See General Directions for Bootie.

SIZES Small (fits 6½″ foot) [medium (7½″ foot)–large (8½″ foot)].

MATERIALS 4 [4–5] ounces blue (color A), 1 ounce orange (B), small amount white (C).

BOOTIE BODY Starting at back seam with color A, cast on 24 sts. Work in seed st for 4¾″ [5½″–6″]. Break off A; attach 1 strand each of B and C.

TOE Follow General Directions for Bootie toe, working ribbing for 1¼″ [1½″–2″].

FINISHING Fold piece in half with gathered toe at one end. Sew edges of toe section tog; sew back seam.

   Ties (make 1 for each bootie) With double strand of B, crochet 27″ chain. Pushing tie between sts along top edge, lace ties as for shoe-laces for about 1½″ [2½″–3½″].

The Dancer

Worked with double yarn for solid footing. Stitches are simple: single and half-double crochet. Basic design is the same for all.

GENERAL DIRECTIONS

MATERIALS Knitting-worsted-weight yarn, amounts and colors given with individual directions, alumi-num crochet hook size J for all 3 versions plus size E for button only on Child's (or international sizes 6:00 and 3:50 mm) **or the size that will give you the correct gauge;** tapestry needle for Child's.

GAUGE With J hook, (ch 1 and sc) 3 times = 2″; 2 rnds = 1″.

NOTE Work with double strand of yarn throughout.

TO MAKE SC DEC Ch 1, draw up lp in each of next 2 sp, yo and draw through all 3 lps on hook.

TO MAKE HDC DEC Yo and draw up lp in next sp, yo and draw up lp in following sp, yo and draw through all 5 lps on hook.

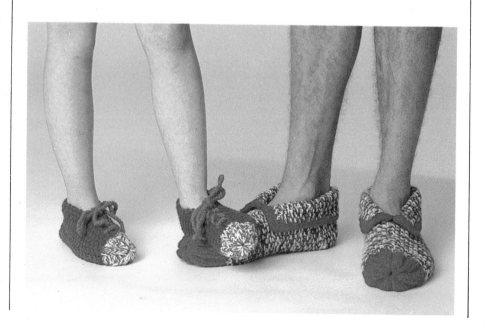

TO INC Work (ch 1 and sc) twice in same sp.

WOMAN'S DANCER

See General Directions for Dancer, above.

SIZES 7 [8–9].

MATERIALS 4 [5–5] ounces pink (A), 1 [2–2] ounces each blue (B) and purple (C).

SOLE Starting at center with color A, loosely ch 12 [14–16]. **1st rnd:** Sc in 2nd ch from hook, * ch 1, sc in next ch *. Repeat from * to * across. Turn piece around with same side facing you and repeat from * to * across opposite side of chain (there should be the same number of sc on each side of chain). Do not join, but work around and around. Mark beg of rnds. **2nd rnd:** Ch 1, sc in 1st sc, * ch 1, sc in next ch-1 sp. Repeat from * around. Mark sc at 1st end of sole for heel and sc at other end for toe. **3rd rnd:** Work in ch 1-sc pattern around, increasing in sp before and after heel and toe markers (4 inc on rnd). Keep toe and heel markers at extreme ends of sole; position of marker for beg of rnds shifts gradually around to side of sole. **4th and 5th rnds:** Work in pattern around and inc 4 sc as before. Break off A; attach B. **6th rnd:** Work in pattern around and inc 4 sc as before. **7th rnd:** Work even in pattern; break off B; attach C.

FOOT UPPER 8th rnd: Work even. **9th rnd:** Work in pattern around, working sc dec before and after heel and toe markers (4 sc dec). Break off C; attach A. **10th rnd:** Repeat last rnd. Do not break off. **11th rnd:** Work to heel and dec 2 sc as before, work in pattern to within 3 sp of toe marker, ch 1, work hdc dec, (ch 1, dc in next sp) 3 times; ch 1, work hdc dec, work pattern to end (2 sc and 2 hdc dec). **12th rnd:** Work to heel and dec 2 sc, work in pattern to within 5 sp of toe marker, ch 1, hdc in next sp, ch 1, work hdc

dec, ch 1, dc in each of next 4 sp, ch 1, hdc dec, ch 1, hdc in next sp, work pattern to end. Break off.

TIES (make 1 for each slipper) With double strand of B, crochet 72″ chain. Weave through sts on last rnd, starting and ending at back. Slippers are worn with chain wrapped around legs as in photograph and tied in front.

MAN'S DANCER

See General Directions for Dancer, above.

SIZES 9 [10–11].

MATERIALS 4 [4–5] ounces orange (color A), 2 [2–3] ounces taupe (B).

SOLE Starting at center with color A, loosely ch 14 [16–18]. Work as for Woman's Dancer through 3rd rnd.

4th through 7th rnds: Work in pattern around and inc 4 sc as before. **8th and 9th rnds:** Work even in pattern. Do not break off.

FOOT UPPER 10th rnd: Work in pattern around, working sc dec before and after heel and toe markers (4 sc dec). Break off A; attach B. **11th rnd:** With B, repeat last rnd. **12th rnd:** Work to heel end and dec 2 sc, work in pattern to within 5 sp of toe marker, work sc dec, hdc dec, ch 1, hdc in each of next 3 sp, ch 1, hdc dec, sc dec, work pattern to end (4 sc and 2 hdc dec). **13th rnd:** Work to heel and dec 2 sc, work pattern to within 6 [7–7] sts of toe marker, hdc in each of next 3 sp, hdc dec, dc in each of next 3 [5–5] sp, work

continued on p. 40

continued from p. 39

hdc dec, hdc in each of next 3 sp, work pattern to end (2 sc and 2 hdc dec). **14th rnd:** Work pattern to within 4 [4–6] sts of toe marker, work 2 [2–3] sc dec, sc in next dc, work 2 [3–3] sc dec, work pattern to end (4 [4–6] sc dec). Break off.

TIES (make 1 for each slipper) With double strand of B, crochet 24″ chain. Weave through sts of last rnd and tie in front. Knot ends of ties.

CHILD'S DANCER (Mary Jane)

See General Directions for Dancer, above.

SIZES Small (fits 6½″ foot) [medium (7½″ foot)–large (8½″ foot)].

MATERIALS 2 [2–3] ounces each red (color A) and black (B).

SOLE Starting at center with J hook and color A, loosely ch 10 [12–14]. Work as for Woman's Dancer through 5th rnd. Break off A; attach B.

FOOT UPPER 6th rnd: Work around in pattern without increasing. **7th rnd:** Repeat 10th rnd of Man's Dancer. **8th rnd:** Work to heel and dec 2 sc as before, work in pattern to within 5 sp of toe marker, ch 1, hdc in next sp, ch 1, work hdc dec, work (ch 1, dc in next sp) 4 times; ch 1, work hdc dec, ch 1, hdc in next sp, work pattern to end (2 sc and 2 hdc dec). **9th rnd:** Work to heel and dec 2 sc, work pattern to within 4 sp of toe marker, work (ch 1, hdc in next sp) twice; dc in each of next 5 sp, hdc in next sp, ch 1, hdc in next sp, work pattern to end (2 sc dec). **10th rnd:** Work pattern to within 1st dc (no heel shaping), hdc dec in next 2 dc, hdc in center dc, hdc dec in next 2 dc, work pattern to end. Break off.

STRAPS Mark center st on one side of slipper. With 2 strands of B, sl st in marked st, ch 12 [13–14], sc in 6th ch from hook for button loop, sc in each remaining ch, sc in same place as sl st. Break off. Work in same manner on other slipper, starting strap on opposite side.

BUTTONS (make 1 for each slipper) With E hook and single strand of A, ch 2. **1st rnd:** Work 6 sc in 2nd ch from hook. **2nd rnd:** Work 2 sc in each sc around (12 sc). **3rd rnd:** * Draw up lp in each of next 2 sc, yo and draw through all 3 lps on hook. Repeat from * around. Break off, leaving 8″ end. Stuff button with bits of yarn. Thread end into needle and draw opening closed. Sew to slipper.

Pomponed Elf Slippers

(Project **12** in group photograph, page **18**)

Perfect for a pixie, and everyone knows one of those! Knitted and crocheted versions.

SIZE Stretches to 9″ long.

MATERIALS Knitting-worsted-weight yarn, 1 (4-ounce) skein makes 2 pairs of either crocheted or knitted slippers; scraps of contrasting color yarn for pompons; aluminum crochet hook size K (or international size 7:00 mm), or knitting needles size 10½ (or English needles size 2) **or the size hook or needles that will give you the correct gauge.**

GAUGE 4 knitted sts = 1″; 3 crocheted sts = 1″.

KNITTED SLIPPERS

Cast on 36 sts. Work in garter st until piece measures 9″ square. Bind off.

Fold in half to form triangle. Sew edges tog along one side for sole, then around point and halfway along other side for heel. Fold free point over as shown in photograph and tack. Curl toe point slightly and tack. Make 1½″-diameter pompon (see page 160) and sew to ankle point.

CROCHETED SLIPPERS

Ch 29. **1st row:** Sc in 2nd ch from hook and in each ch across; ch 1, turn. **2nd row:** Sc in each sc across; ch 1, turn. Repeat last row until piece measures 9″ square. Break off.

Complete as for knitted slippers.

Popcorn Slippers

Somewhat intricate to crochet, but intriguing— and that's what counts. Adults only here.

SIZES Soles measure 9″ [10″].

MATERIALS Knitting-worsted-weight yarn: **For woman's slippers,** 3 ounces lilac (color A), 2 ounces eggshell (B) and 1 ounce red (C); **for man's slippers,** 3 ounces dark turquoise (color A), 3 ounces eggshell (B) and 1 ounce orange (C); aluminum crochet hooks sizes H and I (or international hooks sizes 5:00 mm and 5:50 mm) **or the size that will give you the correct gauge.**

GAUGE With single strand yarn on size H hook, 7 sc = 2″.

SOLE (NOTE Work with 2 strands held tog.) Starting at center with larger hook and color A, ch 22 [25]. **1st rnd:** Work 3 sc in 2nd ch from hook, sc in next 19 [22] ch, 3 sc in last ch; working along opposite side of starting chain, sc in next 19 [22] sc, sl st in first sc. **2nd rnd:** Ch 1 (counts as 1 sc), sc in same sc, (2 sc in next sc) twice; sc in each of next 19 [22] sc, (2 sc in next sc) 3 times; sc in next 19 [22] sc; join with sl st in ch-1. **3rd rnd:** Ch 1, sc in same st, (2 sc in next sc) 5 times; sc in each of next 19 [22] sc, (2 sc in next sc) 6 times; sc in next 19 [22] sc; join. **4th rnd:** Ch 1, sc in next 3 sc, (2 sc in next sc) 4 times; sc in next 27 [30] sc, (2 sc in next sc) 4 times; sc in next 23 [26] sc; join. **5th rnd:** Ch 1; working in back lp only of each st, sc in each sc around; join. Drop A; join C. **6th rnd:** With C, ch 1, sc in each sc around; join. Break off C; pick up A. **7th rnd:** With A, ch 1, sc in each sc around; join. Break off.

TOP (NOTE Work with 1 strand yarn throughout.) Starting at top of cuff with smaller hook and color B, ch 38 [42]. **1st row:** Sc in 2nd ch from hook and in each ch across (37 [41] sc); ch 1, turn. **2nd row:** Sc in each sc across; break off B; join C; ch 1, turn. **3rd row (pc row):** Sc in first 2 sc; work popcorn (pc) as follows: Work 4 sc in next sc, drop lp from hook, insert hook in first sc and in dropped lp, pull lp through (pc made); * sc in next 3 sc, pc in next sc. Repeat from * to last 2 sc, sc in last 2 sc; ch 1, turn. **4th row:** Sc in each sc and pc across (37 [41] sc); break off C; join A; ch 1, turn. **5th row (pc row);** Sc in first sc, * pc in next sc, sc in next 3 sc. Repeat from * across; ch 1, turn. **6th row:** Repeat 4th row; break off A; join B; ch 1, turn. **7th row:** Sc in each sc across; ch 1, turn. Repeat 7th row 6 [8] times more. **1st inc row:** Sc in first 16 [18] sc, 2 sc in next sc, sc in next 3 sc (ankle front), 2 sc in next sc, sc in last 16 [18] sc; ch 1, turn. **2nd inc row:** Sc in first 16 [18] sc, 2 sc in next sc, sc in next 5 sc (ankle front), 2 sc in next sc, sc in last 16 [18] sc; ch 1, turn. Repeat last row 3 times more, working 2 more sc at ankle front on each row (11 sc at ankle front on last row). Break off.

Instep 1st row: With B, skip first 19 [20] sc of last row (side edge), sc in each of next 9 [11] sc (instep); ch 1, turn. **2nd row (pc row):** Sc in first 2 [1] sc, pc in next sc, (sc in next 3 sc, pc in next sc) 1 [2] times; sc in last 2 [1] sc; ch 1, turn. **3rd row:** Sc in each sc and pc across (9 [11] sc); ch 1, turn. **4th row (pc row):** Sc in first 4 [3] sc, pc in next sc, (sc in next 3 sc, pc in next sc) 0 [1] times; sc in last 4 [3] sc; ch 1, turn. **5th row:** Repeat 3rd row. Repeat 2nd through 5th rows once [twice] more, then repeat 2nd and 3rd rows once more. Break off.

FINISHING With smaller hook and B, work 1 row sc evenly spaced along side edge, around instep and along other side edge. Break off. Sew center back seam. With wrong sides tog, pin top to sole. Working through both thicknesses, with A, sl st top to sole.

Cut 16 assorted A, B and C yarns 6″ long and make tassel (see page 160); do the same for the other slipper. To attach, with B, sl st in top of tassel, ch 4, sl st in top of center back seam. Break off.

shawl & stole spectacular

Nowadays, what with lowered winter thermostats and air-conditioned summers, these flatterers are valued as much for their warmth as their charm. Either way, they'd be beautiful buys.

Diamond-pattern Crocheted Shawl

Shoulder-hugging triangle is worked in 2 halves with center-back seam.

SIZE About 20″ deep at center back, 70″ across long edge including border.

MATERIALS Unger's Fluffy Tweed (brushed acrylic sport-weight yarn), 4 (50-gram, 1¾-ounce) balls rose tweed No. 705; aluminum crochet hook size I (or international size 5:50 mm) **or the size that will give you the correct gauge.**

GAUGE 7 dc = 2″; 4 rows = 3″.

NOTE Shawl is worked in 2 halves with seam at center back.

FIRST HALF Starting along center back, ch 68 to measure about 19″.
1st row: Dc in 8th ch from hook, ch 2, skip next 2 ch, dc in next ch, dc in next 3 ch, * (ch 2, skip next 2 ch, dc in next ch) twice; dc in next 6 ch. Repeat from * 3 times more; (ch 2, skip next 2 ch, dc in next ch) twice; ch 4, turn. Mark end of row for shaped edge. Continue as follows (all dec will be made at marked edge, and other edge—neck edge—will remain even).
   2nd row: Skip dc below turning ch, dc in next dc (first sp made); ch 2, dc in next dc (another sp made); * dc in next 6 dc, (ch 2, dc in next dc) twice. Repeat from * 3 times more; dc in next 3 dc, ch 2, dc in next dc, ch 2, skip next 2 ch sts of turning ch, dc in next ch st; ch 5, turn.
   3rd row: Make first sp, ch 2, dc in next dc, dc in next 2 dc, * ch 2, dc in next sp, dc in next dc, dc in next sp, ch 2, skip next dc, dc in next 5 dc. Repeat from * 3 times more; ch 2, skip next dc, dc in next sp, ch 1, dc in sp formed by turning ch; ch 4, turn.

4th row: Skip first sp, dc in next sp, * ch 2, skip next dc, dc in next 3 dc, ch 2, dc in next sp, dc in next 3 dc, dc in next sp. Repeat from * 3 times more; ch 2, skip next dc, dc in next 2 dc, ch 2, dc in next dc, ch 2, dc in 3rd ch of turning ch; ch 5, turn.

5th row: Make first sp, ch 2, dc in next dc, * ch 2, dc in next sp, dc in next 5 dc, dc in next sp, ch 2, skip next dc, dc in next dc. Repeat from * 3 times more; ch 2, dc in next sp, dc in last sp formed by turning ch; ch 1, turn.

6th row: Skip first dc, sl st in next dc, ch 5, make first sp, * ch 2, dc in next 7 dc, ch 2, dc in next dc. Repeat from * 3 times more; work 2 sp; ch 5, turn.

7th row: Work 2 sp, * ch 2, dc in next 7 dc, ch 2, dc in next dc. Repeat from * 3 times more; ch 1, dc in 3rd ch of turning ch; ch 4, turn.

8th row: Skip first sp, dc in next sp, * ch 2, skip next dc, dc in next 5 dc, ch 2, dc in next sp, dc in next dc, dc in next sp. Repeat from * 3 times more, omitting last dc on last repeat; work 2 sp; ch 5, turn.

9th row: Work 2 sp, dc in dc, dc in next sp, * ch 2, skip next dc, dc in next 3 dc, ch 2, dc in next sp, dc in next 3 dc, dc in next sp. Repeat from * twice more; ch 2, skip next dc, dc in next 3 dc, ch 2, dc in next sp, ch 1, dc in last sp; ch 4, turn.

10th row: Skip first sp, dc in next sp, ch 2, skip next dc, dc in next dc, * ch 2, dc in next sp, dc in next 5 dc, dc in next sp, ch 2, skip next dc, dc in next dc. Repeat from * twice more; ch 2, dc in next sp, dc in next 3 dc, work 2 sp; ch 5, turn.

11th row: Working dc over dc and sp over sp, work as for last row, ending with ch 1, dc in last sp; ch 3, turn. **12th row:** Work even in pattern; ch 5, turn.

13th row: Repeat 3rd row, repeating from * once and ending ch 2, dc in next sp, ch 2, skip next sp, dc in next dc; ch 4, turn. **14th**

row: Skip first sp, dc in next sp; repeat from * on 4th row 3 times, ending as for 4th row. **15th row:** Repeat 5th row, repeating from * twice. **16th row:** Repeat 6th row, repeating from * twice. **17th row:** Work even in pattern, ending ch 1, dc in 3rd ch of turning ch; ch 4, turn. **18th row:** Repeat 8th row, repeating from * twice, omitting last dc on last repeat; work 2 sp; ch 5, turn. **19th row:** Repeat 9th row, repeating from * once. **20th row:** Repeat 10th row, repeating from * once. **21st row:** Work even in pattern, ending ch 1, dc in last sp; ch 3, turn. **22nd row:** Work even in pattern; ch 5, turn.

23rd through 32nd rows: Repeat 13th through 22nd rows once more, and as sts dec repeat from * only as many times as necessary.

33rd row: Work 2 sp, dc in next 2 dc, ch 2, dc in next sp, dc in next dc, dc in next sp, ch 2, skip next dc, dc in next 5 dc, ch 2, skip next dc and next sp, dc in next dc, ch 1, dc in next dc; ch 4, turn. **34th through 38th rows:** Work as for 4th, 5th, 6th, 7th and 8th rows, but do not repeat from *. Put a marker at beg and end of 38th row. **39th row:** Work 2 sp, dc in next dc, dc in next sp, ch 2, skip next dc, dc in next 3 dc, ch 2, skip next dc, dc in next sp, ch 1, dc in last sp; ch 4, turn.

40th row: Skip first sp, dc in next sp, ch 2, skip next dc, dc in next dc, ch 2, dc in next sp, dc in next 3 dc, work 2 sp; ch 5, turn.

41st row: Work 2 sp, dc in next 3 dc, work 2 sp; ch 5, turn. **42nd row:** Work even in pattern; ch 5, turn. **43rd row:** Work 2 sp, dc in next 2 dc, ch 2, skip next dc, dc in next dc, dc in 3rd st of turning ch; ch 4, turn. **44th row:** Skip first 2 dc, dc in sp, ch 2, skip next dc, dc in next dc, skip next dc, dc in next dc, work 1 sp; ch 5, turn. **45th row:** Work 3 sp; ch 3, turn. **46th row:** Skip first dc, dc in next dc, work 2 sp; ch 5, turn. **47th row:** Work 1 sp, dc in next dc, ch 3, turn. **48th row:** Dc in 3rd st of

turning ch. Break off. Straight edge should measure about 34".

SECOND HALF Work as for first half.

FINISHING Sew pieces together along starting-chain edge.

Border Work ruffled border on all sides of shawl as follows: Starting at one marker, working toward narrow end, then around narrow end to next marker, work a shell of 4 dc in each dc and in every other sp; then working to next marker (on other half of shawl), work a shell in each dc. Continue in this manner until border is completed. Join with sl st in first dc. Break off.

Ring Ch 18, join with sl st to form ring. Work 1 sc in each ch st around. Join with sl st in first sc and break off. To wear, slip one end of shawl through ring, place on body and slip other end through ring.

43

Lacy Crocheted Shawl

Lightweight protection in its most complimentary form. Openwork wrap works up fast despite the generous size.

SIZE About 22″ x 80″.

MATERIALS Bucilla Pouffe (acrylic and wool brushed yarn), 7 (40-gram, about 1.4-ounce) balls rose No. 8; aluminum crochet hook size I (or international hook size 5:50 mm) **or the size that will give you the correct gauge.**

GAUGE 7 sts = 2″.

Starting at one end, ch 76 to measure about 22″. **1st row:** Hdc in 3rd ch from hook and in each ch across (75 hdc, counting turning ch 2 as 1 hdc); ch 2, turn. **2nd row:** Skip first hdc (directly below ch-2), hdc across and in turning ch; ch 5, turn. **3rd row:** Skip first 2 hdc, tr in next hdc, * ch 3, skip 3 hdc, tr in 5 hdc, ch 3, skip 2 hdc, 3 tr in next hdc, ch 3, skip 2 hdc, tr in 5 hdc, ch 3, skip 3 hdc, tr in next hdc, ch 1, skip hdc, tr in next hdc. Repeat from * across; ch 5, turn. **4th row:** Skip first ch-1 sp, tr in tr, * ch 3, skip tr, tr in 3 tr, ch 3, skip tr, tr in ch-3 sp, tr in next tr, work (tr, ch 3 and tr) in next tr, tr in next tr, tr in ch-3 sp, ch 3, skip tr, tr in 3 tr, ch 3, skip ch-3 sp, tr in tr, ch 1, skip ch-1 sp, tr in tr. Repeat from * across, ending last repeat with last tr in 2nd ch of turning ch; ch 5, turn. **5th row:** Skip first ch-1 sp, tr in tr, * ch 3, skip tr, tr in next tr, skip tr, ch 3, tr in ch-3 sp, tr in 3 tr, work (tr, ch 3 and tr) in ch-3 sp, tr in 3 tr, tr in ch-3 sp, ch 3, skip tr, tr in next tr, ch 3, skip ch-3 sp, tr in tr, ch 1, skip ch-1 sp, tr in tr. Repeat from * across, ending last repeat ch 1, tr in 2nd ch of turning ch; ch 5, turn. **6th row:** Skip first ch-1 sp, tr in tr, * ch 3, skip ch-3 sp and tr, tr in ch-3 sp, tr in 5 tr, work (tr, ch 3 and tr) in ch-3 sp, tr in 5 tr, tr in ch-3 sp, ch 3, skip ch-3 sp, tr in tr, ch 1, skip ch-1 sp, tr in next tr. Repeat from * across, ending last repeat ch 1, tr in 2nd ch of turning ch; ch 5, turn. **7th row:** Skip first ch-1 sp, tr in tr, * ch 3, skip ch-3 sp and tr, tr in 5 tr, ch 3, skip tr, 3 tr in ch-3 sp, ch 3, skip tr, tr in 5 tr, ch 3, skip tr and ch-3 sp, tr in tr, ch 1, skip ch-1 sp, tr in tr. Repeat from * across, ending last repeat ch 1, tr in 2nd ch of turning ch; ch 5, turn. Repeating 4th through 7th rows, work even until piece measures about 80″, ending with a 7th row.

Next row: Skip first tr, hdc in ch-1 sp, hdc in tr, * 3 hdc in ch-3 sp, hdc in 5 tr, hdc in ch-3 sp, hdc in 3 tr, hdc in ch-3 sp, hdc in 5 tr, 3 hdc in ch-3 sp, hdc in tr, hdc in ch-1 sp, hdc in tr. Repeat from * across, ending 2 hdc in turning ch; ch 1, turn. **Following row:** Skip first hdc, hdc in each st across. Break off.

One-piece Triangle Shawl

The shawl at its most sumptuous, crocheted in two yarns and colors.

SIZE 62″-wide x 32″-deep triangle, including ruffle border.

MATERIALS Unger Cozy (acrylic and wool bulky thick-and-thin yarn), 5 (1¾-ounce) balls rust No. 30 (MC) and Unger Scot (mohair, wool and nylon sport-weight yarn), 2 (1⁴⁄₁₀-ounce) balls rose heather No. MC1 (CC); Boye aluminum crochet hook size N, **or the size that will give you the correct gauge.**

GAUGE 2 sts average 1″; 3 hdc rows = 2″; 1 dc row = 1″.

Starting at base of triangle above ruffle, with MC, ch 9. **1st row:** Work 2 hdc in 3rd ch from hook, hdc in next 5 ch, 3 hdc in last ch (11 hdc, counting turning ch as 1 hdc); ch 2, turn. **2nd row:** Work 2 hdc in first hdc (2 sts inc); hdc in each hdc across, working 3 hdc in top of turning ch (2 sts inc); ch 2, turn. **3rd row:** Work hdc in first hdc (1 st inc); hdc in each hdc across, working 2 hdc in turning ch (1 st inc); ch 2, turn. **4th through 6th rows:** Repeat 3rd row (2 sts inc on each row). **7th row:** Work 2 hdc in first hdc; hdc in each hdc across, working 3 hdc in turning ch; ch 2, turn. **8th through 10th rows:** Repeat 7th row (4 sts inc on each row). At end of 10th row drop MC; join CC. With CC, ch 3, turn. **11th row:** Work dc in first hdc, dc in each hdc across, working 2 dc in turning ch; ch 3, turn. **12th row:** Work dc in first dc, dc in each dc across, working 2 dc in turning ch; drop CC, pick up MC. With MC, ch 2, turn.

*Work next 10 rows in hdc, using MC and increasing 4 sts on each row as before. Work next 2 rows in dc, using CC and increasing 2 sts on each row as before. Repeat from * once more; ch 1, turn.

37th row: Sc in each st across; ch 3, do not break off or turn.

RUFFLED BORDER Continue with MC, working across both shaped edges and lower edge (not across straight top edge). **1st row:** Work 2 dc at base of turning ch, * ch 1, working sts in ends of rows, work dc in next row, ch 1, 3 dc in next row. Repeat from * along one shaped edge, then continue across opposite edge of starting ch, working in same manner in each st of foundation ch; then continue same border along other shaped edge, ending with 3 dc in last st; ch 3, turn. **2nd row:** Sk first dc, dc in next 2 dc,* ch 1, sk ch-1, work 2 dc in next single dc of last row, ch 1, sk ch-1, work dc in next 3 dc. Repeat from * across, working last dc in top of turning ch. Break off MC, join CC; ch 1, turn. **3rd row:** With CC, sc in each dc and each ch-1 of last row. Break off.

FINISHING With MC, sc evenly across edge of ruffle and straight edge of shawl. Break off.

Fringed Stole

Luxurious sweep of burnished tones, worked the long way in chain loops and single crochet.

SIZE 16″ x 68″, not including fringe.

MATERIALS Bucilla Melody (50% mohair, 50% acrylic yarn), 3 (1-ounce) balls bronze No. 12 (color B), 2 balls each mink No. 17 (M) and seal brown No. 25 (S); Bucilla Brocade, 2 (100-yard) balls gold (G); aluminum crochet hook size K (or international hook size 7:00 mm) **or the size that will give you the correct gauge.**

GAUGE 3 ch lp = 4″; 4 rows = 1″.

Starting at long edge with color B, ch 202 to measure 68″. **1st row:** Sc in 2nd ch from hook, * ch 3, skip 3 ch, sc in next ch. Repeat from * across (50 ch lp); ch 1, turn. **2nd row:** Sc in 1st sc, * ch 3, sc in next sc. Repeat from * across; ch 1, turn. Repeating 2nd row, work 1 row B, 1 G, 3 S, 1 G, 2 B, 2 S, 1 B, 1 G, 1 S, 1 G, 1 M, 1 G, 1 S, 1 G, 1 B, 2 M, 2 B, 1 G, 3 M, 1 G, 2 B, 2 M, 1 B, 1 G, 1 S, 1 G, 1 M, 1 G, 1 S, 1 G, 1 B, 2 S, 2 B, 1 G, 3 S, 1 G, 4 B. Break off.

Following general directions on page 32, make fringe in matching colors at ends of each row, using three 28″ strands for each tassel.

accessory originals

Perky little pickups for anyone's wardrobe, with particular appeal for the young. They're naturals for making in multiples, so have plenty on display—these are bound to be a bonanza!

Bolero and Cowboy Tie

SIZES (8–10) [12–14]. Vest measures 16″ [18½″] across at underarms.

MATERIALS Bucilla Brocade (metallic/rayon yarn—100-yard balls): **For vest,** 8 [9] balls gold; **for tie,** 3 balls gold. Aluminum crochet hook size J (or international hook size 6:00 mm) **or the size that will give you the correct gauge;** 1″-diameter plastic ring for tie.

GAUGE 3 shells for vest = 4″; 3 hdc for tie = 1″.

NOTE Use 2 strands of yarn held together.

BOLERO

BACK Starting at upper edge of back, ch 54 [62] to measure about 16″ [18½″]. **1st row (base):** Dc in 4th ch from hook and in each ch across (52 [60] dc, counting turning ch as 1 dc): ch 3, turn. **2nd row:** Skip 1st dc (directly below ch-3) and next dc, work (dc, ch 1 and dc) between last dc and next dc (1st shell made); * skip 4 dc, work (2 dc, ch 1 and 2 dc) between last dc and next dc (another shell made). Repeat from * across (13 [15] shells between groups of 4 dc, leaving 2 dc at beg and end of base row); ch 3, turn. **3rd row:** Work a 1st shell in 1st ch-1 sp, * work shell in next ch-1 sp. Repeat from * across; ch 3, turn. Repeating 3rd row for pattern, work even until piece measures 15″ [15½″]. Break off. Mark off 7½″ along each side from shoulder for armhole.

LEFT FRONT 1st row: With right side of upper back edge facing you, work across other edge of base as follows: Sl st in sp between 2nd and 3rd dc, ch 3, work a 1st shell in same sp; skipping groups of 4 dc, work 3 [4] more shells on base for shoulder; ch 3, turn. Work in pattern on 4 [5] shells for 6″, ending at front edge.

1st inc row: (2 dc, ch 1 and 2 dc) in 1st ch-1 sp, work shell in each ch-1 sp across; ch 3, turn. **2nd inc row:** Work shell in each ch-1 sp, ending 2 dc in top of turning ch; ch 3, turn. **3rd inc row:** Dc in each of 1st 2 dc, work shell in each ch-1 sp across; ch 3, turn. **4th inc row:** Work shell in each ch-1 sp, dc in last 2 dc, ch 1, 2 dc in top of turning ch (1 shell inc over 4 rows); ch 3, turn. **5th and 6th rows:** Work pattern on 5 [6] shells. Repeat 1st through 4th inc rows once more; work even on 6 [7] shells until piece measures same as back. Break off. Starting at shoulder, mark off 7½″ along side for armhole.

RIGHT FRONT Skip center 24 dc on base for back neck. **1st row:** Sl st between 24th and 25th dc, ch 3, work a 1st shell in same sp, work 3 [4] more shells across base as for other shoulder; ch 3, turn. Complete to correspond to left front.

FINISHING Sew side seams. With right side facing you, work 1 row sc evenly spaced along edges.

COWBOY TIE

Starting at one end, ch 3. **1st row:** Work 2 hdc in 3rd ch from hook (3 hdc—turning ch 2 always counts as 1 hdc); ch 2, turn. **2nd row:** Hdc in each hdc across, 2 hdc in top of turning ch (5 hdc); ch 2, turn. **3rd row:** Repeat 2nd row (7 hdc). **4th row:** Skip 1st hdc (directly below ch-2), hdc in each hdc across; hdc in top of turning ch (7 hdc); ch 2, turn. Repeat 4th row until piece measures 26″. **Next row:** Skip 1st hdc; dec 1 hdc as follows: (Yo, draw up lp in next st) twice, yo and draw through all 5 lps on hook (1 hdc dec), hdc in each st to last 2 hdc, dec 1 hdc; ch 2, turn. **Following row:** (Dec 1 hdc) twice; ch 2, turn. **Last row:** Dec 1 hdc. Break off.

To wear, pull ends of tie through ring as shown in photograph.

Cummerbund Tie Belt

Popular wide style, designed to tie back or front. Make a range of average sizes (24″, 26″, 28″) and take orders for others.

SIZE 2¾″ wide; length is adjustable.

MATERIALS ¼ yard each of 2 fabrics in contrasting colors (color A for painted piece, B for under piece); ¼ yard medium-weight iron-on interfacing; metallic acrylic paint; small paintbrush.

Cut 3¼″-wide strip from fabric A and 3¾″-wide strip from fabric B, cutting both strips 1″ longer than waist measurement (½″ seam allowance included). For ties, cut two 1″ x 18″ strips from fabric B (¼″ seam allowance included).

Iron belt strips to interfacing; cut away excess interfacing. Press seam

allowances under. With wrong sides together, center and pin narrower strip on wider one.

For ties, press under seam allowances, fold in half lengthwise and press again; topstitch. Sandwich one end of each tie between layers at each end of belt. Topstitch outer edges of narrower belt strip, securing underpiece seam allowance and ties in stitching.

Paint on design shown in photograph (or make up your own).

Lacy Crochet Collar

Complementary to so many styles, it pays to display a dozen in different tints.

SIZE 14″ across neckline—adult medium size.

MATERIALS Coats & Clark's Speed-Cro-Sheen cotton yarn, 1 (100-yard) ball robinette No. 76; steel crochet hook No. 0, **or the size that will give you the correct gauge.**

GAUGE 5 sc = 1″.

NOTE Collar can be worn with opening at front or back. For larger neckline add 6 sts to starting chain and work on 25 lps.

COLLAR Starting at neck edge, ch 71 to measure about 14″. **1st row:** Sc in 2nd ch from hook and in each ch across (70 sc); ch 1, turn. **2nd row:** Sc in first sc, * ch 4, skip 2 sc, sc in next sc. Repeat from * across (23 lps); ch 5, turn. **3rd row:** Sc in first lp, * ch 5, sc in next lp. Repeat from * across; ch 5, turn. **4th row:** Repeat last row, but ch 6 at end, turn. **5th, 6th and 7th rows:** Sc in first lp, * ch 6, sc in next lp. Repeat from * across; ch 6, turn. Omit ch 6 at end of last row. Break off.

FINISHING Join crochet cotton with sl st in first sc of 1st row, ch 5, sl st in same place as first sl st (button loop made); break off. Join crochet cotton with sl st in last sc of 1st row and ch 10; break off, leaving a long end. Twist end of chain around itself until it forms a small ball, then sew ball in place. Use as button to fasten collar around neck.

Quick-and-easy accessories to keep sales moving fast!

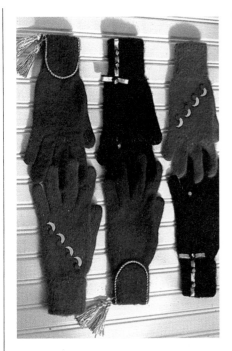

GLAMOUR FOR GLOVES Make elegant fashions of plain purchased knit gloves by transforming them with trims: cords, tassels and ribbons in silver or gold metallic, red plastic hearts, crescent-moon paillettes or whatever finery you fancy.

RIBBON-BELT BEAUTIES To lush velvet ribbons, add the sewn-on sparkle of sequined leaf-and-flower appliqués; hook-and-eye closings turn them into belts.

SEQUIN-SPANGLED COMBS Wrap clear plastic combs with sequins-by-the-yard and glue to hold; ends become streamers, pretty tipped with paillettes.

CLOTHESPIN KEY RINGS Brush bright stripes on clothespins with acrylic artists' paints; coat with high-gloss polyurethane. Glue clamp ends of *spring-type* pins shut around rings; attach rings to *round* pins with tiny screw eye.

TRIM TRICK FOR WEB BELTS Gold trim, handsewn to bought belts, gives a touch of glamour to the webbing belts that everyone's wearing.

DRESS A PLAIN PURSE FOR EVENING A purchased zip bag takes on formal charm when you sew on row after diagonal row of rickrack. One package does up a 5" by 7" purse.

Crocheted Bow Ties

(Project **9** in group photograph, page **18**)

Just the dapper dash of color a young shirt collar needs. Fun to make, fantastic for quantity crocheting.

SIZE About 4½″ wide.

MATERIALS Coats & Clark's Knit-Cro-Sheen cotton yarn, 1 (175-yard) ball main color (MC) makes 4 bow ties, 1 ball contrasting color (CC) trims about 58 bow ties; steel crochet hook size 1, **or the size that will give you the correct gauge;** safety pin or clip for fastener.

GAUGE 5 sc = 1″.

NOTE Work with thread double throughout.

TIE Starting at one end with MC, ch 13. **1st row:** Sc in 2nd ch from hook and in each ch across; ch 1, turn. **2nd row:** Sc in each sc across; ch 1, turn. Repeat last row until piece measures 4″. Break off. **Trim:** With CC, sl st in first sc, (ch 3 for picot, sl st in same sc where last sl st was made, sl st in next 2 sc) 5 times; ch 3, make picot, sl st in last sc. Break off. Work trim at other end of tie.

BAND Starting at one end with MC, ch 5. Work as for tie on 4 sc for 3″. Break off. Wrap band around center of tie and sew ends together. Tack to tie to hold in place. Add safety pin or clip for fastening.

Fringed Muff

Soft in tone and feeling, this mohair beauty is crocheted in one easy piece and self-lined.

SIZE Approximately 9″ x 13″.

MATERIALS Joseph Galler's Majestic Mohair, 4 (40-gram—about 1.4-ounce) balls mink No. 611 (color M), 2 balls each Hawaiian rose No. 604 (R) and copper No. 645 (C); aluminum crochet hook size K (or international size 7:00 mm) **or the size that will give you the correct gauge.**

GAUGE 5 post dc = 2″.

TO MAKE FRONT POST DC (F DC); Yo, insert hook from the front (right side) to back and to front again around vertical post (upright part) of next dc, yo and draw yarn through, yo and complete dc in usual manner.

TO MAKE BACK POST DC (B DC) Yo; reaching over top of piece, insert hook from back (right side) to front and to back again around vertical post of next dc, yo and draw yarn through, yo and complete dc in usual manner.

MUFF With R, starting inside muff, ch 35 to measure 13½″. **1st row (wrong side):** Dc in 4th ch from hook and in each ch across (33 dc); ch 1, turn. **2nd row:** Skip 1st st (directly below ch-1), f dc around each dc across, hdc in top of turning ch; ch 1, turn. **3rd row:** Skip hdc, b dc around each dc across, hdc in turning ch (horizontal ridges formed on wrong side); ch 1, turn. Repeat 2nd and 3rd rows 7 times (piece should measure 8½″). Break off R, attach M. **18th and 19th rows:** Repeat 2nd row twice (forms ridge on right side for fold line). **20th through 59th rows:** Repeat 2nd and 3rd rows in following colors: 2 rows M, 4 C, 1 R, 3 M, 1 C, 3 R, 1 C, 25 M. **60th and 61st rows:** With M, repeat 2nd row twice (forms ridge on right side). **62nd through 78th rows:** With C, repeat 2nd and 3rd rows 8 times, then repeat 2nd row once more. Break off.

FINISHING Fold piece along ridges so that first R section forms front lining and last C section forms back lining. Sew edges of starting ch and last row together on wrong side. With lining sections facing, fold again so ridges meet at lower edge to form muff. With M, sc across ridges through both thicknesses to join. Working through both thicknesses with M, sc around open ends of muff. **Strap:** With M, ch 6. **1st row:** Dc in 4th ch from hook and in each ch across (4 dc); ch 1, turn. Repeat 2nd and 3rd rows of muff until strap measures 32″. Break off. Following photograph, sew ends to muff. **Fringe:** Using 12″ strands of matching yarn, make 2-strand tassel in each row or stitch along front and lower edges (see General Tips, page 160).

Hair Ornaments

(Project **7** in group photograph, page **18**)

Floral trims are crocheted and created of ribbon and embroidered lace; barrettes have painted-on designs.

MATERIALS Coats & Clark's Knit-Cro-Sheen cotton yarn, 175-yard balls in assorted colors; steel crochet hook size 1; combs, barrettes and bobby pins; epoxy glue. **Ribbon ornaments:** ⅜"- to ⅝"-wide satin ribbon for flowers (1 yard makes 4); 1"- to 1¼"-wide satin ribbon for leaves (1 yard makes 14); sewing thread. **Embroidered lace ornaments:** Embroidered Venice lace-by-the-yard with distinct units that can be cut apart. **Painted barrettes:** Acrylic paint; clear nail polish.

CROCHETED ORNAMENTS

Use yarn double throughout.
Large flower Starting at center, ch 4. Join with sl st to form ring. **1st rnd:** Ch 1, work 6 sc in ring; join with sl st to first sc. **2nd rnd:** Ch 1, work 2 sc in each sc around (12 sc); join. **3rd rnd:** Ch 1, work sc around and inc 6 sc evenly spaced (18 sc); join. **4th rnd:** Ch 1, sc around and inc 9 sc (27 sc); join and break off.
Border: With another color, sl st in any sc, * ch 2, sl st in same sc (picot made); sl st in next 2 sc. Repeat from * around until 13 picots have been made; sl st in next 2 sc. Join and break off.
Large leaf Ch 13. Sl st in 2nd ch from hook; across ch work sc, hdc, 2 dc, tr, 2 dc, hdc, sc and sl st. Now turn piece around and work across opposite edge of ch in same manner with sl st, sc, hdc, 2 dc, tr, 2 dc, hdc, sc and sl st. Break off.
Small flower Work as for large flower through 2nd rnd. Break off.
Border: With another color, sl st in any sc, * ch 2, sl st in same sc (picot), sl st in next sc. Repeat from * around (12 picots); join and break off.
Small leaf Ch 9, sl st in 2nd ch from hook; across ch work sc, hdc, 2 dc, sc and sl st. Work across opposite edge of ch in same manner. Break off.
To assemble Following photograph, sew flower and leaves together. Glue to comb or bobby pin.

RIBBON ORNAMENTS

Flowers Cut 8" length of ribbon. Sew running stitches the full length of ribbon close to one edge. Pull up to gather. Roll tightly spiral fashion and sew (flower A), or roll around and around and sew (flower B).
Leaves Cut 2½" length of ribbon. Fold to form triangle (folds on 2 sides of triangle, raw ends of ribbon at base of triangle). Fold sides in again, overlapping bottom corners, and sew.
To assemble motifs Bobby-pin motif: Make 1 flower A with ⅜"-wide ribbon and 2 leaves with 1"-wide ribbon. Following photograph, sew pieces together and then sew motif to bobby pin. **Comb motif:** Make 4 flowers B with ⅜"-wide ribbon and 1 flower A with ⅝"-wide ribbon. Make 2 leaves with 1¼"-wide ribbon. Sew pieces together, then glue to comb.

EMBROIDERED LACE ORNAMENTS

Bobby-pin motif: Cut out 1 small flower and sew to bobby pin.
Comb motif: Cut out lace unit wide enough to fit comb. Glue to comb.

PAINTED BARRETTES

Using small brush and following photograph for designs (or make up your own), paint barrettes. When completely dry, brush on coat of clear nail polish.

Crocheted Flower Pins

(Project **6**, shown on turtleneck collars in group photograph, page **18**.)

These are made the same way as the small crocheted flowers and leaves under Hair Ornaments, left. Assemble as shown in photograph and glue or sew to pin back.

chain &
crochet H

Cable-cord Tote-all

Crocheted carryall in a hold-everything size. Cord makes it sturdy, filet mesh pattern gives a light look.

SIZE Bag measures 15″ square.

MATERIALS Lily Sugar-'n-Cream, 4 (125-yard) balls ecru No. 4; aluminum crochet hook size G (or international hook size 4:50 mm) **or the size that will give you the correct gauge.**

GAUGE 5 sp = 3″.

SIDE PANEL (make 2) Panel is composed of center square and a border.

Center square Starting at lower edge, ch 38 loosely. **1st row:** Work dc in 6th ch from hook, * ch 1, skip next ch, dc in next ch. Repeat from * across (17 sp made—turning ch always counts as 1 sp); ch 4, turn. **2nd row:** Skip 1st sp, dc in next dc, * ch 1, dc in next dc. Repeat from * 3 times more (5 sp); work bl over next sp as follows: Yo, insert hook in next ch-1 sp and draw up lp, yo and draw through 2 lps on hook, yo, insert hook in same ch-1 sp and draw up lp, yo and draw through all 3 lps on hook to complete cl; work dc in next dc (bl completed); work bl over next sp, work sp over each of next 3 sp, bl over each of next 2 sp, sp over each of last 5 sp, working dc in 3rd ch of turning ch to complete last sp; ch 4, turn. **3rd row:** Work 4 sp, 1 bl, then work bl over bl as follows: Yo, insert hook in next cl and draw up lp, yo and draw through 2 lps on hook, yo, insert hook in same cl and draw up lp, yo and draw through 2 lps on hook, yo and draw through all 3 lps on hook to complete cl, dc in next dc (bl over bl completed); work bl over next bl, bl over next sp, sp over next sp, work 4 bl, 4 sp; ch 4, turn. Starting with 4th row on diagram, continue to work sp and bl, completing diagram. Piece should measure about 11″ square. Do not break off but continue for border.

Border Ch 3, turn. **1st rnd:** Work bl in 1st sp, work (1 sp, 1 bl) 8 times, ending in corner sp, ch 2 for corner lp; working along adjacent side of square, work 1 bl in same corner sp (last dc of bl is worked in

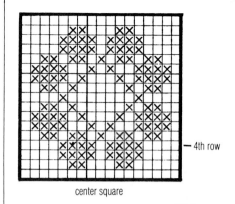

— 4th row

center square

⊠ bl

☐ sp

next st on side of square). * Work along side of square to match 1st side; work corner as before. Repeat from * once more; work 4th side of square as before, ending with ch-2 corner lp; join with sl st to top of ch-3; ch 4. **2nd rnd:** Work (1 sp, 1 bl) 8 times; 1 sp. Over corner lp work (bl, ch 2 and bl) for corner. Continue around in pattern, ending in last corner lp with bl, ch 2 and cl; join to 3rd ch of ch-4; ch 3. **3rd rnd:** Work (1 bl, 1 sp) 9 times; work corner in corner lp. Continue around in pattern, ending with corner and 1 sp; join. Break off.

JOINING 1st row: Work sc in back lp of each st on 3 sides of panel, working 3 sc in 2 corners. Sl st panels tog on the 3 sides where last row was worked. Work rnd of sc in back lp of each st around open edge; join and break off.

HANDLES (make 2) Ch 46 to measure about 14″. **1st row:** Sc in 2nd ch from hook and in each ch across; ch 1, turn. **2nd and 3rd rows:** Sc in each sc across; ch 1, turn. Break off. Sew one end of each handle to wrong side of open edge of bag 1″ from top and about 3″ from joining. Sew other end to corresponding place 3″ from opposite joining on same side of bag.

Crochet-edge Hankies

Give plain white handkerchiefs an edge on the competition with borders of crocheted pearl cotton.

SIZE 1"-wide crocheted edgings.

MATERIALS Purchased 11"-square handkerchiefs with ⅛"-wide plain hems; DMC Pearl Cotton size 8, 1 (95-yard) ball for each hankie; steel crochet hook size 10, **or the size that will give you the correct gauge.**

GAUGE 4 sp = 1".

NOTE Edgings are the same on all hankies in photograph.

1st rnd: Starting at center of one edge, insert hook in hankie at base of hem and work sc over hem, * skip about ⅛" of hem, sc over hem. Repeat from * to within ⅛" of corner, making 44 sc; in corner work 3 sc (corner group). ** Make 87 sc along next edge; work corner group in next corner. Repeat from ** twice more; work 43 sc on remaining half of first edge; sl st in first sc.

2nd rnd: Ch 6, skip next sc, dc in next sc, (ch 3, skip next sc, dc in next sc) 20 times, * ch 3, skip next 2 sc, in next (corner) sc work dc, ch 3, dc (corner shell); ch 3, skip next 2 sc, dc in next sc, (ch 3, skip next sc, dc in next sc) 42 times. Repeat from * twice more; ch 3, complete rnd in pattern, ending ch 3; join with sl st in 3rd ch of ch-6 (44 sp on each side, corner shell in each corner).

3rd rnd: Sl st in next sp, ch 6, dc in next sp, * ch 3, dc in next sp *. ** Repeat from * to * to corner sp; ch 3, work corner shell in corner sp. Repeat from ** 3 times more; complete rnd in pattern; ch 3, join (45 sp on each side, corner shell in each corner).

4th rnd: Repeat last rnd (46 sp on each side, corner shell in each corner).

5th rnd: Sl st in next sp, ch 3; in next sp work 4 dc (group made); dc in next sp, * (ch 1, dc in next dc, ch 1, dc in next sp) 3 times; work group in next sp, dc in next sp *. Repeat from * to * 3 times more, ending last repeat with group; ch 1, in next (corner) sp work (dc, ch 1) 3 times; work group in next sp, dc in next sp. Repeat from * to * 9 times, ending last repeat with group; ch 1, work corner. Complete rnd in pattern, ending sl st in top of ch-3 (10 groups on each side).

6th rnd: Sl st in each of next 2 dc, ch 8, tr in next dc, ch 4, tr in next dc; * skip next dc, sc in next dc, (ch 4, skip next dc, sc in next dc) twice; skip next dc. Make shell as follows: (Tr in next dc, ch 4) 3 times, tr in next dc (shell made). Repeat from * 3 times more; work corner as follows: Sc in next dc, (ch 4, sc in next dc) twice; work shell; skip next dc, sc in next dc. Complete rnd in pattern, working 10 shells on each side and ending ch 4; sl st in 4th ch of ch-8 to complete first shell. Break off.

Minibag Quartet in Crochet

Novel shapes in tiny sizes, to go over the shoulder or around the neck.

WEDGE (BLUE-AND-GOLD) MINIBAG

SIZE About 2½" deep.

MATERIALS DMC Pearl Cotton No. 5, 1 (53-yard) ball blue No. 798; Bucilla Spotlight (polyester/nylon metallic yarn), 1 (0.7-ounce) ball gold; steel crochet hook No. 1, **or the size that will give you the correct gauge.**

GAUGE 17 cotton sts = 2"; 16 rnds = 2".

BAG Hexagon Starting at center with blue, ch 6. Join with sl st to form ring. **1st rnd:** Work 12 sc in ring. Do not join but work around and around spirally. Work in back lp of each st throughout. **2nd rnd:** (Work 3 sc in next sc for corner, sc in next

sc) 6 times (24 sc). Drop blue; attach gold. **3rd rnd:** Sc in each sc around. Drop gold; pick up blue. **4th rnd:** Sc in next sc, (3 sc in next sc for corner, sc in each of next 3 sc) 5 times; 3 sc in next sc, sc in last 2 sc (36 sc). Change yarns and repeat 3rd rnd. Change yarns. **6th rnd:** Sc in next 2 sc, (3 sc in next sc, sc in next 5 sc) 5 times; 3 sc in next sc, sc in last 3 sc (48 sc). Change yarns and repeat 3rd rnd. Change yarns. Continuing to alternate yarns, work 5 more rnds, working 3 sc at each corner on blue rnds (84 sc on last rnd). Sl st in next rnd. Break off. Hexagon should measure about 3½" from corner to opposite corner. Fold hexagon in half, corner to corner (see photograph), and sew sides with blue to form bag.

Top section 1st rnd: With gold, work sc in each sc around top opening. Drop gold; attach blue. **2nd rnd:** Sc in each sc around. Change yarns. Alternating yarns, repeat 2nd rnd 6 times more. Sl st in next sc. Break off.

HANDLE With blue, crochet 30" chain. Sl st in 2nd ch from hook and

in each ch across. Break off. Sew ends of cord inside opening.

TUBE (SILVER) MINIBAG

SIZE 3" long, without tassel.

MATERIALS Bucilla Spotlight (polyester/nylon metallic yarn), 1 (0.7-ounce) ball silver; steel crochet hook No. 0, **or the size that will give you the correct gauge.**

GAUGE 6 sc = 1"; 7 rnds = 1".

BAG Starting at bottom, ch 4. Join with sl st to form ring. **1st rnd:** Work 6 sc in ring. Do not join but work around and around spirally, marking beg of each rnd. **2nd rnd:** Work 2 sc in each sc around (12 sc). **3rd rnd:** Sc in each sc around. Repeat last rnd until piece measures 3". Sl st in next st. Do not break off, but work handle as follows:

HANDLE * Ch 16; holding back on hook the last lp of each dc, work 4 dc in 3rd ch from hook, yo and draw through all 5 lps on hook (cl made). Repeat from * 10 times more, ch 10; sl st in top edge of purse on opposite side from start of handle. Break off.

TASSEL Cut seven 10" strands of yarn. Draw them, one at a time, halfway through bottom of bag. Fold in half and wind tightly with strand of yarn for ½", leaving end long enough to thread in needle. Fasten yarn at top and tuck in end.

CIRCLE (GREEN-AND GOLD) MINIBAG

SIZE 3¾" diameter.

MATERIALS DMC Pearl Cotton No. 5, 2 (53-yard) balls green No. 906; Bucilla Spotlight (polyester/nylon metallic yarn), 1 (0.7-yard) ball gold; steel crochet hook No. 2, **or the size that will give you the correct gauge.**

GAUGE 17 sc = 2"; 17 rnds = 2".

BAG Back Starting at center with gold, ch 6. Join with sl st to form

ring. **1st rnd:** Work 8 sc in ring. Do not join but work around and around spirally, marking beg of each rnd. **2nd rnd:** Work 2 sc in each sc around (16 sc). **3rd rnd:** Sl st in next st, ch 3; holding back on hook the last lp of each dc, work 3 dc in same st where sl st was worked, yo and draw through all 4 lps on hook (1st cl made); * ch 4, skip next sc, work 4-dc cl in next sc. Repeat from * 6 times more, ch 4; join with sl st to top of ch-3. Break off. Piece should measure 1½″ in diameter. **4th rnd:** With green, sl st in any ch-4 lp, ch 3, work 5 dc in same lp, work 6 dc in each of next 7 lps. **5th rnd:** Sc in each dc around, increasing 8 sc evenly spaced (56 sc). Work in back lp of each st from now on. Work 2 more rnds, increasing 8 sc on each rnd (72 sc). Break off; attach gold and work 1 rnd even. Break off; attach green and work until circle is about 3¾″ in diameter, increasing where necessary to keep piece flat. Sl st in next st. Break off.

Front Work as directed for back.

Hold circles tog, wrong sides facing; with green, sl st tog about two-thirds of the way around. Break off.

TASSELS Mark 4 sts, about 1″ apart, centered along lower edge of bag. With gold, ch 4, sl st in a marked st, turn, work 3 sl sts along chain. Break off. Make tassel at end of chain as for Tube Minibag, above, winding with green. Make tassel at each marker.

HANDLE Crochet 30″ chain with double strand of pearl cotton, or cut four 2-yard lengths of pearl cotton and make twisted cord. Sew ends of the handle at ends of joining inside the bag.

SQUARE (RED) MINIBAG

SIZE About 3″.

MATERIALS DMC Pearl Cotton No. 5, 2 (53-yard) balls red No. 666; Bucilla Spotlight (polyester/nylon metallic yarn), 1 (0.7-ounce) ball

silver; steel crochet hook No. 2, **or the size that will give you the correct gauge.**

GAUGE 17 sc = 2″; 17 rnds = 2″.

BAG Starting at bottom with red, ch 30 for base chain. **1st rnd:** Work 3 sc in 2nd ch from hook, sc in each ch across, working 3 sc in last ch; turn piece around with same side facing you and continue to work sc in bottom of each st of base chain. Do not join but work around and around spirally, marking beg of each rnd. **2nd rnd:** Sc in back lp of each sc around. Repeat last rnd until bag measures about 3″. **Next rnd:** Work reverse sc from *left to right* around top edge (see diagram). Break off.

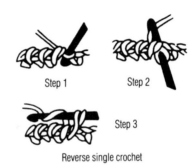

Step 1　　Step 2

Step 3

Reverse single crochet

DANGLE BALL With red, ch 2. **1st rnd:** Work 6 sc in 2nd ch from hook. Work in rnds in back lp of each st. **2nd rnd:** Work 2 sc in each sc around (12 sc). **3rd rnd:** Sc in each sc around. Repeat last rnd twice more. **6th rnd:** * Draw up lp in each of next 2 sc, yo and draw through both lps on hook. Repeat from * 5 times more. Stuff ball with bits of red, then sl st across top to close; ch 11, sl st in top edge of bag on center of one side, then sc in each ch. Break off; thread end in needle and run through ball, fastening at bottom.

HANDLE With metallic yarn, crochet 30″ chain. Sc in 2nd ch from hook

and in each ch across. Break off. Draw ends of ch through purse at sides. Make tassels as for Tube Minibag, above, cutting 5″ strands and winding with red.

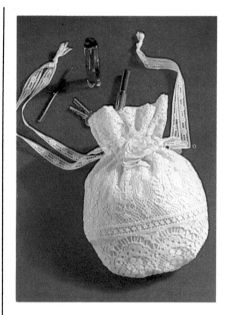

Satin-and-lace Evening Pouch

SIZE 8″ wide x 10″ deep.

MATERIALS ¼ yard 45″-wide white satin; ¼ yard 22″-wide white lace; 1 yard 1″-wide white moiré ribbon; 2 yards ½″-wide lace insertion (straight edges); ⅜ yard 1″-wide lace; white sewing thread; tracing paper.

For pattern, draw 9″ x 11″ rectangle on tracing paper, then curve one corner. Trace same curve on other corner on same 9″ edge. Use pattern to cut 4 satin and 2 lace pieces (½″ seam allowance included on all edges).

Place 2 satin pieces wrong sides together, then baste 1 lace piece on top. Repeat with other 3 pieces. Cut two 9″ lengths of moiré ribbon, turn in ends ½″ and topstitch. Pin ribbons across lace, 3″ down from uncurved edge; topstitch close to long edges to form casing for ties.

With lace sides facing, pin pouch pieces together; stitch sides and bottom; turn. Fold in top edges and topstitch. On inside of pouch, turn in raw edges of seam allowance at each side for 3″ and slipstitch neatly.

Cut lace insertion in half. Starting at one side seam, run one length of the lace through both casings, bringing end out at same side seam. Knot ends together. Repeat with other length, starting at opposite side seam. Pull ties to close pouch.

For rosette, use remaining moiré ribbon. Starting about 1″ from one end, fold, twist and roll ribbon around and around the end to form rosette. Sew to hold shape. Sew running stitches close to one edge of 1″-wide lace, pull up tightly and sew ends together to form circle. Sew lace circle to one side of pouch just below casing and sew rosette to circle.

Calico Conveniences

(Project **11** in group photograph, page **18**)

Purse-size cases for makeup, tissues and eyeglasses. Coordinate a collection (see detail at left) and sell them as sets.

SIZES Makeup kit, 5" x 8"; tissue holder, 3½" x 6¼"; eyeglass case, 4½" x 7".

MATERIALS 45"-wide reversible quilted calico (½ yard makes 4 makeup or 7 eyeglass cases); 45"-wide unquilted calico (⅜ yard each of 2 coordinated prints makes 7 tissue holders); sewing thread to match lining; snap fastener or self-fastening tape circles (1 per makeup case).

MAKEUP KIT

Cut piece of quilted fabric 9¾" x 14¾". For binding effect, turn all edges ¼" to right side and press, then ½" more and topstitch. Fold up one end of piece 5" to form case; topstitch along sides over previous stitching. Sew fastener halves to purse and flap.

TISSUE HOLDER

Cut piece of unquilted outer fabric 6" x 7". Cut piece of lining fabric (which will also form binding) 7¾" x 8½". Form binding effect as for Calico Checkbook Holder, below. Fold ends to meet at center and topstitch along sides over previous stitching.

EYEGLASS CASE

Cut piece of quilted fabric 5¾" x 16". Form binding effect as for Makeup Kit, above. Fold piece in half crosswise and topstitch along sides over previous stitching.

Calico Checkbook Holder

(Project **8** in group photograph, page **18**)

Styled so lining fabric folds back for a crisp binding effect. Coordinate with calico cases for an unbeatable combination.

SIZE 3¾" x 7¼".

MATERIALS 45-wide calico (⅜ yard each of 2 coordinated prints makes 5); sewing thread to match lining and binding print.

Cut piece of outer fabric 7¼" x 10½". Cut lining fabric (which will also form binding effect) to 8¾" x 12". For binding effect, turn lining in and press ¼" on all edges. Then, with wrong sides facing, center and pin outer fabric on lining. Fold edges of lining over edges of outer fabric and topstitch. Fold up one end of piece 3¼" to form case; topstitch along sides over previous stitching lines.

Wooden-key key chains

(Project **10** in group photograph, page **18**)

Simple wooden shapes painted in brilliant colors and threaded with chain. One 2' by 4' piece of ¼" plywood will make about 144.

MATERIALS Scrap ¼"-thick plywood (2' x 4' piece–¼ sheet–makes about 144); acrylic paint and primer; sandpaper; spackle; key chain; coping saw.

Enlarge key shape (see page 158 for enlarging instructions). Make pattern and cut plywood with coping saw. Sand and fill edges with spackle. Drill hole in top. Prime, then paint with 2 coats acrylic paint. Thread chain through hole. See page 161 for general guidance in woodworking.

Each sq. = ½"

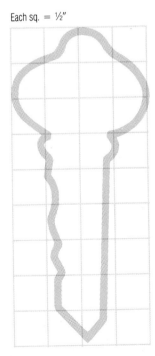

Little
charmers
for
children

Starting at top left: **1.** Bug-eyed moose and giraffe hand puppets, page 79. **2.** Knitted mittens and cap, page 68. **3.** Soft baby blocks, page 73. **4.** Pompon dog, and **5.** Pompon owl, kitty and squirrel, page 77. **6.** Wiggly-snake pull toy, page 86. **7.** Stick-doll puppets, page 85. **8.** Pink-gingham stuffed pig, page 74. **9.** Snowboy and snowgirl sock dolls, page 84. **10.** Pin-striped bunny, page 77. **11.** Checked tabard apron, page 71. **12.** Polka-dot beanbag doll, page 80. **13.** Tooth-fairy pillow, page 85. **14.** Knitted stuffed lion, page 73. **15.** Crocheted baby bootees, page 68. **16.** Autograph cat pillow, page 82. **17.** Tiny finger puppets, page 86. **18.** Wooden push-toy cars, page 87.

Irresistible clothes for kids begins with baby things—the most adorable sweaters, hats and mittens, bootees and buntings, you've ever seen anywhere. Watch the customers cluster around these! They are all knitted or crocheted, as are most of the bigger kids' clothes that follow (the exceptions involve sewing or appliqué). Children old enough to have preferences like lighthearted designs in cheerful colors, so naturally that's what we feature.

Treasure-house of toys emphasizes simple designs because that's the kind of playthings children love best. (They're also easier for unskilled hands to make.) Many will cost you under a dollar to produce, especially if you collect yarn, fabric and wood scraps in quantity and make the toys in multiples. Little ones can help with some of the crafting. Pompon animals, for instance, just seem to be *made* for small hands to handle.

irresistible clothes for kids

There's nothing quite so appealing as a booth brimful of handmades for children, and our designs have especially winning ways. Your needleworkers will adore them, and they'll attract delighted buyers like a magnet.

Crochet Hat and Sacque

Darling outfit is mostly shells, with satin ribbons woven through edgings.

SIZES (6 to 12 months) [(12 to 18 months)]. Hat measures 13″ [13½″] at face edge. Sacque fits loosely and measures 12″ [13″] across back at underarms, 9½″ [10½″] from shoulder to lower edge.

MATERIALS 7 [8] ounces acrylic baby yarn; aluminum crochet hook size F for (6 to 12 months) [size G for (12 to 18 months)] (or international hook size 4:00 mm [size 4:50 mm]) **or the size that will give you the correct gauge;** satin ribbon, 2 yards ½″-wide for hat and 1½ yards ¼″-wide for sacque; sewing needle; matching thread.

GAUGE With size F hook: 9 sc = 2″; 5 sc rows = 1″. With size G hook: 4 sc = 1″; 9 sc rows = 2″.

HAT

Back section Starting at center back, ch 4. Join with sl st to form ring. **1st rnd:** Ch 3, work 6 shells (see 1st row of body for shell pattern, but work in large lp to right of each shell) in ring. Do not join rnds. **2nd rnd:** Work 2 shells in each shell around (12 shells). **3rd rnd:** Repeat last rnd (24 shells). **4th rnd:** * Work 2 shells in next shell, 1 shell in next shell. Repeat from * around (36 shells); ch 3, turn.

Side section Work in rows from now on. **1st row:** Work even in shell pattern across 32 shells, do not work last 4 shells; ch 3, turn. Work even on 32 shells until hat measures 7″ [7½″] from beg of hat. Repeat sleeve border for scallops. Break off.

Cuff Turn back last 1½″ of work to right side and sew at each end (neck edge).

FINISHING Neckband Working in rows of sc, draw in neckband to measure 8″ [8½″]. Work even in sc for 1″, then work 1 more row, working picot between each 4 sc (for picot: ch 3, sc in first st of ch). Break off.

Weaving ribbon through both thicknesses, weave ribbon through spaces between shells ¾″ from folded front edge. With sewing needle and matching thread, sew 3 loops in ribbon at each corner of cuff. Tack ends securely.

SACQUE

Yoke Starting at neck edge, ch 51 loosely to measure about 11″ [12″]. **1st row:** Sc in 2nd st from hook and in next 6 ch for one front, work 3 sc in next ch (2 sc inc); sc in next 7 ch for one sleeve, inc 2 sc in next ch; sc in next 18 ch for back, inc in next ch; sc in next 7 ch for other sleeve, inc in next ch; sc in last 7 ch for other front (8 sc inc on row); ch 1, turn.

2nd row: Sc in first 8 sc, inc in next sc, sc in next 9 sc, inc in next sc; sc in next 20 sc, inc in next sc; sc in next 9 sc, inc in next sc; sc in last 8 sc (8 sc inc); ch 1, turn.

Continue in this manner for 8 rows more, working inc in center sc of each inc group of last row (130 sc); ch 1, turn.

To divide for body and sleeves Sc in first 18 sc, ch 10 for one underarm; sk next 28 sc, sc in next 38 sc, ch 10 for other underarm; sk next 28 sc, sc in last 18 sc; ch 3, turn. Starting with a right-side row, work in shell pattern as follows:

Body: Shell pattern 1st row: Yo, draw up ½″ lp in next sc, yo and draw through 2 lps on hook, (yo, draw up ½″ lp in same sc, yo and draw through 2 lps on hook) 3 times; yo and draw through all lps on hook, ch 1 (shell made); work shell in next sc, (sk next sc, work shell in each of next 3 sc) 4 times (14 shells). Work 5 shells across underarm ch as follows: (Sk 1 sc,

work shell in next ch) 5 times, then mark ch st at base of center shell on underarm. Work across sts of back as follows: Sk first sc, shell in next sc, (sk 1 sc, shell in each of next 2 sc) 12 times (25 shells). Work 5 shells across ch at underarm; work shell in each of next 2 sc, (sk 1 sc, shell in each of next 3 sc) 4 times (14 shells); ch 3, turn.

2nd row: (**NOTE** When working in shells, work in large lp to left, of each shell.) Work shell in first shell, * work shell in next shell. Repeat from * across (shells fall between shells of last row); ch 3, turn.

Repeating 2nd row for pattern, work even on 63 shells until shell section measures 6½″ [7″]. Omit turning ch at end of last row, break off.

SLEEVE Work back and forth in rows, starting and ending each row at marker. Make lp on hook and with right side of work facing you, sl st in marked st at center of underarm.

1st row: Ch 3, work shell in each of next 3 ch-1 sp between shells of body, then work as follows across last sc row of yoke: Yo, insert hook in sc where last shell of body was worked and draw up long lp, yo and draw through 2 lps on hook, yo, draw up long lp in next sc, yo and draw through 2 lps on hook, yo and draw up long lp in next st, yo and draw through 2 lps on hook, yo and draw up long lp in same st, yo and draw through 2 lps on hook, complete shell as before (shell worked over 3 sts); (sk 1 sc, shell in next sc) 13 times, working last shell over last sc and in sc where last shell of body was worked. Work shell in each of next 3 ch-2 sp between shells of body (20 shells in all). Do not join; ch 3, turn.

Repeating 2nd row of shell pattern of body, work even on 20 shells for 2″ [2½″]; ch 3, turn.

Next row (dec row): Work half shell in first shell as follows: Work as for shell, completing after 2 of

the usual 4 steps; work in shell pattern to last st, work half shell in last st; ch 3, turn.

Following row: Sk half shell, work in shell pattern across, work dc in top of half shell; ch 3, turn.

Working on 18 shells, continue in pattern until sleeve measures about 6″ [6½″] from beg of shell pattern, ending with a wrong-side row; ch 1, turn.

Border (right side) Sc in top of first shell, * sk 1 shell, work scallop of 5 sc in next shell, sk 2 shells, work scallop in next shell. Repeat from * across. Join and break off.

Work other sleeve to correspond.

FINISHING Sew sleeve seams. **Border 1st row:** Make lp on hook and, with wrong side facing you, work across opposite edge of starting ch as follows: Sl st in first st, ch 3, dc in each st across for beading; ch 1, turn.

2nd row (right side): Sc in next 4 dc, ch 3, sc in first st of ch (picot made). Continue in this manner across last row. Working in same manner, sc along left front edge of yoke, making picots every ½″, then continue across left front edge, lower edge and right front edge as follows: Sc in edge of work, * sk ½″ of work, work 5-dc scallop in edge of work, sk ½″ of work, sc in edge of work. Repeat from *, working scallop in each corner of work. Work across right front edge of yoke to correspond to left front edge; join with sl st to first st and break off.

Cut 26″ length of ribbon for neck and two 14″ lengths for sleeves. Weave neck ribbon through beading row and tie in front. Starting at top of sleeve and using spaces between last 2 rows of shell pattern on sleeve, weave sleeve ribbons through spaces and tie ends.

Surplice Sweater and Hat

Fun-to-crochet sweater has cable border, straight sleeves; hat is cuffed.

SIZES 6 months (11 to 18 pounds) [12 months (19 to 24 pounds)]. Sweater measures 10½″ [11½″] across back. Circumference of hat is about 15″ [16″].

MATERIALS Brunswick Fore-'n-Aft Sport (acrylic sport-weight yarn). 4 (2-ounce) balls light powder blue No. 60111; aluminum crochet hooks sizes F and H (or international hook sizes 4:00 mm and 5:00 mm) **or the sizes that will give you the correct gauges;** 1 small button; snap fastener.

GAUGES With size F hook: 5 sc = 1″. With size H hook: 4 sts = 1″.

SWEATER

BACK: Ribbed border With smaller hook ch 7 for side edge. **1st row:** Sc in 2nd ch from hook and in each ch across; ch 1, turn. **2nd row:** Working in back lp, sc in each sc across (6 sc); ch 1, turn.

Repeat last row for pattern until border measures 10½″ [11½″] when stretched slightly. At end of last row do not break off; ch 1, turn.

Change to larger hook and, spacing sts evenly, work 43 [47] sc across one long edge of border.

Pattern stitch 1st row (wrong side): Sc in first sc, * hdc in next sc, sc in next sc. Repeat from * across; ch 1, turn. **2nd row:** Sc in each st across.

Repeat 1st and 2nd rows for pattern until piece measures 9½″ [10″] from beg (there is no armhole shaping). Work across first 13 [14] sts only for 2 rows. Break off. Skip center 17 [19] sts, work last 13 [14] sts for 2 rows. Break off. This is shoulder edge.

LEFT FRONT: Ribbed border Marking beg for front edge, work as for back until border measures 8½″ [9½″]; ch 1, turn (this is side edge; put marker at top edge 1″ from other end of border at front edge). Change to larger hook and, with right side of work facing you, work 33 [37] sc evenly across one long edge between side edge and marker; ch 1, turn.

Work in pattern st as for back and *at same time* dec 1 st at front edge only every other row 10 [11] times; then dec at same edge every row 10 [12] times. Work even, if necessary, on 13 [14] sts until piece is same length as back to shoulder. Break off. Leave marker in work for cable border to be worked later.

RIGHT FRONT Work as for left front, reversing shaping. **Shoulder seams:** Holding back and fronts with right side facing you and using crochet hook and yarn, sl st shoulder seams.

SLEEVE For one sleeve put 2 markers at side edge of work, each marker 3¾″ [4″] from shoulder seam. With right side of work facing you and using larger hook, work 31 [33] sc between markers; ch 1, turn.

Work even in pattern st for 5½″ [6½″], ending with right-side row.

Cable border Change to smaller hook. **1st row (wrong side):** Sc across and dec evenly to 28 sts; ch 1, turn. **2nd row (cable row):** Sc in first st, ch 3, skip next 2 sc, sc in next sc, turn; sc in each of 3 ch sts, sl st in first sc, turn; holding ch-3 lp down on right side of work, sc in each of 2 skipped sts, sc in next sc already worked into, * ch 3, skip 2 sc, sc in next sc, turn; sc in each of 3 ch sts, sl st in next sc worked before ch-3, turn; holding ch-3 lp down, sc in each of 2 skipped sts, sc in next sc already worked into. Repeat from * across; ch 1, turn. **3rd and 4th rows:** Sc in each sc across. At end of last row do not break off, sl st along sleeve and side seams. Break off. Make other sleeve in same manner.

FINISHING: Cable border 1st row (right side): Starting at marker above ribbed border on left front, with smaller hook and wrong side of work facing you, sc evenly along left front edge, back neck edge and right front edge to next marker, having a number of sts divisible by 3 plus 1; ch 1, turn. Repeat 2nd, 3rd and 4th rows of cable border of sleeve. Break off.

Sew ends of cable border to top edge of ribbed border.

Button loop Sl st at lower edge of right front ribbed border, ch 5, skip ½″ of border, sc in edge of work. Break off. Sew button near left side seam. Sew snap fastener to point on left front and to right side seam.

HAT

Ribbed border for cuff With smaller hook, ch 15 and, working on 14 sc, work as for ribbed border of back until piece measures 15″ [16″] when stretched slightly. At end of last row do not break off; ch 1, turn.

Cable border 1st row (wrong side): Work 61 [64] sc evenly across one long edge of cuff; ch 1, turn. Repeat 2nd, 3rd and 4th rows of cable border of sleeve. Change to larger hook and, starting with a wrong-side row and working on 61 [64] sts, repeat 1st and 2nd rows of pattern st of back until hat measures 7" [7½"] from lower edge of cuff. **Next row:** * Dec 1 sc over next 2 sts. Repeat from * across, work last 1 [0] sc; ch 1, turn. Repeat last row once more. Break off. Gather last row worked and sew opening closed, then with right side of work facing you, sl st back seam of hat. Break off. Turn half of ribbed cuff to right side.

Ties (make 2) With larger hook and using yarn double, crochet ch 10" [11"] long. Break off. Spacing ties evenly apart, sew one end of each to cuff of hat 1" from fold. Knot ends.

Two-tone Helmet and Mitts

Sweet set is a snap to knit.

SIZE Fits 17" to 18" head.

MATERIALS Bucilla Winsom (acrylic sport-weight yarn), 1 (2-ounce) skein each royal No. 292 (color R) and blue heather No. 313 (B); 1 set (4) size 9 dp needles (or English needles size 4) **or the size that will give you the correct gauge;** ½"-diameter button; aluminum crochet hook size F (or international hook size 4:00 mm).

GAUGE 4 sts = 1".

HELMET

Starting at top with color B, cast on 6 sts; divide evenly on 3 needles. **1st rnd:** K around. **2nd rnd:** Inc in each st around (12 sts). K 1 rnd. **4th rnd:** (K 1, inc in next st) 6 times (18 sts). K 1 rnd. **6th rnd:** (K 2, inc in next st) 6 times (24 sts). K 1 rnd. Repeat last 2 rnds, working 1 more st between incs on each inc rnd until there are 78 sts on needles. K 4 rnds. Break off B; join R. P 1 rnd. Work in k 1, p 1 ribbing for 6 rnds. Piece should measure about 5½" from beg.

Next rnd: Work 57 sts in ribbing; bind off remaining 21 sts for face opening. Work back and forth in rows as follows: **1st row:** K 3, sl 1, k 1, psso, rib to last 5 sts, k 2 tog, k 3. **2nd through 4th rows:** Keeping first and last 3 sts in garter st and working remainder in ribbing, work 3 rows even. Repeat last 4 rows twice more (51 sts).

To shape lower back edge Work short rows in established pattern as follows: **1st row:** Work across. **2nd row:** Work 20 sts; turn. **3rd row:** Sl 1, work to end. **4th row:** Work 15 sts; turn. **5th row:** Repeat 3rd row. **6th row:** Work 10 sts; turn. **7th row:** Repeat 3rd row. **8th row:** Work 5 sts; turn. **9th row:** Repeat 3rd row. Repeat 1st through 9th rows once more (short rows will be at opposite end). Bind off all sts.

FINISHING Sew button at lower left front corner. **Chin strap** With crochet hook sl st at lower right front corner, ch 20. **1st row:** Sc in 2nd ch from hook and in each ch across; sl st in edge of hat; turn. **2nd row:** Sc in first 2 sc, (ch 3, skip next 3 sc, sc in next sc) 3 times; ch 3, skip next 3 sc, sc in last 2 sc; ch 1, turn. **3rd row:** Sc in each sc and ch st across; sl st in edge of hat. Break off. (Four buttonholes are for adjustable fit.)

MITTS

Starting at cuff with R, cast on 26 sts; divide evenly on 3 needles. Join, being careful not to twist sts. K 1, p 1 in ribbing for 2¼". K 2 rnds.

To shape thumb 1st rnd: K 12, place marker on needle, inc in next 2 sts, place marker on needle, k 12. K 1 rnd. **3rd rnd:** K 12, sl marker, inc in next st, k 2, inc in next st, sl marker, k 12. K 1 rnd. Repeat last 2 rnds, having 2 more sts between inc sts, until there are 12 sts between markers (36 sts in all). Work in rows as follows: **1st row:** K 23. **2nd row:** P 10. **3rd row:** K 10. **4th row:** P 10. Repeat 3rd and 4th rows once more. **7th row:** (K 2 tog) 5 times. **8th row:** P 1, (p 2 tog) twice. Break off, draw end through remaining sts, pull up tight and secure. Sew edges of rows tog to form thumb.

Join yarn and work in stockinette st in rnds on remaining 26 sts until piece measures 4½" from beg. Break off R; join B. P 1 rnd, then work even in stockinette st until piece measures 6" from beg.

To shape tip 1st rnd: * (K 2, k 2 tog) twice; k 3, k 2 tog. Repeat from * once more. **2nd rnd:** K around. **3rd rnd:** * (K 1, k 2 tog) twice; k 2, k 2 tog. Repeat from * once more. **4th rnd:** K around. **5th rnd:** * (K 2 tog) twice; k 1, k 2 tog. Repeat from * once more. Break off, draw end through remaining sts, pull up tight and secure.

No-thumbs Mittens and Bonnet

Knitted mittens and bonnet; crocheted topknot, ties and edging.

SIZE Bonnet fits 15″ to 16″ head.

MATERIALS 3 ounces knitting-worsted-weight yarn; 1 set (4) size 7 dp needles (or English needles size 6) **or the size that will give you the correct gauge;** aluminum crochet hook size F (or international hook size 4:00 mm).

GAUGE 5 sts = 1″.

MITTENS

Starting at wrist, cast on 24 sts. Divide sts evenly on 3 needles. Join, being careful not to twist sts. Working in rnds, k 1, p 1 in ribbing for 1½″. **Next row (beading row):** (Yo, k 2 tog) 12 times. **Following rnd:** K, inc 4 sts evenly spaced (28 sts). Work even in stockinette st for 2″. **To shape tip 1st rnd:** (K 2, k 2 tog) 7 times. K 1 rnd. **3rd rnd:** (K 1, k 2 tog) 7 times. K 1 rnd. **5th rnd:** (K 2 tog) 7 times. Break off, leaving 8″ end. Thread end in tapestry needle, draw through remaining sts, pull up tight and fasten off. **Drawstring** With crochet hook make 20″ chain. Sc in 2nd ch from hook and in each ch across. Break off. Weave through holes on beading row. Tie in bow.

BONNET

Starting at lower edge of back, cast on 47 sts. Work back and forth in rows on 2 needles. **1st row (short row):** K 1, p 1, k 1, place marker on needle, p and k in next st, p 1, k 1; turn. **2nd row (short row):** (P 1, k 1) twice; sl marker, p 1, k 1, p 1. **3rd row (short row):** K 1, p 1, k 1, sl marker, k and p in next st, k 1, (p 1, k 1) 3 times; turn. **4th row (short row):** P 1, (k 1, p 1) 4 times; sl marker, p 1, k 1, p 1. **5th row:** K 1, p 1, k 1, sl marker, p and k in next st, p 1, (k 1, p 1) 20 times; k and p in next st, place marker on needle, k 1, p 1, k 1. **6th row (short row):** P 1, k 1, p 1, sl marker, (k 1, p 1) twice; turn. **7th row (short row):** K 1, p 1, k 1, p and k in next st, sl marker, k 1, p 1, k 1. **8th row (short row):** P 1, k 1, p 1, sl marker, p 1, (k 1, p 1) 4 times; turn. **9th row (short row):** (K 1, p 1) 4 times; k and p in next st, sl marker, k 1, p 1, k 1. **10th row:** P 1, k 1, p 1, sl marker, k 1, (p 1, k 1) 23 times; sl marker, p 1, k 1, p 1 (53 sts). **11th row:** K 1, p 1, k 1, sl marker, k and p in next st, work in ribbing to 1 st from marker, p and k in next st, sl marker, k 1, p 1, k 1. **12th row:** P 1, k 1, p 1, sl marker, rib to marker, sl marker, p 1, k 1, p 1. **13th row:** K 1, p 1, k 1, sl marker, p and k in next st, rib to 1 st from marker, k and p in next st, sl marker, k 1, p 1, k 1. **14th row:** Repeat 12th row. Repeat 11th through 14th rows once more (61 sts). **19th row:** K 1, * p 1, k 1. Repeat from * across; cast on 25 sts (86 sts). Divide sts evenly on 3 needles.

Working in rnds on 4 needles, work in k 1, p 1 ribbing for 7 rnds. **8th rnd:** P around and dec 16 sts as evenly spaced as possible (70 sts). K 1, p 1 in ribbing for 4 rnds more.

To establish petal pattern 1st rnd: * K 1, p 4, p 1 and place marker on this st, p 4. Repeat from * 6 times more. **2nd rnd:** (K 1, p 9) 7 times. Repeat 2nd rnd twice more. **5th rnd:** * K 1, p 3; work petal as follows: Yarn to back, insert point of right-hand needle into marked st, yo needle as if to k behind work, draw lp through marked st on first row and up to height of 5th row; yarn to front (first petal made); p 2, make 2nd petal, p 2, make 3rd petal, p 2. Repeat from * 6 times more. **6th rnd:** * K 1, p 2; skip next st, insert point of right-hand needle into petal st and into skipped st and k 2 sts tog, (p 1, skip next st, k petal st and skipped st tog) twice; p 2. Repeat from * 6 times more. **7th through 10th rnds:** Repeat 2nd rnd 4 times. **Next rnd:** (P 2 tog, p 8) 7 times (63 sts). K 5 rnds. **Following rnd:** P around and dec 11 sts as evenly spaced as possible (52 sts). K 3 rnds. **Next rnd:** P around, dec 8 sts as evenly spaced as possible (44 sts). K 1, p 1 in ribbing for 4 rnds. **Following rnd:** P 2 tog around (22 sts). K 1, p 1 in ribbing for 4 rnds. **Next rnd:** K 2 tog around. Break off, leaving 12″ end. Thread end in tapestry needle, draw through remaining 11 sts, pull up tight and fasten.

FINISHING Topknot With crochet hook make 16″ chain. Sc in 2nd ch from hook and in each ch across. Break off. Tie in single knot at center. Sew to top of hat. **Ties and Lower back edging** Sl st at lower front corner, make 11″ ch; sc in 2nd ch from hook and in each ch across; sl st at same corner; sc across lower back cast-on edge; make 2nd tie as for first. Break off. **Upper front edging** Work 1 row sl st across upper front cast-on edge. Break off.

Two-piece Bunting

Rug-snug crocheted combination of hooded jacket and blanket-bright bunting.

SIZES Jacket: 6 months [1 year]. Jacket measures 11″ [12″] across back. **Bunting:** One size, 20″ long and 14″ wide.

MATERIALS Use Bucilla Winsom (acrylic sport-weight yarn), 2-ounce skeins, for both. **For jacket:** 3 [4] skeins lapis blue No. 310 (color B); 5 red heart-shaped buttons. **For bunting:** 2 skeins winter white No. 330 (color W), 1 skein each brick red No. 332 (R), lapis blue No. 310 (B), sun gold No. 334 (S) and emerald green No. 297 (G); 5 red heart-shaped buttons; self-fastening tape (such as Velcro) or large snaps for front opening. **For both:** Aluminum crochet hook size G (or international hook size 4:50 mm) **or the size that will give you the correct gauge.**

GAUGE (for both) 2 cl = 1″; 10 rows = 3″.

JACKET

Back Starting at lower edge with B, ch 45 [49] to measure 11″ [12″]. **1st row (right side):** In 3rd ch from hook work (1 sc and 1 dc—cl made); * skip 1 ch, work cl in next ch. Repeat from * across (22 [24] cl); ch 1, turn. **2nd row:** Skip 1st dc, sc in next sc, * sc in dc, sc in sc. Repeat from * across (43 [47] sc); ch 1, turn. **3rd row:** Work cl in 1st sc, * skip next sc, work cl in next sc. Repeat from * across (22 [24] cl); ch 1, turn.

Repeating 2nd and 3rd rows for pattern, work even until piece measures 5½″ [6″] from beg, ending with 2nd row, then ch 19 [21] for right sleeve; turn. With another strand of blue, ch 17 [19] and join to beg of last row worked for left sleeve.

Sleeves and back Next row (right side): Starting at right sleeve, work cl in 3rd ch from hook, (skip 1 ch, work cl in next ch) 8 [9] times; working across back, work cl in 1st sc, * skip next sc, work cl in next sc. Repeat from * across back. Working across other ch for left sleeve, work cl in 1st ch, (skip next ch, work cl in next ch) 8 [9] times; ch 1, turn.

Work even on 40 [44] cl for 4½″ more. Piece should measure 10″ [10½″] from beg. On last row mark center 12 cl for back neck. Break off.

Left front Starting at lower edge, ch 23 [25]. Keeping in pattern as for back, work even on 11 [12] cl (21 [23] sc) to beg of sleeve, ending at side edge. Ch 19 [21] for sleeve; turn. Work even as for back on 20 [22] cl for 4½″ more. Break off. On last row, mark 6 cl for front neck edge.

Right front Work to correspond to left front, reversing sleeve shaping. Mark 6 cl for front neck edge.

FINISHING With crochet hook and B, join pieces with right side of work facing you, forming a ridge on right side, as follows: Leaving marked cl at neck edges open, sl st across top sleeve seam between markers and wrist edge. Repeat for side seams and lower sleeve seams.

Hood 1st row (right side): Starting at right front neck edge, work 49 [53] sc evenly spaced across right front neck, back neck and left front neck; ch 1, turn. **2nd row:** Work across in sc, increasing 6 sc evenly spaced (55 [59] sc); ch 1, turn.

3rd row: Work as for 3rd row of back (28 [30] cl). **4th row:** Work as for 2nd row of back (55 [59] sc). Repeat last 2 rows until hood is 7″ [7½″] from beg. Do not break off. Fold last row in half and, with right side facing you, sl st across top edge. Break off.

Sleeve border 1st rnd: Sc evenly around lower edge of sleeve; join with sl st. **2nd rnd:** Sc in 1st sc, * ch 1, skip 1 sc, sc in next sc. Repeat from * around; join. Break off. **Ties (make 2)** For each sleeve, crochet 16″ chain. Starting at top edge, weave chain in and out of lps formed on 2nd rnd. Gather to fit and tie ends in bow.

Front borders For boy, work right front border first; for girl, work left front border first. **First border: 1st row:** Sc evenly spaced across front edge; ch 1, turn. Work even in sc for 3 more rows. Break off. Mark border for 5 buttons, the 1st one ¾″ from lower edge, the last one ½″ below neck edge, the others spaced evenly between. **Second border: 1st row:** Repeat 1st row of first border. **2nd row:** Continue to work in sc and, at the same time, work buttonhole at each marker as follows: Ch 2, skip 2 sts, work to next marker. **3rd row:** Keeping in sc pattern, work 2 sc in each ch-2 sp. Complete as for 1st border.

Lower edging Starting at right side seam, with right side of work facing you, sc evenly along lower edge, front edge, face edge of hood, other

continued on p. 66

continued from p. 65

front edge and lower edge of front and back, working 3 sc in each corner. Join. Break off. Sew on buttons.

BUNTING

NOTE When not in use, carry color W loosely along side of work. Attach and break off other colors as needed. **To change colors** Work to end of row with old color, attach new color and use for turning ch.

Back Starting at lower edge with W, ch 51 to measure 12½". **1st row (right side):** Work as for 1st row of jacket back (25 cl). **2nd row (inc row):** Skip 1st dc, work 2 sc in sc, * sc in dc, sc in sc. Repeat from * to last 2 sts, sc in dc, work 2 sc in sc (51 sc); drop W but do not break off; attach R, ch 1, turn. **3rd row:** Repeat 3rd row of jacket back (26 cl). **4th row:** Repeat 2nd row (inc row) of bunting (53 sc). Break off R; with W, ch 1, turn.

5th row: Work cl in 1st sc, * skip next sc, cl in next sc. Repeat from * across (27 cl); ch 1, turn. **6th row:** Skip 1st dc, sc in next sc, * sc in dc, sc in sc. Repeat from * across (53 sc). Drop W; attach B, ch 1, turn.

Repeating 5th and 6th rows for pattern, work even in striped pattern of 2 rows each * B, W, S, W, G, W, R and W. Repeat from * until back measures 20" from beg, ending with 2 rows W. Break off.

Front Work as for bunting back for 9" (15 stripes completed).

To divide for front opening Keeping in stripe pattern as established, work until 13 cl are completed; ch 1, turn. Working on these sts only, work to correspond to back. Break off.

Skip center 2 (W) sts (1 cl) on last complete row worked on front; attach yarn and complete second side of front to correspond to first side.

FINISHING Edging With W, work 1 row sc evenly spaced along sides and lower edges of back and front.

Joining With wrong sides together, pin front to back, matching stripes. With W, working through both thicknesses, work 1 row sc evenly along both side edges and lower edge of bunting, leaving top edge open. With B, sc in each sc of last row. Break off.

Front borders Starting with a right-side row with B, work 4 rows sc along each edge of front opening. Sew buttons on right front border for girl, left front border for boy, with snaps or tape on underside. Lap one end over the other at lower edge and sew in place.

Top border Working both rows from right side of work with B, work 2 rows sc across top edge of bunting front and back.

Bunny Bootees

Crocheted comfort in a choice of three sizes. Kids will love the funny features.

SIZES Small (fits 6½" foot), medium (7½" foot) and large (8½" foot).

MATERIALS Knitting-worsted-weight yarn, 3 [4–5] ounces white, 1 ounce pink; scrap blue felt; white glue; aluminum crochet hook size J (or international hook size 6:00 mm) **or the size that will give you the correct gauge;** tapestry needle.

GAUGE 3 sts = 1"; 3 rows = 1".

Foot Starting at heel, working ver- tically, ch 21 [25–29] to measure about 7" [7½"–8"]. **1st row:** Sc in 2nd ch from hook and in each ch across (20 [24–28] sc); ch 1, turn. **2nd row:** Sc in each sc across; ch 1, turn. Repeat 2nd row until piece measures 6½" [7½"–8"]. Break off, leaving 15" end. To form toe, thread end in tapestry needle, run through lps of last row, pull up tight and secure. To form instep, sew adjacent side edges tog for 3" [4"–5"]. Break off. Fold other end in half and sew edges tog to form heel.

Cuff 1st rnd: Work 24 [26–28] sc evenly spaced around opening. **2nd rnd:** Sc in each sc around. Repeat 2nd rnd 3 times more; sl st in next st. Break off.

Ears (make 2) Ch 2. **1st rnd:** Work 8 sc in 2nd ch from hook. Mark beg of rnds but do not join rnds. **2nd through 5th rnds:** Sc in each sc around. **6th rnd:** (Skip next sc, sc in next sc) 4 times. Break off, leaving 6" end. Thread end in tapestry needle, run through lps of last rnd, pull up tight and secure.

FINISHING Make two 1½"-diameter white pompons for cheeks and one 1"-diameter pompon for nose (see General Tips, page 160, to make pompon). Cut out two ½"-diameter felt circles for eyes. Following photograph, sew ears, cheeks and nose securely in place. Glue or sew on eyes. For each tie cut four 20" lengths pink yarn. Hold tog and knot ends. Weave through sts around lower edge of cuff. Tie in bow at front.

Striped Sweater and Hat Set

Everything's coming up cozy in this quick-to-knit garter-stitch set.

SIZES 1 year [2 years]. Sweater measures 10″ [11″] across chest.

MATERIALS Bernat Berella "4" (acrylic 4-ply knitting-worsted-weight yarn), 1 [2] (4-ounce) balls white No. 8942 (color W), 2 balls baby blue No. 8944 (B); 1 pair 14″ No. 6 knitting needles (or English needles No. 7) **or the size that will give you the correct gauge;** aluminum crochet hook size E (or international size 3:50 mm); 8 buttons; stitch holders; tapestry needle.

GAUGE 5 sts = 1″.

SWEATER

NOTE Body is worked in 1 piece without side seams. Entire sweater is worked in garter st.

BODY Starting at lower edge with color B, cast on 96 [106] st. * K 8 rows B, 8 rows W. Repeat from * 3 times more. K 8 rows B, 7 rows W. Piece should measure 7½″.

To divide for fronts and back 1st row (wrong side): With W, k 22 [24] and slip sts to holder for 1 front. Bind off next 2 [3] sts for underarm; k until there are 48 [52] sts on needle, slip these sts to another holder for back. Bind off next 2 [3] sts for underarm, k to end for other front (22 [24] sts). Break off; attach B and use for all yoke sections.

Front yoke K across sts for 1 front for 3″ [3½″], ending at front edge. **To shape neck:** At front edge bind off 3 [4] sts once, then dec 1 st at same edge every other row 3 times. Work even, if necessary, on 16 [17] sts until armhole measures 4″ [4½″] from beg, ending at armhole edge. **To shape shoulder: 1st row:** Bind off 8 [9] sts, k to end. K 1 row. Bind off 8 remaining sts.

Place sts for other front on needle. Attach B and work to correspond to 1st front.

Back yoke Place 48 [52] sts for back on needle. K even for 4″ [4½″]. **To shape shoulders:** Bind off 8 [9] sts at beg of next 2 rows, then bind off 8 sts at beg of following 2 rows. Bind off remaining 16 [18] sts.

SLEEVES Starting at lower edge with B, cast on 40 [45] sts. K even in stripe pattern as for back until sleeve measures 6½″ [7¼″], ending with a complete stripe. Bind off.

FINISHING Sew shoulder and sleeve seams. Sew sleeves in place.

Front borders 1st border: With B, cast on 6 sts. K until border, stretched slightly, fits along front edge of sweater to neck. Bind off. Sew this border to right front of boy's sweater or left front of girl's sweater. With pins mark positions for 8 buttons. **2nd border:** Work as for 1st border, but make buttonhole opposite each marker as follows: K 3, yo, k 2 tog, k 1. Complete as for 1st border and sew in place.

Edging With right side facing you, with B, crochet 1 row sc across front and neck edges. Break off. Sew on buttons.

HAT

Starting at cuff with W, cast on 80 [84] sts. K 8 rows W, 8 rows B, 9 rows W, ending on right side of cuff.

For crown, change to k 1, p 1 ribbing and, starting with a right-side row, work 8 [12] rows B, 8 rows W, 8 rows B, 7 rows W.

To shape top 1st row: With W, p 2 tog across (40 [42] sts). With B, work even in k 1, p 1 ribbing for 7 rows, then p 2 tog across (20 [21] sts). **Next row:** With B, k 2 tog across, k last 0 [1] st. Cut yarn, leaving 12″ end. Thread end in tapestry needle and draw through remaining sts. Pull up tight and sew back seam from wrong side, then sew cuff seam from right side.

Earlaps (make 2) Starting at top edge with B, cast on 16 [18] sts. K even for 1″, then dec 1 st at beg and end of every 4th row until 2 sts remain. Bind off.

Border and Tie Starting at beg of earlap, with crochet hook and B, sc evenly across shaped edge to point of earlap, crochet 8″ chain for tie, then sl st in 2nd ch from hook and in each st of ch; sc evenly across other shaped edge of earlap. Break off.

Turn cuff to right side. Sew earlaps to inside of hat about 2½″ [2¾″] from back seam.

Crocheted Baby Bootees

(Project 15 in group photograph, page 58)

Double-weight toddler-size slippers, sturdier and warmer than most.

SIZE About 6″ long.

MATERIALS Knitting-worsted-weight yarn, 3 ounces main color (MC) and 1 ounce contrasting color (CC) make 1 pair; aluminum crochet hook size I (or international size 5:50 mm) **or the size that will give you the correct gauge.**

GAUGE 3 sc = 1″; 3 rnds = 1″.

NOTE Use yarn double throughout, unless otherwise specified.

SOLE Starting at center of sole with MC, ch 10. **1st rnd:** 2 sc in 2nd ch from hook (inc made); sc in next 7 ch, 4 sc in next ch (working around end of ch). Turn work around and work 7 sc along opposite edge of ch, make inc in last st (22 sc). Do not break off, but mark beg of each rnd. **2nd rnd:** Working in each sc around, make inc in next sc, sc in next sc, inc in next sc, work 7 sc, inc in next sc, work 2 sc (mark this end for heel), inc in next sc, work 7 sc, inc in next sc, sc, inc in next sc (30 sc). **3rd rnd:** Sc around, increasing 4 sc around toe and 2 sc around heel, spacing inc so that sole lies flat (36 sc). **4th rnd:** Sc around, increasing 2 sc around toe (38 sc). Sole is completed. Do not break off but ch 1 and turn work with wrong side facing you. **5th rnd:** Mark this rnd. Sc in each sc around; join. Break off.

TOP Turn work with right side facing you. Mark center st at toe and heel. **1st rnd:** Starting at center heel st with MC, sc in each sc to 2 sts before toe marker, draw up lp in each of next 2 sts, yo and draw through all 3 lps on hook (1 sc dec); sc in marked st (transfer marker to new st), dec 1 sc, sc in each sc to end. Repeat last rnd 3 times more. (**NOTE** If center marked st tends to move off center after a few rnds, adjust by transferring marker to new center st and continue to dec each side of new st as before.) Break off. **6th rnd:** Work as for last rnd, decreasing 2 sts each side of toe marker (24 sc). Repeat last rnd once more (20 sc). Break off.

Ankle cuff Mark center 2 sts at edge of instep on last rnd. **1st row:** With right side facing you, sc in st after 2nd marked st, sc in next 17 sc; ch 1, turn. **2nd row:** Sc in 18 sc; ch 1, turn. Repeat last row twice more. Do not ch 1 or turn, but work sc evenly around front cuff opening, then sc around top edge of cuff; join. Break off.

FINISHING With single strand MC, work sc around marked rnd separating sole from top, adding 2 or 3 sc around toe if rnd cups; join. Break off.

Tie With 2 strands CC, crochet 28″ chain. Lace through instep and tie in bow (see photograph).

Knitted Mittens and Cap

(Project 2 in group photograph, page 58)

SIZE Child. Length of mittens is adjustable.

MATERIALS Coats & Clark's Red Heart Knitting Worsted, **for mittens** 1 ounce eggshell No. 111 (main color, MC) and ½ ounce dark turquoise No. 515 (contrasting color, CC), **for cap** 2 ounces dark turquoise (MC) and 1 ounce eggshell (CC); 1 pair size 8 knitting needles (or English needles size 5) **or the size that will give you the correct gauge;** tapestry needle.

GAUGE 4 sts = 1″.

MITTENS

Work as for adult Two-tone Knitted Mittens, page 28, with the following changes:

Cast on 26 sts for cuff. On 9th row of thumb shaping, work k 12 (instead of 15). Work thumb shaping until there are 34 sts on needle. For thumb, k 13 and place sts on holder, k next 8 sts for thumb, place remaining sts on another holder. Work on thumb sts for 1″ and finish as for adult mittens.

For hand, work on 26 sts until entire mitten measures 7½″ (or 1″ less than desired length).

Shape tip and finish as for adult mitten.

CAP

Work as for adult Two-tone Knitted Hat, page 21, with the following changes:

Cast on 17 sts. Work pattern until there are 12 stripes each MC and CC. For cuff, pick up 72 sts and work for 2½″.

With MC, make 3″-diameter pompon (see page 160) and sew to top of cap.

"Shearling" Vest

Knitted in one piece (no side seams). Crocheted edging and curly-yarn collar add the fleecy look.

SIZES Child's size 3–4 [(5–6)—(7–8)]. Vest measures 10¼" [12¼"–14"] across back at underarms.

MATERIALS Unger's Roly Poly (acrylic knitting-worsted-weight yarn), 1 [2–2] (3½-ounce) ball red No. 864; Unger's Roly Sport (acrylic sport-weight yarn), 1 [2–2] ball camel No. 4557; Unger's Kurlie (loopy-texture acrylic/polyester yarn), 1 [2–2] (1½-ounce) skein white No. 200; 1 pair No. 8 knitting needles (or English needles No. 5) **or the size that will give you the correct gauge;** aluminum crochet hook size F (or international size 4:00 mm); stitch holders.

GAUGES With 1 strand each Roly Poly and Roly Sport: 4 sts = 1". With 1 strand Kurlie: 3 sts = 1".

BODY Vest is made in 1 piece without side seams. Starting at lower edge with 1 strand red and 1 strand camel held together, cast on 82 [98–110] sts for entire lower edge of vest. Work even in garter st for 6½" [7"–7½"].

To divide work K across 1st 16 [18–19] sts, place on holder for one front; bind off next 8 [12–16] sts for 1st underarm, k until there are 34 [38–40] sts on right-hand needle, place these sts on another holder for back; bind off next 8 [12–16] sts for 2nd underarm (place marker at end of underarm), k to end of row for other front (16 [18–19] sts).

FRONTS Working on sts of last front only, continue in garter st and dec 1 st at front edge every other row 4 [5–6] times. Place marker at front edge for collar placement. At same edge dec every inch 4 times. Work even on 8 [9–9] sts for 2 [4–6] more rows. Bind off. Attach yarn at 1st underarm and work sts on holder for other front to correspond.

BACK Attach yarn at marker on 2nd underarm, place sts from holder onto needle and work even on 34 [38–40] sts for 5" [5¼"–5½"]. **To shape shoulders:** Bind off 8 [9–9] sts at beg of next 2 rows. Bind off remaining 18 [20–22] sts.

COLLAR Starting at neck edge with 1 strand Kurlie, cast on 39 [42–44] sts. **1st row:** K across. **2nd row (inc row):** K 12 sts, inc 1 st in next st, k to within last 13 sts, inc in next st, k to end (2 sts inc). Repeat last 2 rows once more. K across (43 [46–48] sts).

Continue in garter st and bind off 2 sts at beg of next 8 rows, then bind off 3 sts at beg of next 4 rows. Bind off remaining sts.

FINISHING Sew shoulder seams. Sew cast-on edge of collar to neckline between markers. Work all trim with wrong side of work facing you. With Kurlie, crochet 2 rnds sc around each armhole. Starting at one marker at neck edge, crochet 1 row sc evenly along front, lower edge and other front edge to other marker, working 3 sc in each corner.

Ties (make 2) With 2 strands red, crochet 12" chain. Make pompon as follows: Wrap red yarn about 70 times around 2½"-wide piece of cardboard. Cut yarn along 1 edge of cardboard and tie strands tog tightly at center. Trim to shape pompon. Sew a pompon to one end of each tie. Sew other end of tie to front edge at beg of neck shaping.

Zippered Jackets and Matching Pompon Hats

SIZES Child's size 4 [6–8–10]. Jacket measures about 12½" [13½"–14½"–15½"] across back at underarms, 9½" [10½"–12½"–14½"] from underarms to lower edge.

MATERIALS For girl's set: Bucilla Softex Win-Knit (acrylic knitting-worsted-weight yarn), 3 [3–4–4] (4-ounce) balls light rust No. 73 (MC), 1 ball light beige No. 68 (CC). **For boy's set:** 3 [3–4–4] balls blue-frost No. 65 (MC), 1 ball light beige No. 68 (CC). **For both sets:** 1 pair size 8 knitting needles (or English needles size 5) **or the size that will give you the correct gauge;** crochet hook; 12" [12"–14"–16"] separating-type jacket zipper; 1 cable needle.

GAUGES In garter st or stockinette st: 9 sts = 2". In cable pattern: 5 sts = 1" when stretched.

JACKET

BACK Starting at lower edge with CC, cast on 50 [54–60–64] sts. **Lower border pattern: 1st and 2nd rows:** K across. P 1 row, k 1 row. **5th row:** K across. Drop CC, join MC. **6th and 7th rows:** K across. K 1 row, p 1 row. **10th and 11th rows:** K across. Drop MC, pick up CC.

Using CC for 6 rows, then MC for next 6 rows, repeat 6th through 11th rows until there are 5 stripes in border. Break off CC (lower border completed).

Next row (right side): Using MC, k across and inc 12 [14–14–16] sts as evenly spaced as possible. Working on 62 [68–74–80] sts, change to cable pattern as follows:

Cable pattern 1st row (wrong side): * K 2, p 4. Repeat from * across, ending k 2. **2nd row:** * P 2, k 4. Repeat from * across, ending p 2. **3rd row:** Repeat 1st row. **4th row (right side):** * P 2, sl next 2 sts onto cable needle and hold at back of work, k 2, k 2 sts from cable needle. Repeat from * across, ending p 2. **5th row:** Repeat 1st row. **6th row:** Repeat 2nd row. Repeat these 6 rows for cable pattern until back measures 9½" [10½"–12½"–14"] from beg or desired length to underarm. Put a marker at each end of last row to indicate beg of armholes, then continue in cable pattern until the back is 13" [14½"–16¾"–18½"] from beg, ending with a right-side row. **Next row (dec row):** With MC, p across and dec 12 [14–14–16] sts as evenly spaced as possible (50 [54–60–64] sts). Drop MC, join CC.

Upper border Repeat 6th through 11th rows of lower border 3 times, working 6 rows each CC, MC and CC. Bind off. Put a marker on 16th [17th–19th–20th] st from each end of last row (ends of shoulders).

RIGHT FRONT With CC, cast on 26 [28–31–33] sts. Work 5 border stripes as for back. Break off CC. Using MC, k 1 row and inc 6 [10–7–11] sts evenly.

Change to cable pattern and, working on 32 [38–38–44] sts, work even until front measures same as back to armhole marker, put marker in work at side edge, then continue in cable pattern to beg of upper border, ending with a right-side row. With MC, p 1 row and dec 6 [10–7–11] sts evenly spaced (26 [28–31–33] sts).

Neck shaping and upper border Repeat 12 rows of back upper border and, at same time, shape neck as follows: At front edge, bind off 3 [4–5–6] sts once, then bind off 3 sts every other row twice. Work 1 row even, then dec 1 st at neck edge once. Work even on 16 [17–19–20] sts until 12th row of border is completed. Bind off.

LEFT FRONT Work to correspond to right front.

SLEEVES Starting at wrist edge, with

CC, cast on 40 [42–44–46] sts. Working as for lower back border, work 1 CC stripe, 1 MC stripe and 1 CC stripe. Break off CC. Change to stockinette st and, with MC, work even until sleeve is 10½″ [11½″–12½″–13½″] or desired length to underarm. Bind off.

FINISHING Sew shoulder seams. Pin bound-off edge of sleeve between markers and sew. Sew side and sleeve seams. **Right front border:** With CC and right side of work facing you, pick up and k sts across right front and neck edge. K next 3 rows. Bind off. **Back border and left front border:** Working as for right front border, pick up sts across back neck, left neck and front edge. Complete as for right front border. Sew border shoulder seam. Sew in zipper.

CAP

CUFF With CC, cast on 86 [86–92–98] sts. K 4 rows, drop CC, join MC. Repeat 6th through 11th rows of lower border of jacket back with MC, then repeat with CC (last row is a wrong-side row). Break off CC, use MC for rest of cap. Mark last ridge for fold line. P 1 row.

CROWN Change to cable pattern and, starting with 2nd row, work even until cap measures 6½″ [6¾″ –7″–7¼″] from beg, ending with a wrong-side row.

Next row (dec row): * P 2 tog, (k 2 tog) twice. Repeat from * across, ending p 2 tog. Continue in new rib pattern of k 1, p 2 on wrong-side rows and p 1, k 2 on right-side rows for 1½″. **Last row:** Work 2 sts tog across. Break off, draw end through needle, draw up tightly and sew.

FINISHING Sew back seam. Turn up cuff on fold line and, with crochet hook and CC, work 1 rnd sl st on marked ridge. Break off. With CC, make a 3″ pompon (see General Tips, page 160); sew to top of cap.

Checked Tabard Apron

(Project **11** in group photograph, page **58**)

Gingham apron for young work or play, with a bright new idea in bias trim.

SIZE About 19″ long.

MATERIALS 45″-wide gingham (1⅛ yards make 3); 45″-wide reversible red quilted fabric (⅜ yard makes 5 hearts); 1″-wide bias tape (4½ yards bind 1 apron—we joined assorted colors, end to end).

Follow dimensions on diagram and cut out 2 apron pieces (½″ seam allowance is included at shoulders; other edges will be bound). Cut vertical 6″ slit at center back neck. Cut four 2½″ x 9″ pieces for side ties. Make 7¼″-high x 10¾″-wide heart pattern (see photograph for shape). Cut out heart from quilted fabric, adding ½″ to all edges for seam allowance.

Stitch shoulder seams. Bind side and lower edges and edges of back slit. Cut neck binding 20″ longer than neck edge. Center binding on neck and bind edge, allowing ends to extend for ties. Slipstitch folded edge of binding to neck edge and along tie extensions as well. (Or pin full length of binding and topstitch from right side, stitching "in the ditch" along neck edge. Stitching will catch other side of binding.) Knot ends of ties.

Turn edges of heart ¼″, then ¼″ more; topstitch. Pin and topstitch to apron front, leaving section at each lobe open at top to form pocket.

Fold each side tie in half lengthwise, wrong side out. Stitch ¼″ seam on long edge and one end; turn. Sew a tie to wrong side at each dot, front and back.

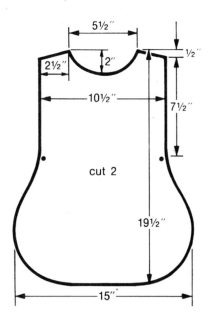

treasure-house of toys

Toys sure of a "welcome home" wherever there are children! Soft squeezables for little ones, with the accent on the animals they all adore . . . wooden push- and pull-toys to play along with toddlers. A dream display in the making, and an easy and inexpensive one : techniques and materials are both simple.

Basketful of Kittens and Bunnies to Knit

KITTENS

SIZE About 9″ tall.

MATERIALS (for one cat) Knitting-worsted-weight yarn, 1 ounce color A, ½ ounce each B and C; 1 pair size 8 knitting needles (or English size 5) **or the size that will give you the correct gauge;** 12″ length ½″-wide ribbon; scraps yarn to embroider face; polyester fiberfill for stuffing.

GAUGE 4 sts = 1″.

LEGS, BODY AND HEAD (made in one piece) 1st leg: Starting at toe with color A, cast on 12 sts. K 6 rows. Cut A; join B. K 18 rows. Cut B. Push leg to needle end. **2nd leg:** Work as for 1st leg.

Body Join C. **1st row:** K across sts of 2nd and 1st legs (24 sts). K 9 rows more. Cut C; join A.

Neck and head (K 1 row, p 1 row) twice, then k 18 rows. **To shape ears: 1st row:** Bind off 2 sts; k until there are 8 sts on right needle (1st ear); bind off 4 sts; k until there are 8 more sts on right needle (2nd ear); bind off 2 sts. Fasten off. Work each ear separately as follows: **2nd row:** Join A, k across. **3rd row:** K 2 tog, k to last 2 sts, k 2 tog. Repeat last 2 rows once more (4 sts). Cut yarn, leaving 10″ end. Thread end in needle, draw through remaining sts, pull up tight and fasten off.

ARMS Starting at hand with A, cast on 12 sts. K 6 rows. Drop A; join C. K 6 rows. Bind off.

FINISHING Fold legs/body/head with side edges at center back. Sew inner leg and center back seams; stuff, then sew top of head. Fold each arm in half and sew, leaving top end open; stuff and sew in place. Embroider face as shown (for stitch choices, see page 159). Tie ribbon around neck.

BUNNIES

SIZES Small about 8″ [large—11″] tall.

MATERIALS (for one bunny) Knitting-worsted-weight yarn, 1 [1½] ounce color A, small amounts colors B and C; 1 pair size 8 knitting needles (or English size 5) **or the size that will give you the correct gauge;** scraps ribbon; scraps yarn to embroider face; polyester fiberfill for stuffing.

GAUGE 4 sts = 1″.

LEGS, BODY AND HEAD (made in one piece) 1st leg: Starting at toe with color A, cast on 12 [15] sts. K 18 [24] rows. Cut A. Push leg to end of left needle. **2nd leg:** Work as for 1st leg.

Body Join B. **1st row:** K across sts of 2nd and 1st legs (24 [30] sts). K 1 row. Drop B; join C. (K 2 rows C, 2 rows B) 2 [3] times. Cut B and C. Join A.

Neck and head With A, (k 1 row, p 1 row) 2 [3] times, then k 12 [20] rows. **To shape ears: 1st row:** Bind off 2 [3] sts; k until there are 8 [9] sts on right needle (1st ear); bind off next 4 [6] sts; k until there are 8 [9] more sts on right needle (2nd ear); bind off remaining sts. Fasten off. Work each ear separately as follows in stockinette st (start with k row) for small bunny and in garter st (k each row) for large bunny: Work 8 [10] rows. **Next row:** K 2 tog, k to last 2 sts, k 2 tog. **Following row:** Work across. Repeat last 2 rows twice more (2 [4] sts). Cut yarn, leaving 10″ end. Thread end in needle, draw through remaining sts, pull up tight and fasten off.

ARMS Starting at hand with A, cast on 12 sts. K 4 [6] rows. Cut A; join B and C. K 2 rows each B and C 2 [3] times, then 2 more rows B. Bind off.

FINISHING Complete as for Kitten, attaching 2″ color-A pompon (see page 160) on back for tail.

Soft Baby Blocks

(Project **3** in group photograph, page **58**)

Cotton calico on soft foam cubes—safe and stimulating for infants.

SIZE 4″ cube.

MATERIALS 45″-wide calico, ½ yard makes 8; matching sewing thread; 4″-thick polyurethane foam, 20″-square piece makes 25; serrated bread knife.

Following dimensions on diagram, make cardboard pattern (¼″ seam allowance included on all edges). Cut out fabric.

Fold up side and top sections of cross on broken lines, wrong side out, and stitch 2 seams. Fold up lower long section and sew to side sections, forming box with open flap. Turn right side out. Insert foam cube and hand-sew flap closed.

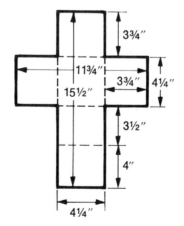

Knitted Stuffed Lion

(Project **14** in group photograph, page **58**)

Simple knit rectangle, seamed and stuffed.

SIZE About 10″ tall.

MATERIALS Ombré knitting-worsted-weight yarn, 3 ounces per lion; 1 pair size 10½ knitting needles (or English needles size 1) **or the size that will give you the correct gauge;** medium-size aluminum crochet hook to knot mane; scrap of black yarn; polyester fiberfill for stuffing; tapestry needle.

GAUGE 7 sts = 2″.

Starting at lower edge of back, cast on 18 sts. Work in garter st for 52 rows (26 ridges) to top of head. Continue by working 28 rows in stockinette st for face. Work front of body in garter st until front is same length as back when piece is folded at top of head. Bind off.

Following photograph, with black yarn embroider mouth with straight sts and eyes and nose in satin st. (Stitch diagrams, page 159.) Fold piece in half and sew side seams. Stuff softly; close opening.

Make four 2″-diameter pompons for legs (see page 160) and sew in place. Cut twelve 12″-long strands yarn, hold together and draw halfway through st at center bottom of lion. Fold in half, braid and tie, leaving 2″ tassel. For ears, pinch 1″ of top corners and sew around. Run strand of yarn through sts around body just below face, pull up to form neck; fasten.

For mane around face and all over back of head (see photograph), cut 5″ strands of yarn. One at a time, fold a strand in half; with hook, draw fold through a st, ends through lp and pull tight.

Pink-gingham Stuffed Pig

(Project **8** in group photograph, page **58**)

Great tot or teen gift, big enough to hug.

SIZE About 18″ long.

MATERIALS 45″-wide pink and white gingham (1¼ yards make 3); ⅜″-wide satin ribbon (1 yard trims 3); polyester fiberfill for stuffing; white and black sewing threads.

Enlarge pig diagram (see How to Enlarge Patterns, page 158) and make pattern. Cut out 2 gingham pieces (reverse pattern for one), adding ¼″ seam allowance to all edges. Mark details on one piece. Using black thread, machine-embroider all detail lines with ⅛″-wide zigzag stitches, filling in toes with rows of stitches. With right sides facing, stitch pig halves together, leaving tummy open. Clip curves, turn and stuff. Sew opening closed. Make bow from 12″ ribbon; sew to head as shown.

Each sq. = ½″

Animal Pals

Bear, bunny and cat all duded up in for-the-fun-of-it colors.

SIZES Bunny measures 8″ x 18″. Bear and cat measure 8″ x 14″.

MATERIALS For bear: ⅜ yard 60″-wide purple knitted velour; scraps blue, green, orange, gold and fuchsia felt. **For bunny:** ⅜ yard 45″-wide gold polka-dot fabric; scraps pink striped and solid-color fabric; scraps blue, green and orange felt. **For cat:** ⅜ yard 60″-wide blue knitted velour; scraps pink striped fabric; scrap purple velour; scraps gold, green and fuchsia felt; blue embroidery floss. **For all:** Polyester fiberfill for stuffing; white glue.

BODY Enlarge pattern (see How to Enlarge Patterns, page 158). See individual directions to cut pieces from fabrics, adding ½″ seam allowance to all but felt edges. To sew and stuff pieces, see General Tips, page 157.

BEAR

Cut purple velour body and arms. Cut green felt tie and glue on blue and yellow stripes. Cut ⅝″ x 12″ fuchsia collar and nose, orange mouth and blue ½″-diameter eyes. Stitch, then stuff arms and sew to body. Stitch and stuff body. Glue on features, collar and tie.

BUNNY

Cut polka-dot body, arms and 3″-diameter nose. Cut two striped 1¼″-wide inner ears and two solid pink 2″-diameter circle cheeks. Cut orange felt carrot, four green ⅝″ x 2½″ carrot tops and three blue ⅜″ x 5½″ whiskers and two blue ½″-diameter eyes.

With machine zigzag stitch, sew inner ears and cheeks to one body piece. Stitch, then stuff arms and sew to body; stitch and stuff body. Stitch and stuff carrot, leaving opening at upper end. Insert tops and sew opening closed; tack carrot under arm. Sew running stitches around nose circle ½″ from edge; stuff; pull up stitches to form ball.

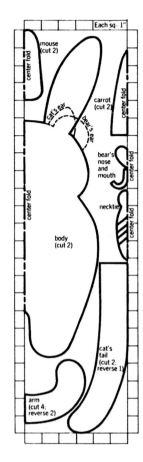

Sew to face, tacking whiskers underneath. Glue on eyes.

CAT

Cut blue velour body, arms and tail. Cut 3″-diameter purple velour nose. Cut striped mouse. Cut two 1¼″-diameter gold felt ears. Cut green crescent-shaped felt cat's mouth, ¼″ x 3½″ mouse tail and three ⅜″ x 5½″ fuchsia whiskers. Stitch, then stuff arms and sew to a body piece. Stitch and stuff body and tail. Sew tail to back. Stitch and stuff mouse, catching tail in stitching and leaving opening at head. Pleat each ear, insert in opening and sew opening closed. Embroider straight-stitch eyes. (Stitch diagram, page 159.) Tack mouse under arm. Make and attach nose and whiskers as for bunny. Glue on mouth.

76

Felt Pets

SIZE Each about 14″ x 14″.

MATERIALS ½ yard 36″-wide felt for each; bulky yarn in contrasting color for blanket-stitch joining; polyester fiberfill for stuffing; large-eyed tapestry needle; awl.

Enlarge patterns (see How to Enlarge Patterns, page 158), and cut out of felt (do not add seam allowance). Following stitch diagram, page 159, with tapestry needle and yarn work French knot for eye on each piece. On one felt

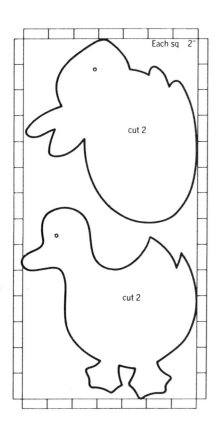

piece, with pencil mark dots all around about ⅜″ apart and ¼″ in from edge. Pin felt pieces together and, with awl, poke holes through dots. Work blanket stitch (stitch diagram, page 159) around edges to join pieces, leaving about 6″ open. Stuff; close opening with blanket stitch.

Terry Teddy

SIZE 20″ tall.

MATERIALS (for 1 bear) 22″ x 30″ piece brown terry cloth (1¼ yards 45″-wide fabric make 3 bears); 4½″ square white plush or terry; black embroidery floss; 1 yard ⅝″-wide ribbon; polyester fiberfill for stuffing.

Enlarge bear body diagram (see How to Enlarge Patterns, page 158) and make pattern. Adding ½″ seam allowance, cut out 2 bear shapes (back and front) from brown terry cloth; 1 muzzle and 2 ears from white. Sew body pieces together, leaving opening for stuffing. Clip curves; turn. Stuff; sew opening closed. Sew muzzle to front, turning edge under and padding. Sew white circles to front of ears. Embroider eyes and nose with satin stitch and mouth with outline stitch (stitch diagrams, page 159). Tie ribbon around neck.

Each sq. = ½″

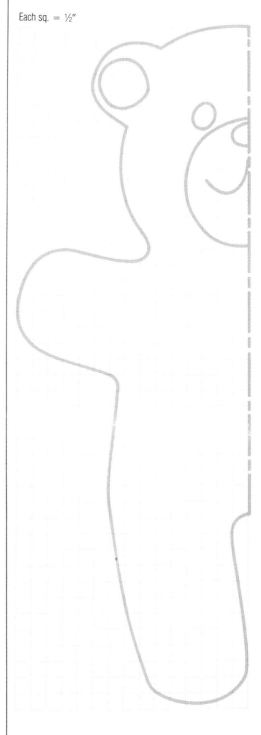

Pompon Dog

(Project **4** in group photograph, page **58**)

SIZE About 8″ tall to top of head.

MATERIALS Knitting-worsted-weight yarn (3 ounces yellow and 1 ounce each orange and bright pink make 1); 45″-wide felt (¼ yard makes 27 ears, ¼ yard makes 10 ties); scraps of felt for features; white glue.

See General Tips, page 160, for pompon instructions.

With yellow yarn, make 4½″-diameter pompon head and with yellow, orange and pink yarns make 5½″-diameter pompon body (cut 1½″-diameter hole in cardboard circles to make pompons). Tie and glue pompons together.

For ears, cut two 3″ x 4½″ felt ovals. Pleat one end of each and sew to hold pleat. Glue pleated ends to head. Cut 1″ x 1½″ oval tongue; pleat and glue to face. Cut ¾″-diameter nose and ½″-diameter eyes; glue to face. For tie, cut 2″ x 7″ strip for bow and 1″ x 13″ band. Fold bow strip crosswise, overlapping ends at center; sew. Cut 3″ strip from band and wrap around bow; sew, then sew bow to center of band. Wrap band around neck and sew ends together at back.

Pompon Owl, Kitty and Squirrel

(Project **5** in group photograph, page **58**)

MATERIALS Rug yarn or knitting-worsted-weight yarn (2 ounces make 1 owl, 1 ounce makes kitty or squirrel); scraps of felt for features; white glue.

See General Tips, page 160, to make pompons (4½″ diameter for owl, 3½″ diameter for kitty or squirrel).

For kitty: Make 7″ braid for tail with 3 strands yarn and tie to pompon. Make two ¾″ pompons for inside ears. Make tiny pompon for nose. Cut four 1″-wide x 1½″-high pointed ears; glue ear piece pairs together.

For owl or squirrel: Cut out 3½″-diameter felt circle for feet; shape into fat heart shape. Cut ¾″ x 1″ oval ears, ¾″- or 1″-diameter circle nose. **For eyes:** Cut 1″-diameter felt circles, or ¾″ x 1″ ovals, and smaller pupils. Glue all features in place.

Pin-striped Bunny

(Project **10** in group photograph, page **58**)

A dapper little dandy, with his pin-striped suit and suave expression.

SIZE About 21″ tall.

MATERIALS 45″-wide striped fabric (¾ yard makes 2); 1″-wide grosgrain ribbon (1 yard trims one); polyester fiberfill for stuffing; black sewing thread and thread to match fabric.

Enlarge bunny (see How to Enlarge Patterns, page 158) and make full pattern. Make bunny in same manner as Pink-gingham Stuffed Pig, page 74, filling in nose with rows of stitches and tying 36″ length of ribbon around neck.

Each sq. = ½″

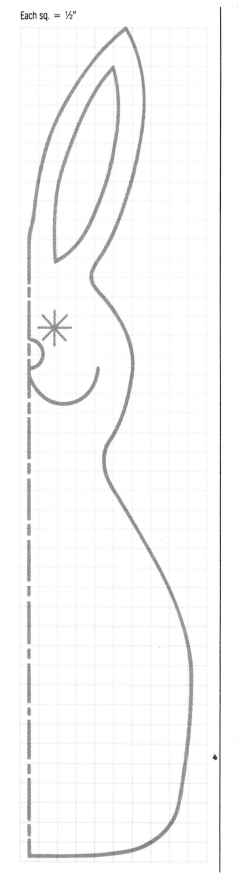

Crocheted Mama Cat and Kittens

Very easy, very basic pattern works for big and little kitties.

SIZES Cat is about 12½″ square and kittens are about 7½″ x 8½″, not including tail.

MATERIALS Bernat Berella "4" (acrylic knitting-worsted-weight yarn), 2 (4-ounce) balls Roman gold (tan) No. 8907 (color T), 1 ball each camel No. 8913 (C) and old gold No. 8909 (G) for cat and both kittens, 3 ounces camel and 2 ounces old gold for striped-leg kitten, 3 ounces Roman gold, 2 ounces camel and ½ ounce old gold for striped-body kitten; aluminum crochet hook size G (or international hook size 4:50 mm) **or the size that will give you the correct gauge;** polyester fiberfill stuffing; felt scraps for facial features; white glue.

GAUGE 3 sts = 1″; 4 rows = 1″.

NOTE To change colors, work with color in use until 2 lps of last sc remain on hook; join new color, yo and draw through both lps on hook.

MAMA CAT

BODY BACK Starting at hind end with color T, ch 24 to measure about 8″. **1st row:** Sc in 2nd ch from hook and in each ch across (23 sc); ch 1, turn. **2nd row:** Sc in each sc across; ch 1, turn. Repeat 2nd row until 53 rows have been completed (about 12½″.) Break off.

BODY FRONT Work as for back for 32 rows.

FACE Continuing in sc, work colors as follows: **1st row:** Work 9 T, 5 C, 9 T. **2nd row:** Work 8 T, 7 C, 8 T. **3rd row:** Work 7 T, 9 C, 7 T. **4th row:** Work 6 T, 11 C, 6 T. Repeat 4th row 11 times more. **16th row:** Repeat 3rd row. **17th row:** Repeat 2nd row. With T, work 4 rows. Break off.

LEGS (make 4) Starting at foot with C, ch 2. **1st rnd:** Work 4 sc in 2nd ch from hook. Mark beg of rnds but do not join rnds. **2nd rnd:** Work 2 sc in each sc around (8 sc). **3rd rnd:** Repeat 2nd rnd (16 sc). **4th rnd:** Sc in each sc around, increasing 7 sc evenly (23 sc). Work 4 rnds even. Break off C; join T. Work even until piece measures 6″ from beg. Break off.

TAIL Starting at tip, work as for leg through 3rd rnd. Working even on 16 sc, work 2 more rnds C; join T and work 6½″ tail. Break off.

EARS (make 4) With C, ch 4. **1st row:** Sc in 2nd ch from hook, sc in next ch, 3 sc in next ch; working along opposite side of ch, sc in next 2 ch; ch 1, turn. **2nd row:** Sc in first 2 sc, 2 sc in next sc, sc in next sc, 2 sc in next sc, sc in last 2 sc; ch 1, turn. **3rd row:** Sc in first 4 sc, 3 sc in next sc, sc in last 4 sc. Break off.

For each ear, sl st 2 pieces tog.

FINISHING Sew back and front together along upper and side edges. Stuff body, legs and tail. Sew legs to body back and front. Close body. Sew tail and ears in place. Cut out and glue or tack felt features in place.

STRIPED-LEG KITTEN

BODY BACK With color C, ch 16 to measure about 5″. **1st row:** Sc in 2nd ch from hook and in each ch across; ch 1, turn. **2nd row:** Sc in each sc across; ch 1, turn. Repeat 2nd row until 30 rows have been completed. (Piece should measure about 7½″.) Break off.

BODY FRONT Work as for back until 16 rows have been completed.

To work face Continuing in sc, work colors as follows: **1st row:** Work 6 C, 3 G, 6 C. **2nd row:** Work 5 C, 5 G, 5 C. **3rd row:** Work 4 C, 7 G, 4 C. **4th through 7th rows:** Repeat 3rd row 4 times more. **8th row:** Repeat 2nd row. **9th row:** Repeat 1st row. With C, work 5 rows. Break off.

LEGS (make 4) Starting at foot with G, ch 2. **1st rnd:** Work 4 sc in 2nd ch from hook. Mark beg of rnds but do not join rnds. **2nd rnd:** Work 2 sc in each sc around (8 sc). **3rd rnd:** Sc in each sc around, increasing 6 sc as evenly spaced as possible (14 sc). Join C. Working even, work 1

rnd C, 1 rnd G until piece measures 4½", ending with a C rnd. Break off.

TAIL With C, ch 2. **1st rnd:** Work 4 sc in 2nd ch from hook. **2nd rnd:** Work 2 sc in each sc around. Working even, work 1 rnd each C and G until piece measures 4", ending with C. Break off.

EARS (make 2) With G, ch 3. **1st row:** Sc in 2nd ch from hook, 3 sc in next ch; sc in next ch on opposite side of ch; ch 1, turn. **2nd row:** Sc in 2 sc, 3 sc in next sc, sc in last 2 sc. Break off.

FINISHING See Mama Cat.

STRIPED-BODY KITTEN

BODY BACK AND FRONT Work as for Striped-leg Kitten, substituting 1 row each T and C for C.

LEGS Work as for Striped-leg Kitten, working 3 rnds C, 1 rnd each T and C, ending with T.

TAIL Work as for Striped-leg Kitten, working 1 rnd each C, T and C, ending with T.

EARS Work as for Striped-leg Kitten, substituting T for G.

FINISHING See Mama Cat.

Bug-eyed Moose and Giraffe

(Project **1** in group photograph, page **58**)

Hand puppets, ideal for kids who like to make up their own games.

SIZE About 11" long.

MATERIALS 45"-wide felt (¾ yard red or yellow makes 8 bodies, ¾ yard pink makes 12 mouths), scraps of black and white and other colors for details; white glue; polyester fiberfill for stuffing.

For body, cut two 5½" x 12" felt pieces. Cut 5½" x 7" pink rectangle for mouth. Cut four 2"-diameter white circles for eyes and two ½"-diameter black circles for pupils. Cut 1" circles or 1½" x 1¾" ovals for spots. Enlarge diagrams for giraffe ear and 3-pronged moose antler (see How to Enlarge Patterns, page 158). Make patterns and cut 4 felt antlers, 2 ears and four 1½" x 3" straight horns.

Pin body pieces together and round corners at one end. Separate pieces. Round all 4 corners of mouth to match. Fold mouth in half and pin between body pieces; stitch rounded ends with ½" seam; clip seam. Stitch side seams on body. Turn.

Stitch pairs of pieces for eyes, antlers and horns together with ¼" seams, leaving base open on each. Clip curves and turn. Stuff firmly and sew opening closed. Following photograph, sew antler, horns, eyes and ears (pleat) to face. Glue pupils and spots in place.

Each sq. = ½"

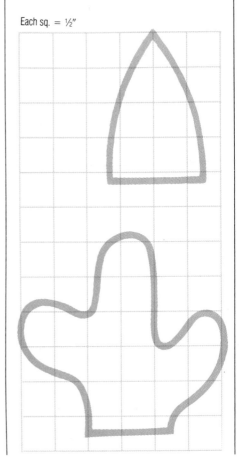

Each sq. = ½″

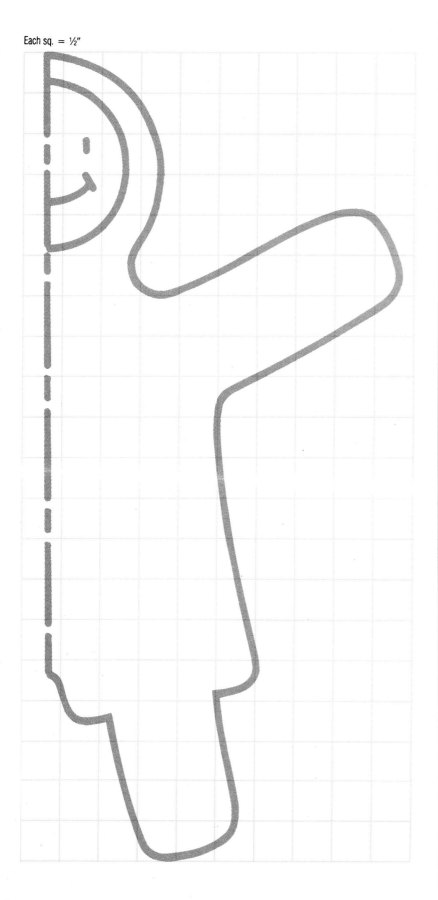

Polka-dot Beanbag Doll

(Project **12** in group photograph, page **58**)

Acrobat's body is stuffed with dried peas so she's nice and flip-floppy.

SIZE About 10″ tall.

MATERIALS 45″-wide polka-dot fabric (¾ yard makes 4); scrap of white fabric; ½″-wide ribbon or bias tape (1 yard trims 3); red, white and blue sewing threads; scraps of yellow and red yarn; 3 buttons; polyester fiberfill and dried peas for stuffing.

Enlarge diagram (see How to Enlarge Patterns, page 158) and make full pattern. Cut out 2 fabric pieces, adding ¼″ seam allowance to all edges. For face, cut out 2¼″-diameter white fabric circle. Using ⅛″-wide machine zigzag stitch, appliqué face to one body piece, then add red mouth and blue eyes. Cut 2 pieces of ribbon for belt halves. Topstitch one across front and one across back. With right sides facing, stitch doll halves together, leaving 3″ open. Clip curves and turn. Stuff head, arms and legs with fiberfill, then topstitch across neck, arms and legs where they join body. Stuff body with peas. Sew opening closed.

For hair, cut eighteen 4″ lengths of yarn. Spread across top of head and sew through middle. Sew on buttons. Cut two 10″ lengths of red yarn. Hold together and tie in bow. Sew to neck.

Winter Sports Dolls

Dolls have quilted bodies; muslin faces with embroidered smiles and crayonned cheeks.

SIZE About 18″ tall.

MATERIALS 45″-wide cotton-blend quilted fabric, ⅜ yard for each doll body (or ¾ yard for 3 dolls); scrap unbleached muslin for head; ¼ yard 45″-wide brushed jersey for cap, scarf, mittens and boots; crewel or fingering yarn for hair and embroidered features; matching sewing thread; pink crayon for cheeks; polyester fiberfill for stuffing.

Enlarge patterns, (see How to Enlarge Patterns, page 158), adding ½″ seam allowance to all edges. Cut out fabric pieces.

FACE On one head piece, embroider eyes in satin stitch, nose and mouth in backstitch (see stitch diagrams, page 159). Color cheeks with crayon.

ASSEMBLING With right sides facing, stitch a head piece to neck of a body piece, a mitten piece to each arm (thumbs toward body) and a boot piece to each leg (toes turned outward). Stitch doll halves together, leaving 4″ opening at one side leg. Turn, stuff (except ears) and close opening. Topstitch on broken lines at base of ears.

HAIR Girl: Cut yarn into 9″ lengths. Fold in half and, with matching sewing thread, sew folded ends across top seam line of head from ear to ear, distributing yarn evenly. **Boy:** Thread needle with sewing thread to match yarn. Wind yarn 6 or 7 times around a pencil. Without cutting yarn, carefully slide loops from pencil and sew to head close to one ear. Continue making curls,

sewing them across top of head from ear to ear. Add more curls to back of head but don't make them too thick or cap may not fit.

CAP Using pattern, cut out crown pieces from fabric. For brim, cut two 2½″ x 7″ strips with grain running lengthwise. With right sides facing, stitch crown pieces together. Stitch ends of brim pieces together to form ring. Stitch wrong side of brim to right side of crown around edge. Trim seams. Roll up brim and tack hat to head.

SCARF Cut 4½″ x 29″ fabric strip. Stitch ¼″ finished hems on all edges. Tie scarf around neck.

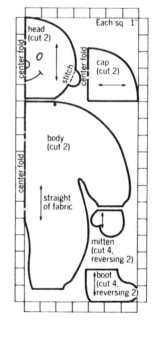

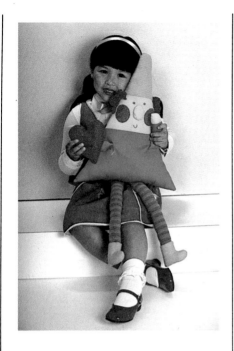

Triangle Pillow Doll

Jolly little elf made soft to sit on laps.

SIZE 29″ high.

MATERIALS 45″-wide cotton-blend fabric, ¼ yard each turquoise (color A) and yellow (B), scrap of pink; ¼ yard green felt (C); two 6″-square pieces orange felt for heart; ¼ yard striped jersey; matching sewing threads; pink and green embroidery floss; few yards of orange yarn; polyester fiberfill for stuffing.

CUTTING Enlarge patterns (see How to Enlarge Patterns, page 158). Adding ½″ seam allowance to all edges, cut pieces from fabrics. Make triangular body pattern 14″ x 19″ x 19″ and cut into 3 sections parallel to 14″ edge: 7½″ bottom, 4½″ middle and 5½″ top. Adding ½″ to all edges, cut 2 bottom pieces from A, 2 middle pieces from B and 2 top pieces from C. Cut two 5″ x 11½″ jersey strips for legs, two 2″-diameter pink cheeks and two 2″ x 2¼″ B ovals for nose.

STITCHING Stitch hand to each arm. Stitch matching arm/hands together, leaving top open. Stitch nose sections together with ¼″ seams, leaving 1″ open. Stitch hearts together, leaving 3″ open. Fold legs in half lengthwise; stitch long edges. Stitch matching boots together, leaving tops open. Turn all pieces and stuff; close nose and heart openings.

Topstitch cheek circles with machine zigzag stitch to a B body piece. Embroider pink outline-stitch mouth and green satin-stitch eyes. (Stitch diagrams, page 159). Tack nose to face.

Turn in top edges of arms and topstitch to one A body piece. Turn in top edges of boots and slide onto ends of legs; slipstitch.

Stitch A, B and C pieces together to form 2 triangles. Stitch triangles together, rounding top point and leaving 5″ open at center of lower edge. Turn. Stitch legs to front body at bottom. Stuff body. Turn in back open edge and slipstitch opening closed. Make about 20 loops of yarn and sew along seam at each side of head. Sew heart to doll's hand.

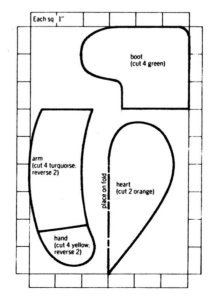

Autograph Cat Pillow

(Project **16** in group photograph, page **58**)

Cat-shaped canvas; main body lines drawn on with felt pens.

SIZE About 14″ tall.

MATERIALS 45″-wide unbleached muslin (1¼ yards make 4); red and pink waterproof felt-tipped markers for fabric; ½″-wide grosgrain ribbon (1½ yards trim 2); polyester fiberfill for stuffing; ballpoint pen with clip.

Enlarge and cut out diagram pattern (see How to Enlarge Patterns, page 158). Cut out 2 muslin pieces (reverse pattern for one), adding ¼″ seam allowance to all edges. Mark details on one piece. For base, cut 2″ x 8½″ oval. Using red marker, trace over all detail lines. Fill in nose with pink. With right sides facing, stitch half of oval along bottom edge of front cat piece, then stitch cat halves together, leaving other side of oval open like a flap. Clip curves and turn. Stuff cat and sew other side of oval to back of cat. Tie 27″ length of ribbon around neck. Clip on pen.

Each sq. = ½″

84

Stuffed Cat and Mouse

SIZES Cat, 12″ tall; mouse, 5″ tall.

MATERIALS Cat: ⅜ yard plush fabric (¾ yard makes 3); two ⅝″-diameter buttons; ½ yard ½″-wide grosgrain ribbon; scraps felt and red embroi-

dery floss. **Mouse:** 7″ x 9″ piece plush fabric (¼ yard makes 5); two ⅜″-diameter buttons; ¼ yard ¼″-wide ribbon; scraps felt and embroidery floss. For both: white glue; polyester fiberfill for stuffing.

Enlarge cat and mouse body shapes (see How To Enlarge Patterns, page 158) and make patterns. Cut out 2 body pieces for each animal, adding ¼″ seam allowance. **For mouse ears,** cut two 2″-diameter felt circles. Pleat slightly and pin pleated edge to body front, right sides facing. With right sides facing (mouse ears will be sandwiched between), stitch body pieces together, leaving opening at bottom for tail. Turn right side out.

For cat's tail, cut 2″ x 15″ strip. **For mouse's tail,** cut 1½″ x 6″ strip. Fold each strip in half lengthwise; stitch long edge and one end with ¼″ seam; turn right side out. Stuff tail and body. Insert tail in opening and sew opening closed. Bend tail to desired shape and tack to hold.

Sew on button eyes, embroider whiskers and glue on felt nose. (**NOTE** Substitute embroidered or felt eyes if toy is for small child.) Tie ribbon bow to each tail. Cut out and glue felt heart on cat.

Each sq. = ½″

Snowboy and Snowgirl Sock Dolls

(Project **9** in group photograph, page **58**)

Softies made of tubular stretch socks.

SIZE About 12″ tall.

MATERIALS Tubular sport stretch socks with striped cuffs, 1 sock per doll; scraps of felt for scarf; embroidery floss or yarn for features; scraps knitting-worsted-weight yarn for braids and ties; polyester fiberfill for stuffing.

Following photograph, starting at toe, mark one 2½″ vertical line on sock foot to separate legs, and two 2″ lines to outline arms. Topstitch along these lines. Stuff sock firmly until area from bottom of cuff to toe is stretched to 12″ long. Sew tightly closed at bottom of cuff, then wind thread around several times and knot to fasten. About 5″ below, sew row of running stitches around doll and draw up to form neck; fasten.

Embroider 2 straight stitches for eyes and one French knot for nose (Stitch diagrams, page 159.) For scarf, cut 2″ x 16″ felt strip. Fringe or pink ends. Decorate with glued-on heart or stripes. Tie around neck.

For braids, cut about six 18″ strands of yarn. Knot together in middle, fold in half and braid. Tie with bit of contrasting yarn. Tack a braid to each side of head. Fold cuff, wrong side out, over head, then fold half up to form cap. For boy's bangs, sew loops of red yarn to inside at cuff.

Tooth-fairy Pillow

(Project **13** in group photograph, page **58**)

A familiar shape, pocketed for that all-important visit.

SIZE About 8½″ x 9½″.

MATERIALS 45″-wide white cotton-blend fabric or sheeting (1⅛ yards make 8); scraps of yellow fabric (¼ yard makes 24 stars); ⅜″-wide blue satin ribbon (1 yard trims 6); waterproof fine-point felt-tipped fabric marker; polyester fiberfill for stuffing.

Enlarge and cut out diagram patterns (see How to Enlarge Patterns, page 158). Cut 2 fabric teeth, adding ¼″ seam allowance all around. Cut one star, adding ¼″ seam allowance. Turn in seam allowance on star, cutting notch at each inner point and trimming outer points; fold, press and topstitch hem. With marker, write "tooth fairy pillow" on star. Cut 6″ length of ribbon. Pin ribbon and star to one tooth piece. Following previous stitching line, topstitch bottom and sides of star, leaving top open for coin pocket. Topstitch both edges of ribbon. With right sides facing, stitch tooth pieces together, leaving 4″ open. Clip curves, turn and stuff. Sew opening closed.

Each sq. = ½″

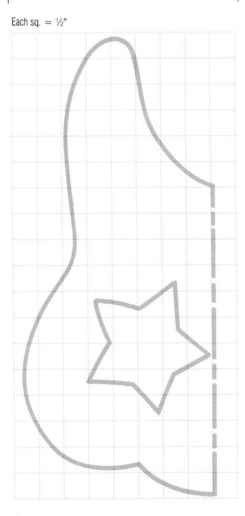

Stick-doll Puppets

(Project **7** in group photograph, page **58**)

SIZE About 13½″ tall.

MATERIALS 45″-wide calico and white cotton, 1⅜ yards calico for 2 dolls, 1 yard white cotton for 6 dolls; contrasting-color sewing thread; 2½″-diameter plastic ball; ¼″ x 1″ lattice, 12″ length for 1 doll; ¼″-wide ribbon, ¾ yard for 1 doll; scraps of ⅜″- to ½″-wide ribbon or hem tape for wig base; scraps of felt for features; 1 ounce knitting-worsted-weight yarn for wigs for 2 dolls; acrylic paint and primer; white glue; rubber bands, pinking shears.

Cut 12″ length of lattice; prime and paint. Cut ½″-deep slit in plastic-foam ball, fill with glue and insert end of lattice. Let dry thoroughly.

From calico, cut 24″-diameter circle. Topstitch ¼″ finished hem with machine zigzag stitch in contrasting color. From white cotton, cut two 10½″-diameter circles with pinking shears. Center and drape calico over plastic ball head. Hold white cotton circles together and center on top of calico. Pinch together below head and fasten tightly with rubber band. Cut out felt features (see photograph) and glue to face. Cut 19″ length of ribbon and tie around neck in bow, covering rubber band.

For hair, cut yarn into 7″ lengths. Cut 4½″ length of scrap ribbon and spread about 90 strands of yarn across it, covering ribbon completely. Topstitch down center. Glue ribbon across head from top to back neck. Clip a few strands of yarn for bangs. Make bow and glue to head.

Tiny Finger Puppets

(Project **17** in group photograph, page **58**)

Miniatures made for pennies of intriguing bits and pieces.

SIZE About 3½″ tall.

MATERIALS Scraps of yarn to make pompon heads and features (or use 1¼″-diameter balls from ball fringe); scraps of felt and trims such as lace, baby rickrack and fake flowers; tiny moveable animal eyes; white glue; heavy sewing thread for whiskers.

Cut 2½″ x 3¼″ felt piece. Overlap 2½″ edges to form cone with about 1¼″-wide opening at bottom and ½″ at top; glue edges together, trimming them straight. Make 1¼″-diameter pompon for head. (General pompon instructions, page 160.) Cut felt ears (see photograph) and glue to head. Make nose, cheeks or mouth pompon by tying tightly together several ½″-long strands of yarn and trimming them to form a tiny ball (or trim ball from ball fringe). For whiskers, cut three 1″-long strands of heavy thread, brush with glue and let dry to stiffen, then glue to back of nose. For mouth, wrap and glue a thin strand of yarn tightly around tiny pompon. Glue mouth, nose or cheeks and eyes to head. Push top of cone up into head pompon and glue. When dry, decorate neck with flowers or bits of lace or rickrack as shown.

Flying Disk

Soft toss toy, safe to throw or catch.

SIZE 14″ diameter.

MATERIALS ½ yard each of red and blue shiny fabric; ¼ yard silver metallic fabric; matching sewing threads; polyester fiberfill for stuffing.

Cut 1 red and 1 blue 15″-diameter circle. Cut 1 red and 1 blue 10″ square. Reversing colors, topstitch a square centered on each circle. Cut 2 silver 7¼″ squares and topstitch following photograph. Stitch circles together, right sides facing, with ½″ seam, leaving small opening for turning. Clip seams, turn and stuff lightly so that disk remains flat. Sew opening closed.

Wiggly-snake Pull Toy

(Project **6** in group photograph, page **58**)

Sections of poles and dowels strung together with cord.

SIZE 28″ long.

MATERIALS 18″ length 1½″-diameter pole and 9″ length ¾″-diameter dowel (make 1); 1½ yards cord; acrylic paints; sandpaper. For general woodworking guidance, see page 161.

From pole, cut one 2″ section and sixteen 1″ sections. From dowel, cut eighteen ½″ sections. Sand pieces, rounding edges. Paint dowel pieces 2 colors (9 of each). Drill 2 cone-shaped eyes in 2″ pole section (head) ½″ apart, about ¼″ deep. Cut ¼″-deep slash across end of head for mouth. Paint eyes and mouth. Drill small hole lengthwise through center of each piece. Cut 1½-yard length of cord; knot one end. Starting with dowel, string pieces alternately on cord, ending with head. Make knot near head and 2nd one 2″ from end. String remaining dowel piece on end for pull and make 3rd knot.

Wooden Push-toy Cars

(Project **18** in group photograph, page **58**)

SIZE 7″ to 9″ long.

MATERIALS Scraps 2 x 2 and 2 x 4 pine; 1½″-diameter pole (4″ make 4 wheels); ¼″-diameter dowel (5″ make 2 axles); primer and acrylic paints; polyurethane finish; wood glue. For general woodworking guidance, see page 161.

Enlarge car diagrams (see How to Enlarge Patterns, page 158) and make patterns. Cut low-slung car from 2 x 2 and other 2 cars from 2 x 4. Drill holes for windows. Drill holes slightly larger than ¼″ for axles. Cut pole into four 1″ lengths for wheels; cut dowel into two 2½″ lengths for axles. Drill ¼″ hole halfway through center of each wheel. Sand car and wheels smooth. Prime, paint and finish car and wheels. Insert axles through car; glue wheel on both ends of each.

Each sq. = ½″

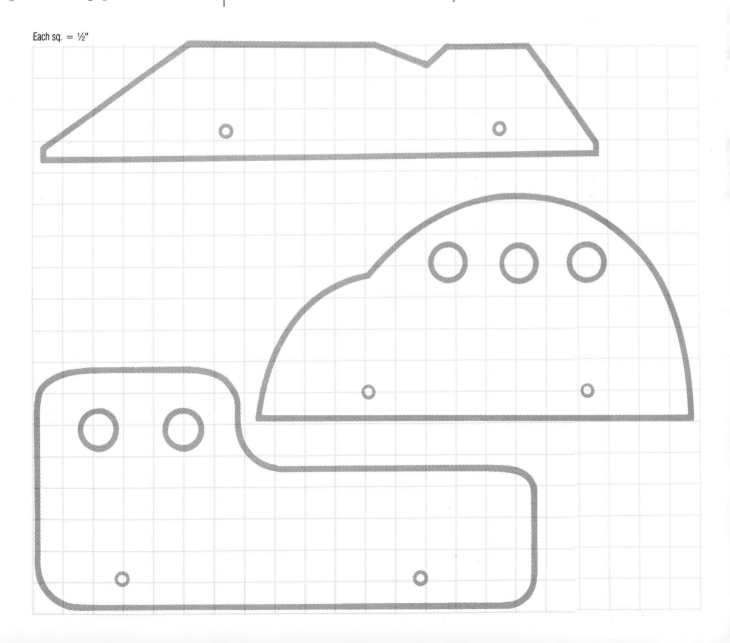

Designs to do a house proud

treats for cooking & dining

Starting at top left: **1.** Sweet shapes (cookie, cupcake and ice-cream-cone) refrigerator magnets, page 101. **2.** Appliquéd aprons, page 98. **3.** Quilted tea cozy with teapot appliqué, page 92. **4.** Wooden-teapot paper-napkin caddy, page 92. **5.** Quilted cook's mitts, page 94. **6.** Quilted place mats with polka-dot napkins and rings, page 105. **7.** Bouquet garni packets (mix of cooking herbs) in decorated jar, page 102. **8.** Crocheted potholders, page 91. **9.** Crocheted kitty-cat pad and pencil holder, page 98. **10.** Quilted covers for blender and toaster, page 95. **11.** Fruit-appliquéd potholders, page 93.

Designs to do a house proud is the name we've given to the three sections that follow. (The others begin on pages 106 and 116.) Each group is aimed at a particular facet of living, and they're all colorfully coordinated to appeal to the home decorator in every passerby.

Treats for cooking and dining begin with brighteners for the kitchen, from aprons to cook's mitts, appliance covers to tea cozies. Practical help for the cook takes many forms: hanging notepad, refrigerator magnets, a canister, a breadboard. The hostess who likes to set a handsome table will love quilted place mats with matching napkins, and some new accessory ideas for showing off candles and flowers.

treats for cooking & dining

A cheerful kitchen and a smartly set table—that's every woman's dream. How satisfying to coin money by making it come true! With these designs, the fun and the profits are both in the fabrics: striking but simple; coordinated for you; easy for unskilled hands to work with.

Padded Watermelon Potholders

For matching place mats and napkins, see page 104.

SIZE About 5″ x 10″.

MATERIALS ⅜ yard green print, ¼ yard each pink print and quilt batting make 4 potholders; scrap ⅜″-wide grosgrain ribbon; appropriate sewing threads, including red for zigzag stitching.

From green print cut out 11″-diameter circle. From pink print cut 8½″-diameter half circle; from batt, cut 10″-diameter half circle. Turn under straight edge on pink piece; center and pin to half of green piece. Appliqué folded edge with slipstitch. Center and baste batt to wrong side of half of holder. Fold holder in half, wrong side out. Stitch curved edge, leaving opening for turning. Turn right side out; sew opening closed, inserting ribbon loop in opening. Using red zigzag stitch, machine stitch over raw curved edge of pink.

Crocheted Potholders

(Project **8** in group photograph, page **88**)

SIZE About 7″ square.

MATERIALS Coats & Clark's Rug Yarn (rayon and cotton), 1 (70-yard) skein white (W) makes centers for 3 potholders, 1 skein blue (B) trims 6 potholders or 1 skein each green (G) and yellow (Y) trims 12 potholders, 1 skein red (R) borders 5 potholders; aluminum crochet hook size G (or international size 4:50 mm) **or the size that will give you the correct gauge.**

GAUGE 7 sc = 2″; 4 rows = 1″.

CENTER With W, ch 17. **1st row:** Sc in end ch from hook and in each ch across; ch 1, turn. **2nd row:** Sc in each sc across; ch 1, turn. Repeat last row 15 times more (or until piece is square). Break off.

INNER TRIM 1st rnd: With B or G, work 15 sc on each edge of W square and 3 sc in each corner (72 sc). Either break off G and join Y or continue with B. **2nd rnd:** Sc in each sc around, working 3 sc in each corner sc (80 sc). Break off.

BORDER Starting in 3rd sc of a 3-sc corner group, with R repeat 2nd rnd of inner trim, ending with 3 sc in last corner sc (88 sc). **2nd rnd:** *Sk next sc, sc in next sc, sk next sc, in next sc work shell of (sc, dc and sc). Repeat from * around to within last 3-sc corner group (21 shells), sk next sc, sc in next sc, ch 6 for hanging lp, sc in next sc; join. Break off.

Bandanna Potholders

SIZE About 7″ square.

MATERIALS 2 contrasting-color bandannas 18″ square will make 4 potholders; 7″ square ¼″-thick quilt batting and 1¼″-diameter plastic ring for each.

Cut out two 7½″ squares of each color for each potholder. Cut in half to form 8 triangles. Cut out 1¾″ x 4″ strip for loop. Stitch triangles together as shown to form two squares. With right sides facing, stitch squares together, leaving opening for turning along center of one side.

For loop, fold strip in half lengthwise, wrong side out. Stitch ¼″ from long raw edges. Turn right side out. Insert through ring. Baste ends together to form loop.

Turn squares right side out; insert batt; pin loop in opening and sew opening closed. Machine stitch through all thicknesses to form quilt pattern.

Smile Potholders

SIZE About 8″ in diameter.

MATERIALS (for 1) Coats & Clark's Red Heart Cotton Knit and Crochet Yarn, 1 (2.5-ounce) skein each yellow No. 265 (MC) and turquoise No. 519 (CC); aluminum crochet hook size F (or international size 4.00 mm) **or the size that will give you the correct gauge;** large-eyed crewel needle.

GAUGE 4 sc = 1″.

CIRCLE (make 2) With MC, ch 2. **1st rnd:** Work 6 sc in 2nd ch from hook. Mark beg of rnds; do not join rnds. **2nd rnd:** Work 2 sc in each sc around (12 sc). **3rd rnd:** (Sc in next sc, 2 sc in next sc) 6 times (18 sc). **4th rnd:** (2 sc in next sc, sc in next 2 sc) 6 times (24 sc). Continue in this manner, increasing 6 sc evenly spaced on each rnd and being careful not to work incs over previous incs, until piece measures about 7½″ in diameter; join. Fasten off.

With wrong sides facing and using CC, sc around outer edges, working through both thicknesses; join; ch 12 for loop; sl st in next st. Fasten off.

Eyes (make 2): With CC, work 1st and 2nd rnds of circle; join. Fasten off, leaving 15″ end. Thread end in crewel needle and sew in place. With CC, embroider chainstitch mouth (stitch diagram, page 159).

Quilted Tea Cozy

(Project 3 in group photograph, page 88)

SIZE 11″ high x 12″ wide.

MATERIALS 45″-wide reversible quilted fabric, two 12″ x 13″ pieces per cozy (2 yards make 9); 6″ x 7½″ piece contrasting unquilted fabric for appliqué, matching one side of quilted fabric, if possible (1 yard makes 36 appliqués); 1″-wide bias tape, ¾ yard per cozy (one 3-yard package trims 4 covers); sewing thread to match tape.

From quilted fabric, cut two 12″ x 13″ pieces. Round one corner. Cut cardboard pattern of rounded corner and use to round opposite corner of 12″ edge and 2 corners on other piece.

Enlarge teapot diagram (see How to Enlarge Patterns, page 158) and make pattern. Cut fabric teapot without adding seam allowance. Pin to center of one cozy piece and machine appliqué with narrow zig-zag stitch.

With right sides facing, stitch cozy together around sides and rounded end; turn. Bind open edge.

Wooden-teapot Paper-napkin Caddy

(Project 4 in group photograph, page 88)

SIZE 6″ x 7¼″.

MATERIALS ¼″ plywood, 7¼″ x 12¼″ piece for one holder (2′ x 4′ plywood—¼ sheet—makes 10); ½″-thick scraps pine for base; nails (4 per holder); spackle; primer; acrylic paint; coping saw; sandpaper; polyurethane or shellac finish.

Enlarge teapot diagram (see How to Enlarge Patterns, page 158) and make pattern. Cut 2 pieces from plywood with coping saw. Sand edges and fill with spackle, sanding again if necessary. Cut 1¼″ x 3″ piece scrap pine for base; sand edges. Nail a teapot to each side of base. Prime all surfaces, then apply 2 coats paint and 1 coat finish.

Each sq. = ½″

Appliquéd Potholders

(Project **11** in group photograph, page **88**)

SIZE 7½″ square.

MATERIALS 45″-wide cotton-blend fabrics, 8½″ x 17″ piece for 1 potholder (1 yard makes 10), 6″ x 7″ piece for one appliqué (1 yard makes 36 oranges or 42 apples or 60 pears); scraps green fabric for stems and leaves; sewing thread to match potholder and black for appliqués; 7½″-square quilt batting to pad one potholder (1⅛-yard square pads 25 potholders); plastic ring.

Cut two 8½″ squares fabric and one 7½″ square batting. Enlarge apple, pear and orange stem diagrams (see How to Enlarge Patterns, page 158) and make patterns. Draw free-form circular orange pattern about 6″ x 6½″. Cut pieces from fabric without adding seam allowance. Pin a fruit and stem to center of one potholder piece; machine appliqué with narrow zigzag stitch and black thread. Center batting on wrong side of appliquéd piece; pin two together through right side. With right sides facing, stitch front and back of potholder together, leaving 3″ open for turning. Turn; close opening. Topstitch ½″ in from edge of potholder and around appliqué about ⅛″ from edge. Sew ring to corner.

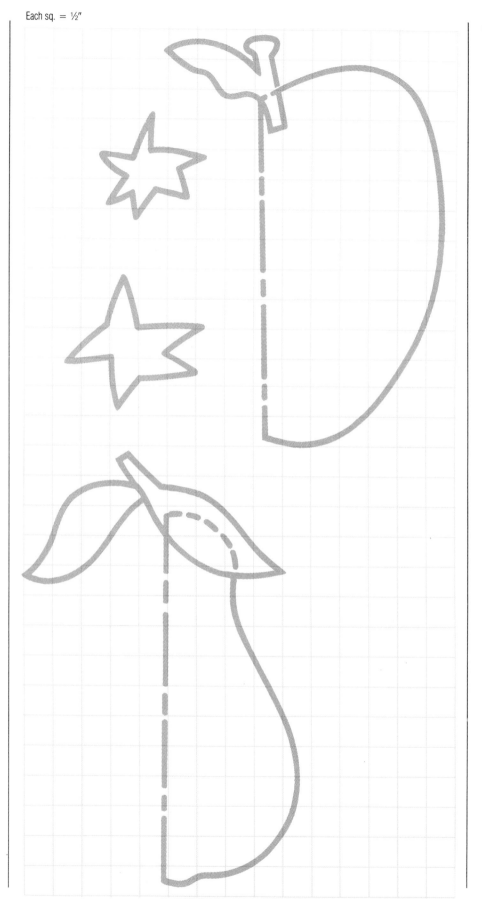

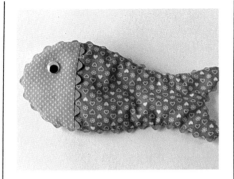

Quilted Fish Potholder

SIZE About 6″ x 11″.

MATERIALS ½ yard each of 2 different print fabrics make 5 potholders; 12″ square of quilt batting makes 2 potholders; 1½ yards jumbo rickrack and 1 paste-on 20-mm moveable animal eye per potholder.

Enlarge fish diagram (see How to Enlarge Patterns, page 158) and make pattern, being sure to mark dividing line. Adding ¼″ seam allowance, cut out two head sections and two body sections. Cut out whole fish shape from batting, omitting seam allowance.

On right side, baste rickrack on seam line of straight edge of each body section. With right sides facing, stitch head sections to body sections to form front and back. Press seam allowances toward head sections. Baste rickrack along seam line around outer edge of front.

Each sq. = ½″

Stitch front to back, leaving opening for turning. Turn right side out, insert batting piece and sew opening closed. Topstitch across head section close to seam line. Paste on eye.

Quilted Cook's Mitts

(Project **5** in group photograph, page **88**)

MATERIALS 45″-wide reversible quilted fabric, four 8″ x 11½″ pieces for 1 mitt (2 yards make 7); 1″-wide bias tape, 30″ per mitt (two 3-yard packages make 7 mitts); sewing thread to match tape.

NOTE A free-arm sewing machine is necessary to machine stitch inner band trim on mitts. To hand-sew, use closely spaced, invisible stitch.

To make cardboard pattern, draw around your hand in mitten shape, adding about 1″ for ease to fingers and thumb edges and forming straight edges to wrist as shown in photograph. Pattern should be about 11″ long and 6″ wide. From fabric, cut out 4 pieces for each double-thick mitt, reversing two and adding ¼″ seam allowance to all but wrist edges.

With right sides facing, stitch pairs of mitts together, clipping seams at curves. Turn. Cut 2 strips tape to fit around wrist of mitt, plus ½″. Bind wrist edge with one strip, then fold other strip in half lengthwise and stitch around mitt along both edges 1½″ from wrist binding. To make multiple hanging loops (1 for each mitt), fold length of tape in half lengthwise and topstitch along both edges. Cut into 3″ strips. Fold in half and sew ends inside mitts.

Mouse Pot-handle Cover

SIZE About 3″ x 7″, not including tail.

MATERIALS ½ yard each white fabric, calico fabric and ½″-thick quilt batting make 10 covers; three ¼″-diameter buttons and 4½″ length ½″-wide single-fold bias tape per cover.

Enlarge mouse body diagram (see How to Enlarge Patterns, page 158) and make pattern, being sure to include inner lines. For front and back, cut out 2 whole body pieces each from calico fabric and from quilt batt and, for lining, cut out 2 whole body pieces from white fabric, adding ¼″ seam allowance to all pieces. From white, cut out one face piece and 4 ears, adding ¼″ seam allowance.

To make ears, stitch pairs together, leaving straight edge open. Turn right side out, press and pleat at center of straight edge. For face, press under ¼″ edges that face toward body. Pin to right side of top body, matching raw edges of snout and sandwiching ears between; topstitch.

Baste batting piece to wrong side of top body and one to bottom body. To form tail, fold tape in half crosswise, right side out, and pin to top body, with raw edges matching and loop toward center. With right sides facing, stitch body edges together, leaving front open. Stitch lining pieces together in same manner, leaving 2″ opening at lower end. Turn right side out.

With right sides facing, pin open edges of body to lining at face edge; stitch. Turn right side out through opening in lining. Sew opening closed. Push lining inside body.

Quilted Appliance Covers

(Project **10** in group photograph, page **88**)

SIZES 6½″-high x 10½″-wide x 6″-deep toaster cover; 7½″-wide x 15½″-high x 7½″-deep blender cover.

MATERIALS 45″-wide reversible quilted fabric, 14″ x 23″ piece for toaster cover (1 yard makes 4), 16″ x 37″ piece for blender cover (1¼ yards make 3); 1″-wide bias tape (1¼ yards per toaster cover or 3-yard package for 2 covers, 3 yards per blender cover); sewing thread to match tape.

TOASTER COVER From fabric, cut two 7″ x 11″ pieces for sides and one 6½″ x 23″ piece for boxing strip. On a side piece, round one corner. Cut cardboard pattern of rounded corner and use to round corners on top edges of both side pieces. With wrong sides facing, pin boxing strips along sides and top edge of a side piece; trim strip to fit if necessary. Bind pinned edge. Pin and bind other edge of boxing strip to other side piece. Bind lower edge of cover.

BLENDER COVER From fabric, cut two 8″ x 16″ pieces for sides and one 8″ x 37″ piece for boxing strip. Finish as for toaster cover, using same pattern to round corners.

Each sq. = ½″

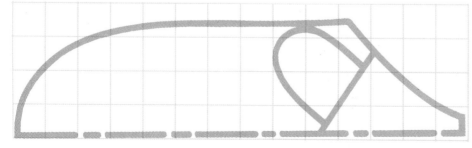

Smocked Apron

SIZE About 19″ long.

MATERIALS 1 yard 45″-wide cotton or cotton-blend fabric; contrasting-color pearl cotton size 5; large-eyed crewel needle.

APRON Cut fabric 23″ long x 31″ wide. For ties, cut two 4″ x 22″ strips. Make ¼″ finished hem at upper and side edges of apron piece, and 3″ hem at lower edge.

SMOCKING Starting 1″ below upper edge, with ballpoint pen mark 4 rows of dots ½″ apart on right side of apron. Thread length of pearl cotton in needle and knot one end.

Row 1: Starting at upper right dot (dot 1, on Diagram 1), insert needle from wrong to right side and draw through, then make stitch over dot as shown. Insert needle through fabric at 2 (on Diagram 2) halfway between dots 1 and 3, draw through. Insert through dots 3 and 4, pulling them together, then make stitch over dots. Insert through 5. Insert through dots 6 and 7, pulling them together, then make stitch over them (Diagram 3). Insert through 8 and continue across in pattern. Fasten off.

Row 2: Make stitch at dot 1 on Diagram 4. Insert through 2. Make stitch just below stitch 3. Insert through 4. Insert through dots 5 and 6, pulling them together, then make stitch over them. Insert through 7. Make stitch just below stitch 8. Continue across in pattern. Fasten off.

Row 3: Starting where you started Row 2, work as for Row 1 once more.

FINISHING Fold each tie strip in half lengthwise, wrong side out. Stitch raw edges and one end of each. Turn right side out. Turn in remaining raw ends, and topstitch to sides of apron at ends of smocking.

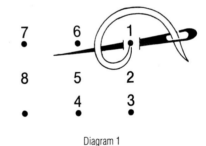

Diagram 1

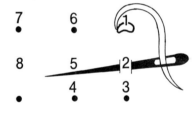

Diagram 2

Diagram 3

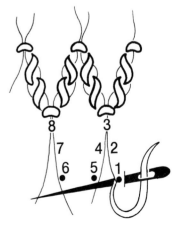

Diagram 4

Double-pocket Apron

MATERIALS 1½ yards 45"-wide cotton-blend printed fabric; 2¾ yards Wrights® Extra Wide double-fold bias tape; matching sewing thread.

From fabric cut 21" x 36" skirt, two 9" squares for bib and lining, 8½" x 13½" pocket back, 8½" x 10" pocket A (inner pocket), 6½" x 8½" pocket B (outer pocket), two 3" x 38" strips for ties-waistband and 3" x 28" strip for neckband.

Topstitch narrow hem on 21" edges of skirt. Bind one 36" edge (bottom) with tape (encase raw edge in folded tape and topstitch).

With tape bind one 8½" edge (top edge) each on pockets A and B. With wrong sides facing up, place pocket A on pocket B and pocket B on pocket back, matching 8½" raw edges on all three. Taking ½" seam allowance, stitch through all 3 layers along 8½" edge (bottom of pocket). Turn right side out. Bind sides with tape to form 2 pockets. Pin inverted box pleat at center top of pocket back so piece measures 5" across.

Gather top of apron skirt to measure 13". Pin top of pocket to top of skirt about 1½" from right edge.

Pin bib and lining together, right sides out. Bind 3 edges with tape. Center bib and pin to wrong side of skirt, matching raw edges. Stitch ends of ties-waistband together to form one long band. Turn in long edges ½" and press. Center, fold lengthwise and pin band over tops of pocket, skirt and bib. Topstitch the whole length of band and across band ends. Turn bib up. Topstitch top edge of band along width of bib.

Turn in and press edges of neckband; topstitch. Sew ends to back of bib, adjusting length.

Handywoman Apron

SIZE 16½" wide x 14" long.

MATERIALS ½ yard 45"-wide blue denim; red sewing thread; 6¼" self-fastening tape.

Cut 14" x 17¾" denim for apron. Mark each 14" edge 11½" down from top corner. Starting at marks, cut diagonally to form point at lower edge. Cut 13" x 21¾" denim for pocket. Mark 10½" down each 13" side and cut to point at lower edge (⅝" seam allowance is included on both pieces).

Pin sides of pocket to apron. Following photograph, pin four 1" box pleats in pocket. Trim pleats at lower edge of pocket. Unpin pocket from apron and press pleats. Turn upper edge of pocket in ¾"; re-form pleats and stitch hem ⅛" and ⅝" from edge, holding pleats in position. Place pieces together, with right side of pocket facing wrong side of apron, and pin along side and lower edges; stitch. Turn pocket right side out, slashing apron seam allowance at upper edge of pocket.

Baste side hems of apron, above pocket, to top edge of apron. Topstitch side and lower edges ½" from edge. Make vertical line of stitching between pleats.

To make band, cut denim 3" x waist measurement plus 6½". Turn under raw edges ½" and press. Fold in half lengthwise, right side out, and pin edges together leaving center open to insert apron. Insert and baste. Topstitch ⅛" from all edges. Sew fastening strips to overlapping ends of band.

Appliquéd Aprons

(Project **2** in group photograph, page **88**)

SIZE 25″ wide x 32½″ long.

MATERIALS 45″-wide heavy-weight unbleached muslin (or similar fabric), 1 yard for 1 apron (1½ yards make 2); 6″ x 7″ cotton-blend fabric for orange or tomato appliqué (1 yard makes 45); scraps green fabric for appliqué stems; 1″-wide bias tape, 1 (3-yard) package per apron; sewing threads to match tape and apron and black thread for appliqué; 2-D-rings to fasten neck tie.

Following broken lines on diagram, draw and cut out cardboard patterns to shape top and lower corners of apron. Following dimensions on diagram and using patterns for shaping, cut apron from fabric. Cut 6¾″ x 7¼″ pocket, three 2½″ x 24″ long ties and one 2½″ x 4″ short tie.

Bind all apron edges with tape. For appliqué, cut out free-form circular tomato or orange about 6″ to

Each sq. = ½″

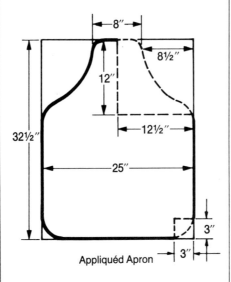

Appliquéd Apron

7″ diameter (or cut cardboard pattern first). Enlarge large stem and center stem diagrams (see How to Enlarge Patterns, page 158) and make patterns. Cut from fabric but do not add seam allowance. Pin to apron bib and machine appliqué with narrow zigzag stitch and black thread.

Fold one 6¾″ edge of pocket in 1″ and topstitch (top edge). Fold in and press other edges ¼″. Pin pocket to apron; topstitch.

Fold in and press long edges of ties ¼″; fold in half lengthwise and topstitch both edges. Zigzag stitch close to ends of ties. Topstitch 2 long ties to sides of apron about 13″ from top of bib, and remaining long tie to right corner of bib. Slide D-rings on short tie, fold tie in half and topstitch ends to left corner of bib.

Crocheted Kitty-cat Pad and Pencil Holder

(Project **9** in group photograph, page **88**)

SIZE About 12½″ tall, without tail.

MATERIALS Knitting-worsted-weight yarn, one (3½-ounce) skein each orange (color O) and red (R) makes 2 holders; aluminum crochet hook size F (or international size 4:00 mm) **or the size that will give you the correct gauge;** tapestry needle; 2 moveable animal eyes; white glue; notepad 4″ to 5″ square; pen or pencil.

GAUGE 9 dc = 2″; 2 rnds = 1″.

BODY Starting at center with color O, ch 4. Join with sl st to form ring. **1st rnd:** Ch 3, work 14 dc in ring; join with sl st in top of ch 3. **2nd rnd:** Ch 3, dc in top of sl st, work 2 dc in each dc around (30 dc, counting ch-3 as 1 dc); join. **3rd rnd:** Ch 3, work 2 dc in next dc, * dc in next dc, 2 dc in next dc. Repeat from * around (45 dc); join. **4th rnd:** Ch 3, 2 dc in next dc, * dc in each of next 2 dc, 2 dc in next dc. Repeat from * around, ending dc in last dc (60 dc); join. **5th rnd:** Ch 3, dc in each of next 2 dc, 2 dc in next dc, * dc in each of next 3 dc, 2 dc in next dc. Repeat from * around (75 dc); join. Break off. Body measures about 6″ in diameter. Make another body with R.

Pad-holder band With R, ch 24. **1st row:** Sc in 2nd ch from hook and in each ch across; ch 1, turn. **2nd row:** Sc in each sc across; ch 1, turn. Repeat last row once more, do not break off.

Pin body circles tog. Place band across circle O, ends of band at edges of circle. Join end of band to circles by working 3 sc through band and both circles tog; then continue around circles, joining them by working sc in pairs of sc around to other end of band. Join end of band as before; complete joining of circles; sl st in first sc. Break off.

HEAD Make 1 circle each of O and R, working through 4th rnd of body.

Pencil-holder band With R, ch 13. Repeat 1st and 2nd rows of pad-holder band. Repeat 2nd row 6 times more or until band, when folded into lengthwise tube, will form a firm holder for pencil. Sl st long edges of tube tog. Break off, leaving 8″ end. Thread end in tapestry needle and sew tube to circle O. With R, sc head circles tog as for body.

Ears Mark center 17 sc at top of head. **1st row:** With right side facing you, using R, sc in first 6 sc of the marked 17; ch 1, turn. Work 2 rows of 6 sc each. **4th row:** Draw up lp in each of first 2 sc, yo and draw through all 3 lps on hook (1 sc dec); sc in each of next 2 sc, 1 sc; ch 1, turn. **5th row:** (Dec 1 sc) twice (2 sc). Break off (1 ear completed). Sk next 5 sts (top of head). Working across next 6 sts, work as for other ear. Break off. With right side facing you, sc around edge of first ear, sc in first sc of the 5 free sc at top of head, ch 5 for hanging lp, sk 3 sc, sc in next sc, sc around edge of other ear; sl st in next st. Break off.

FINISHING Butting edges of circles, sew head to body for 2¼″ neck. **For whiskers:** Cut eight 3″ strands R. Hold tog and sew around middle to head above pencil holder. Glue on eyes. **For bow tie:** Cut four 15″ strands R, hold tog and tie around neck. **For tail:** Cut six 22″ strands R. Hold tog and draw halfway through 2 sts at bottom of body. Make 3″ braid. Tie ends in overhand knot and then tie bow.

Slip cardboard backing of notepad over pad-holder band of hanging holder.

Hexagonal Coffee-canister

Made of mitered molding and a drawer knob; just fits a standard can.

SIZE 8⅜″ x 7½″ high.

MATERIALS 6′ of 1¾″ x 5¾″ mantel molding; 12″ square of 3/16″ plywood; scrap ¾″-diameter dowel; 1½″-diameter wooden knob; 1¼″ No. 8 FH wood screw; wood glue; Minwax® green wood stain/varnish. For general woodworking guidance, see page 161.

Cut 6 pieces molding for sides with 60° miters as shown in diagram. Assemble with glue and hold tight in position with many wraps of string or clamps until dry. Cut base from plywood; sand and glue in place.

Cut 6 pieces molding for top lid as shown. Assemble with glue and clamp until dry. With piece securely clamped in place, counterbore a ¾″-diameter spotface at center to attach dowel knob. Cut ½″ of ¾″-

diameter dowel. Glue to base of knob and glue and screw dowel/knob assembly to lid. Cut plywood bottom for lid, sand, bevel edges and glue in place.

Finish with green stain/varnish.

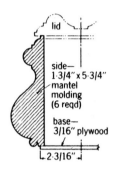

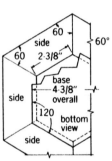

Body assembly

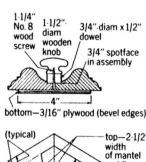

bottom—3/16″ plywood (bevel edges)

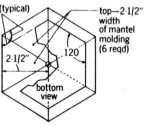

Lid assembly

Felt "Food" Magnets

SIZE About 2″ to 3″ long.

MATERIALS Scraps felt in appropriate colors; small magnets (available at hardware stores); white glue; epoxy adhesive.

Enlarge outlines (grape cluster, orange slice, watermelon slice, apple, fried egg) and make patterns. Following photograph, cut out and glue felt pieces together, using white glue and layering pieces from the largest base piece to the smallest uppermost piece. **NOTE** Grape cluster has small circles of grapes glued on base; watermelon is in 3 layers with black felt seeds added; for fried egg and apple only, glue 2 base pieces together to create desired stiffness.) With epoxy, glue magnet to back of each.

Each sq. = ½″

BREADBOARD Enlarge whale diagram (see How to Enlarge Patterns, page 158) and make pattern. Cut four 12″ lengths of pine; stack; nail in excess. Mark whale diagram on top piece. Clamp and drill for eye, then cut out with jig, coping or saber saw. Sand smooth. Seal with clear sealer.

HOLDER Enlarge wave pattern for sides of holder. Mark twice on pine; cut out. Cut 2⅛″ x 6½″ piece for bottom. Assemble holder with glue. Let dry. Sand smooth. Stain blue; when dry, apply coat of sealer.

Whale-of-a-breadboard

Cut in stacks of 4—an easy job with jig, coping or saber saw.

SIZE About 9″ long x 5½″ high.

MATERIALS 6′ of ½ x 6 pine wood; glue; blue stain; clear sealer. For general woodworking guidance, see page 161.

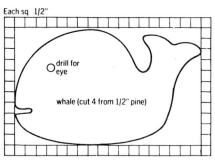

Each sq 1/2″

drill for eye

whale (cut 4 from 1/2″ pine)

Whale pattern

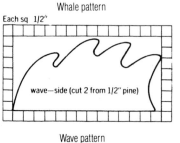

Each sq 1/2″

wave—side (cut 2 from 1/2″ pine)

Wave pattern

Sweet Shapes Refrigerator Magnets

(Project **1** in group photograph, page **88**)

Easy-to-cut wood shapes—cookie, cupcake, cone—with magnets glued to the back.

MATERIALS Scraps ¼″ plywood (2′ x 4′ plywood–¼ sheet–makes about 96 shapes); spackle; small magnets (available at hardware stores); epoxy adhesive; primer; acrylic paints; coping saw; sandpaper; spackle; polyurethane or shellac finish.

Enlarge the 3 shapes to be cut (see How to Enlarge Patterns, page 158) and make patterns. Cut out of plywood with coping saw. Sand and fill edges with spackle; sand again if necessary when dry. Prime all surfaces, then apply 2 coats paint and 1 coat finish. Glue magnet to back of each shape.

Each sq. = ½″

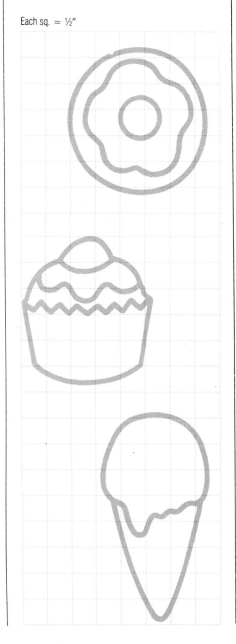

Each sq. = ½"

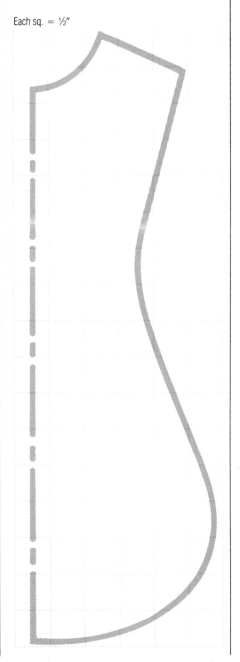

Detergent-bottle "Apron"

SIZE Fits 11"-high detergent bottle.

MATERIALS ¼ yard fabric makes 3 aprons; 2½ yards ½"-wide single-fold bias tape per cover.

Enlarge apron outline (see How to Enlarge Patterns, page 158) and make pattern. Use to cut out 2 pieces, adding ¼" seam allowance at shoulders. Stitch shoulder seams. Encase all raw edges with tape; topstitch. For ties, cut four 6½" lengths tape. Fold in half lengthwise; topstitch. Stitch an end of each tie to waist at front and back of apron (it ties tabard style—see photograph).

Bouquet Garni (Mixed Herbs) Packets

(Project **7** in group photograph, page **88**)

MATERIALS Jelly jar with lid; cheesecloth; 1 ball thin white crochet cotton; self-stick labels; red felt-tipped marker; 45"-wide gingham (1 yard covers about 36 jar lids); 3 yards bias tape or ribbon (for about 12 lids); pinking shears; rubber bands. **Herbs for garni:** Mixtures of assorted dried herbs such as thyme, bay leaf, basil, celery leaf, tarragon, rosemary, savory, etc. A good mixture for beef stew is bay leaf (crumbled), thyme, rosemary and oregano.

Mix herbs in bowl. Use 2 or 3 layers cheesecloth and cut into 4"-diameter circles. Spoon 1 teaspoonful of herb mixture onto center of each circle. Cut crochet cotton into 7" lengths and use 2 or 3 to tie each cheesecloth circle into a little pouch.

Drop pouches into jar and cover with lid. To cover jar lid, cut circular cardboard pattern about 3" larger in diameter than jar lid. Using pattern, cut gingham circles with pinking shears. Center one circle on lid and secure with rubber band. Tie with ribbon or tape. Mark label and apply to jar front.

Unusual kitchen helpers from ordinary things

APRON-ON-A-HOOP The apron is a dish towel; cotton print (stitched into thirds) supplies three pockets and the strip that folds over the waist-hugging plastic hoop.

PICTURE-PRETTY RECIPE BOX Decorate with decals or glue on seed catalog pictures; spray on clear acrylic for shine and protection.

BLOSSOMING MESSAGE BOARD Paint the frame of a bought blackboard with a bright-colored acrylic. When paint is dry, add multicolor flowers.

CLEVER COOKIE JAR Cover an inexpensive apothecary jar with 2 coats of white acrylic paint; brush with varnish and add letters and picture while it's still wet. Coat with more varnish, then spray on clear acrylic.

Watermelon Place Mats and Napkins

A match to padded potholders, page 90.

SIZE Place mat About 10½" x 21".

Napkin About 17" diameter.

MATERIALS Place mats ⅝ yard green print, ¼ yard pink print and ⅜ yard thin quilt batting make 2 mats.

Napkins ½ yard each green and pink fabrics make 2 napkins. Appropriate sewing threads, including red for zigzag stitching.

PLACE MAT From green print cut out 22"-diameter circle. From pink print cut out 17½"-diameter half circle. From batting cut out 21"-diameter half circle. Make as for Padded Watermelon Potholder, page 90, omitting loop.

NAPKIN From green print, cut out 18"-diameter circle, then cut 2¼"-wide ring from circle. From pink print, cut out 14½"-diameter circle. Lap pink over the inner edge of green ring and work machine zigzag in red along raw edge of pink. On wrong side, trim seam allowance of green close to stitching. Make ¼" finished hem on outer edge.

Place-setting-size Potted Violets

MATERIALS For one pot: ¼ yard 45"-wide purple taffeta; ½ yard green velvet or velveteen; 1½"-wide bonding net (such as Stitch Witchery); white glue; 4"-diameter clay pot; scrap cardboard; sharp scissors; thirty-five 12"-long 26-gauge green-paper-covered wires; floral tape; green plastic foam to fit pot; 40 artificial yellow stamens (available at some craft- and party-supply stores).

CUTTING Make cardboard patterns as follows: For small leaf, cut 1¾" x 2¼" oval. For large leaf, cut 2½" x 3¼" oval. For petal, cut 1½"-diameter circle. On wrong side of velvet, trace 14 small leaves and 16 large leaves. Cut out.

PETALS Cut 1½" x 45" length taffeta. Cut fifty 5" lengths of wire. Line up as many wires as will fit 1½" apart across edge of larger piece of taffeta, having ¾" of wire on fabric and the rest extending beyond. Spread strip of bonding net over wire ends, then lay 1½"-wide length of taffeta on mesh (be sure net doesn't extend beyond fabric). Iron to bond fabric layers together with wire ends sandwiched between. Using circle pattern, draw circles around each wire with end of wire at center of circle. Cut out, then trim to slight heart shape with point at wire, varying sizes of petals

from about ¾" to 1¼". Repeat to make 50 petals in all.

Cut 5" length of wire and hold 4 stamens at 1 end; wrap with tape for 1". Cut off tape. Hold 5 petals together with stamens at center. Starting at base of petals, wrap wires with tape to form stem.

LEAVES For each leaf, take 2 ovals and 7" piece of wire. Glue ovals together with wire sandwiched lengthwise between (this produces leaf vein). Wrap wire that extends beyond edge of oval with floral tape. When "sandwich" is dry, cut wavy edges around leaves.

Cut plastic foam to fit inside pot and insert stems in foam, following photograph for arrangement.

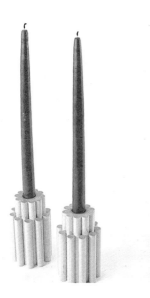

Columnar Candlesticks

Simply constructed of long and short dowels glued around a piece of pole.

SIZE 4½″ tall.

MATERIALS (for a pair): Four 3′ lengths ½″-diameter dowel; 1′ of 1⅛″-diameter pole; white glue; clear polyurethane. For general woodworking guidance, see page 161.

From dowel, cut twenty 4½″-long and twenty 3⅜″-long pieces. Divide into groups of 10 each. Cut two 4½″ pieces of pole.

For each candlestick, glue 10 longer dowel pieces around a pole piece, following photograph. Hold with rubber bands until dry (wipe away any excess glue immediately). Glue 10 shorter lengths around center unit, as pictured. Hold until dry with rubber bands.

In top of each pole, center and drill one ⅞″-diameter hole ¾″ deep. Finish entire unit with 2 or 3 coats polyurethane.

Pine Vases

Easy to cut, glue and waterproof. Two versatile sizes.

SIZE Large vase is 2¾″ x 5⅜″ x 10″; smaller two are 1¾″ x 2¾″ x 5″.

MATERIALS To make all three: 8′ of ½ x 3 and 2′ of ½ x 6 pine; wood glue; clear polyurethane; clear polymer decoupage finish or clear bathtub caulking in squeeze tube. For general woodworking guidance, see page 161.

For large vase, mark off and cut two 5⅜″ x 10″ sides, two 2¾″ x 10″ sides and one 1¾″ x 4⅜″ bottom (bottom must make very snug fit). Rip long edges of each side for mitered joints. Test-fit bottom with sides. Assemble sides with glue around bottom. Clamp until dry.

Coat inside, bottom and outside with 3 coats polyurethane, sanding lightly between coats.

To waterproof vase, caulk inside all joints or pour decoupage sealer into all joints and spread with piece of scrap cardboard.

Follow same procedure for small vases, making all sides 2¾″ x 5″ and bottom 1¾″ x 1¾″.

Quilted Place Mats with Polka-dot Napkins and Rings

(Project **6** in group photograph, page **88**)

SIZE 12″ x 18″.

MATERIALS 45″-wide reversible quilted fabric for mats, 12″ x 18″ piece for 1 mat (1 yard makes 6); 45″-wide coordinated printed, unquilted fabric for napkins and binding, 18″-square piece for 1 napkin (1 yard makes 4), 1½″ x 60″ strip to bind 1 mat (1 yard binds 12 mats with minimum piecing); sewing thread to match napkins and binding.

PLACE MAT

Cut 12″ x 18″ rectangle from quilted fabric. Round one corner. Cut cardboard pattern of rounded corner and use to shape other corners. Cut 1½″-wide bias strips of coordinated fabric for binding and piece to fit around mat; bind mat edge.

NAPKIN AND RING

Use coordinated fabric. To make multiple napkin rings (1 for each mat), make a length of binding from strips as for mat, allowing 5″ for each ring. Fold in half lengthwise and topstitch both edges. Cut into 5″ strips, form each into a ring, overlapping ends ¼″. Sew to mats about 2¼″ from one end (see photograph), with lapped ends on underside.

For each napkin, cut 18″ square and topstitch ¼″-wide finished hem on each edge.

comforts
for bed
and bath

Starting at top left: **1.** Matching calico-covered trinket and tissue boxes, page 109. **2.** Padded basket and lidded box covered with flowered fabric, page 108. **3.** Fancy handkerchief boudoir pillows, page 110. **4.** Butterfly sachets on hang cords, page 112. **5.** Calico-trimmed guest towels, page 109. **6.** Picture-frame mats of crocheted lace and calico, page 113. **7.** Hanging mini-sachets on D-ringed ribbons, page 110. **8.** and **9.** Matching pussycat sachets, page 112, and doggy hot-water-bottle cover, page 114. **10.** Scented-soap wall hangers of D-ringed ribbons, page 111. **11.** Circular sachets with eyelet borders and hang loops, page 110. **12.** Fabric-wrapped coat hangers accented with bows, page 109.

Comforts for bed and bath are the little luxury touches that make relaxing so very pleasant. It's a pennywise kind of luxury, though; nothing involved but cleverness with fabric. Sometimes it's simple calico, transforming ordinary necessities like coat hangers or hot water bottles into things of beauty. Or it may be scraps of ribbon, eyelet or lace, used to surround sachets, trim a pillow, or hold scented soaps.

comforts for bed and bath

It's in their private lives, at the end of a busy day, that people most relish life's little luxuries. When you make them affordable, as this collection does, the response may astonish you. It's amazing what can be done with bits of ribbon and fabric when they are well chosen and ingeniously used.

Padded Basket and Lidded Box

(Project **2** in group photograph, page **106**)

MATERIALS 45"-wide printed fabri (1¼ yards make 3 baskets, ¾ yar covers three 4"-square x 2"-ta cardboard boxes). **For basket:** ¼ wide satin ribbon (2½ yards tri 1); polyester fiberfill for stuffing; small decorative buttons; fusibl iron-on bonding net. **For box** Cardboard box; Elmer's Glue-all and brush; small amount cotto batting for padding; thick sewin needle.

PADDED BASKET Following dimen sions on basket and handle dia grams, cut 2 fabric pieces of each Hold basket pieces together, righ sides facing. Stitch ¼" seams a around, leaving one end open a specified. Clip inner corners and turn. Stuff sides A, B and C, the topstitch along broken lines X Stuff bottom (D) and topstitcl remaining broken lines. Stuff sid E and slipstitch opening closed.

Stitch handle pieces together leaving ends open; turn. Cut rib bon to fit top seam and, using fusi ble net, iron ribbon over seam Stuff handle.

Using thick needle, poke hole through dot at each corner. Cu four 18" lengths ribbon. Fold up sides of basket and run ribbor length through holes at each cor ner; tie in bow. Turn under ends o handle and sew to sides of basket. Sew button to center of each han dle end.

LIDDED BOX Follow directions fo covering boxes, page 157 of Gen eral Tips for Bazaar Projects.

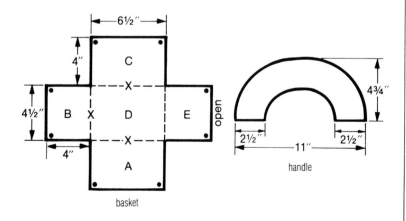

basket   handle

Calico-trimmed Guest Towels

(Project **5** in group photograph, page **106**)

MATERIALS Purchased terry guest towels; 45″-wide calico to match (½ yard trims 11 towels); sewing thread to match fabric.

Cut two 2″ x 16″ lengths fabric. Fold in half lengthwise, wrong side out. Stitch one end and long edge closed with ¼″ seam allowance; turn. Fold in open end and slipstitch. Press flat. Starting at one side about 2½″ from end of towel, pin one band ¼″ less than halfway across towel, leaving end long enough to tie bow. Repeat from other side with other band. Tie ends in neat, flat bow.

Fabric-wrapped Coat Hangers

(Project **12** in group photograph, page **106**)

MATERIALS 45″-wide calico (1½ yards cover 15); ¼″-wide satin ribbon (1 yard trims 2); white glue; ⅝″ nails (2 per hanger); wooden hangers.

Cut two 3″ x 26″ strips calico. Wrap one around arm of hanger to test-fit (there should be about ½″ seam allowance). Fold strip in half lengthwise, wrong side out; seam long edge and one end; turn. Fold in open end about ½″; push and gather cover onto arm of hanger. Add dab of glue near base of hook to hold, then hammer small nail into end of arm on underside to hold cover in place. Cover other arm in same manner.

Cut 18″ length ribbon and tie in bow around hook.

Calico-covered Trinket and Tissue Boxes

(Project **1** in group photograph, page **106**)

MATERIALS 45″-wide calico (⅝ yard covers two 3″-cube cardboard boxes, ¾ yard covers 4 standard tissue boxes). **For box:** Cardboard box; Elmer's Glue-All® and brush; small amount cotton batting for padding. **For tissue-box cover:** Plain fabric for lining (same amount as for cover); 1″-wide bias tape (3 yards trim 1); matching sewing thread.

TRINKET BOX

To cover box and lid, follow directions for covering boxes, page 157 of General Tips for Bazaar Projects.

TISSUE COVER

Following dimensions on tissue box cover diagrams, cut one cover piece and 2 end pieces from calico and lining. Baste matching lining and calico pieces together, wrong sides facing, and treat as single fabric.

Bind edges X on each end piece and shaped edges on cover piece.

Place curved edge of end piece between dots and pin (see assembly diagram 1). Cut two 18″ lengths tape, center each over a pinned edge and topstitch as in assembly diagram 2, stitching along loose ends (ties). Knot ends of ties around box of tissues.

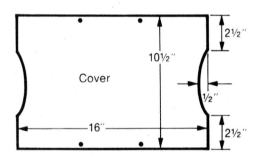

Tissue-Box Cover

end piece

X

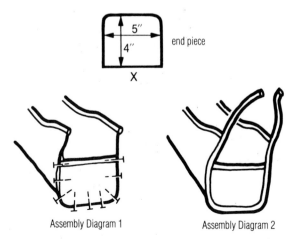

Assembly Diagram 1

Assembly Diagram 2

Fancy Handkerchief Boudoir Pillows

(Project **3** in group photograph, page **106**)

SIZE About 14″ square, including ruffle.

MATERIALS 45″-wide white cotton fabric (1 yard makes backings for 12 pillows); one decorative hanky, about 14″ square, per pillow; 1″-wide ruffled eyelet trim (1⅛ yards trim 1 pillow); ⅝″-wide decorative ribbon (1⅜ yards for 1 pillow); polyester fiberfill.

From white cotton, cut 10″ square. Lightly mark 9″ square centered on wrong side of hanky. Place cotton square on center of wrong side of hanky and turn in 3 edges to marked lines; stitch and stuff. Turn in open edge and baste. Topstitch eyelet trim around stitching line on right side, closing basted edge. Cut decorative ribbon into four 12″ lengths. Tack center of each length to corner as shown; tie in bow.

Circular Sachets

(Project **11** in group photograph, page **106**)

SIZE About 4½″ in diameter.

MATERIALS 45″-wide white cotton-blend fabric or sheeting (¼ yard makes 10); 1″-wide eyelet ruffled lace (1 yard trims 3); ¼″-wide satin ribbon (1¼ yards trim 2); Venice lace (strips of embroidered lace motifs that can be cut apart—1 motif per sachet); cotton batting or polyester fiberfill for stuffing; potpourri and oil essences.

Make 3½″-diameter circular cardboard pattern and cut out 2 fabric circles, adding ¼″ seam allowance. With edges matching, stitch eyelet lace around right side of one circle; sew ends together. With right sides facing and lace sandwiched between, stitch circles together, leaving 2″ opening. Clip edges and turn. Sprinkle potpourri and oil essences on stuffing, and fill sachet. Cut 7″ length ribbon, insert ends in sachet opening and slip-stitch closed.

Run needle and thread back and forth 2 or 3 times through center of sachet, pull up tight and fasten but do not break off. Form 4-loop bow from 15″ length ribbon and sew, with embroidered motif on top, to center of sachet.

Hanging Mini-sachets

(Project **7** in group photograph, page **106**)

SIZE 19″ long.

MATERIALS 45″ wide calico (½ yard makes 60 sachets); 1½″-wide velvet gift-wrap ribbon (2½ yards make 4 hangers); regular size rickrack (1 yard trims 1 hanger); ⅛″-wide ribbon (1¼ yards tie 3 sachets); bunches small fake flowers; potpourri for sachets; cotton balls and oil essences (optional); white glue; D-ring; pinking shears.

FOR HANGER Cut 22″ length velvet ribbon; notch one end. Cut two 18″ lengths rickrack and, starting at notched end, glue to edges of velvet side (wrong side) of ribbon so that rickrack points extend about ¼″. Fold excess 4″ at top of ribbon through D-ring and tack to wrong side.

FOR SACHETS With pinking shears, cut 3½″-diameter circles from calico. Cut ⅛″-wide ribbon into 13″ lengths and separate flowers. Cut 2 holes, side by side and about ⅜″ apart, in center of velvet ribbon 6″ from notched end. Draw ends of a ribbon length through holes from wrong to right side. Sprinkle potpourri and oil essences on 2 cotton balls and place on center of a calico circle, or pour potpourri directly onto center of circle. Fold up 2 opposite sides, then other 2 sides, to form neat packet. Lay 1 or 2 sprigs flowers against packet and wrap twice with ribbon extending from holes. Knot and tie in bow. Attach 2 more sachets to hanger, spacing evenly.

Scented-soap Wall Hangers

(Project **10** in group photograph, page **106**)

A charming way to present a feminine favorite.

SIZE About 18″ long.

MATERIALS 1½″-wide Velvette® ribbon (stiff velour-type ribbon with satin back) (1½ yards make 1); bunches of tiny artificial stamens or flowers; 1 or 2 bars scented soap; one D-ring; stapler; white glue.

SINGLE-SOAP HANGER Following Diagram 1, start at end X, slide on D-ring and make first fold in direction of arrows. Continue to fold ribbon as shown, stapling at dots. Notch ribbon end.

Overlap ends of stamen or flower bunches and tape together. Cut 3″-long ribbon piece for roll, wrap it around bunch and glue. Glue roll to ribbon. Insert soap in loop as indicated and staple back.

DOUBLE-SOAP HANGER Follow Diagram 2 and directions for Single-Soap Hanger.

Ribbon Sachets

MATERIALS (for 3 each of 5 sachets shown): Ribbons: Taffeta picot, 1 yard 2″-wide pink, 1½ yards 1½″-wide lavender; 2½″-wide gingham taffeta, 1 yard blue; 1½″-wide gingham taffeta, 3¾ yards pink, 3¼ yards blue and 3 yards purple; 1½″-wide satin, 2¾ yards blue and 1¾ yards pink; ⅛″-wide satin, 2 yards blue, 1 yard each pink and lavender. **Other materials:** ¼ yard sheer fabric; potpourri.

To make potpourri packet for square sachets Cut 2 squares lightweight fabric to fit sachet (see below); sew together, leaving opening; turn; stuff with potpourri; close opening.

3″-square checkerboard sachet Cut four 5″ strips each from pink or blue 1½″-wide satin and 1½″-wide gingham. Weave 2 strips each together for front and back; stitch all around ¾″ from edges to hold. With right sides together, stitch 3 sides ¼″ inside previous stitching; turn. Make and insert potpourri packet; sew closed.

4″-square envelope sachet Cut two 14″-long strips from purple gingham and one from lavender picot. Topstitch picot, overlapped ⅛″ lengthwise, between the 2 gingham strips. Stitch one end under ¼″, then fold under 2¼″ for flap; fold opposite end under 1″, then 4″ for pocket. Topstitch sides of pocket and flap. Make and insert potpourri packet. Tie 12″ length ⅛″-wide ribbon in bow; tack to flap.

Long sachets Cut 12″ of widest gingham or picot; cut same length 1½″-wide satin or gingham. Topstitch narrower ribbon along center of wider ribbon. Press ends under 1″; fold wrong sides together with ends matching; topstitch sides. Stuff with potpourri. Insert 6″-long loop ⅛″-wide ribbon in center top if desired; topstitch top closed. For rosette, gather one edge of 18″ length 1½″-wide gingham; tack to center top of sachet. Tack ⅛″-wide ribbon bow to center of rosette.

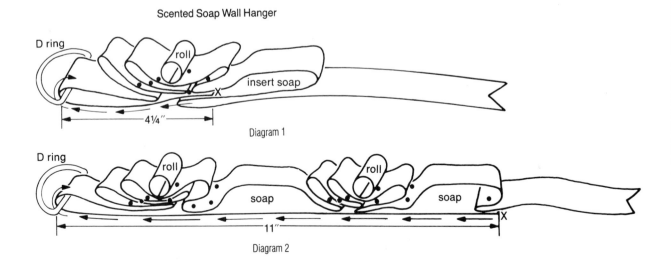

Scented Soap Wall Hanger

D ring · roll · insert soap · X · 4¼″ · Diagram 1

D ring · roll · roll · soap · soap · X · 11″ · Diagram 2

Pussycat Sachets

(Project **8** in group photograph, page **106**)

SIZE About 4″ x 5″.

MATERIALS 45″-wide calico (⅜ yard makes 9); cotton batting or polyester fiberfill for stuffing; potpourri and oil essences; 2 black beads; 1 spool black button-and-carpet thread; scraps ¼″-wide satin ribbon (1 yard trims 4); large-eyed needle.

Enlarge cat diagram (see How to Enlarge Patterns, page 158) and make pattern. Cut out 2 pieces calico (reversing pattern for one) for each sachet, adding ¼″ seam allowance to all edges. Following photograph, sew 2 bead eyes on one piece. Run 2 strands carpet thread through needle; double and knot 1″ from end. Draw needle from right to wrong side of fabric ¼″ below

one eye (knot and ends form whiskers). Draw thread through right side ¼″ below other eye. Make knot and cut thread, leaving 1″ ends on other cheek.

With right sides facing, stitch 2 halves of sachet together, leaving bottom open. Clip curves and turn. Sprinkle potpourri and oil essences on stuffing and stuff sachet. Sew opening closed. Cut 7″ length ribbon. Tie in bow and tack below whiskers.

Butterfly Sachets

(Project **4** in group photograph, page **106**)

Sachets on the wing are just fabric squares tied with ribbon.

MATERIALS 45″-wide calico (½ yard makes 5); ⅛″-wide satin ribbon (1½ yards tie 1); ½″-wide ruffled lace (1 yard trims 1); potpourri.

For each sachet, cut two 8″ squares fabric. Pin lace on right side of one piece, edges matching. With right sides facing and lace sandwiched between, stitch squares together, leaving 6″ opening. Turn. Fill loosely with potpourri and sew closed. Cut 18″ length ribbon and tie tightly in bow around middle. Run remaining ribbon through center ribbon and tie ends, making loop to slip over hanger handle.

Each sq. = ½″

Dotted-Swiss Potpourris

Another unusual shape, these tubes covered with lace and tied with ribbon.

SIZE About 8″ long.

MATERIALS For each sachet 7½″ square of closely woven fabric; ½ yard 1¼″- or 1½″-wide lace, lace-trimmed decorative ribbon or ribbon-beaded lace to go around sachet; ¼ yard 1½″-wide satin ribbon and embroidered appliqué (optional, on one sachet only); ¾ yard 1″-wide lace for ends of sachet; ¾ yard ¼″-wide satin ribbon to tie ends; potpourri to fill sachet.

For sachet with appliqué Cut 1½″-wide ribbon and 2 strips lace 7½″ long. Hand-sew lace to each edge of ribbon; topstitch ribbon along edges across center of fabric square. Sew appliqué to center of ribbon.

For other sachets Cut 2 strips lace-ribbon trim 7½″ long and topstitch, about 1″ apart, across fabric square.

For all sachets Topstitch ¼″ finished hems on fabric edges parallel to trim. Cut lace for ends in half and gather each length to fit hemmed edge of square; topstitch to edge. Fold square in half wrong

side out, raw edges matching. Stitch with ½″ seam allowance to form tube; turn. Run basting thread through one end of tube ½″ from fabric edge. Draw up tight and fasten. Fill tube with potpourri; gather open end. Cut ¼″-wide ribbon in half and tie ends of case as shown.

Picture-frame Mats of Crocheted Lace and Calico

(Project **6** in group photograph, page **106**)

SIZE Frames are 5¼″ x 7¼″, outside measurement.

MATERIALS Coats & Clark's Knit-Cro-Sheen (cotton yarn), 1 (175-yard) ball for about 11; steel crochet hook size 3; purchased frame about 5¼″ x 7¼″ (paint with acrylics if desired); 45″-wide calico (¼ yard for 8); ⅛″-wide satin ribbon (1 yard trims 2); Elmer's Glue-All® and brush.

FABRIC MAT Cut calico ¼″ larger on all sides than cardboard backing in frame. Glue fabric to cardboard, folding excess to wrong side.

CROCHETED MAT Starting at inner edge, ch 72. Join with sl st to form ring. **1st rnd:** Ch 4 (counts as 1 dc and 1 ch), sk 1 ch, work (dc, ch 1 and dc) in next ch (V st made); (ch 1, sk 1 ch, V st in next ch) twice; * (ch 1, sk 1 ch, dc in next ch, ch 1, sk 1 ch, dc in next ch, ch 1, sk 1 ch, V st in next ch) twice; (ch 1, sk 1 ch, dc in next ch) 3 times; (ch 1, sk 1 ch, V st in next ch, ch 1, sk 1 ch, dc in next ch, ch 1, sk 1 ch, dc in next ch) twice *; (ch 1, sk 1 ch, V st in next ch) 3 times. Repeat from * to

* once more, omitting last ch-1 and last dc, ending ch 1, sk last ch; join with sl st in 3rd ch of starting ch.

2nd rnd: * Work 2 sc in next ch-1 sp, sc in next ch-1 sp. Repeat from * around; join.

3rd rnd: * Ch 4, sk 2 sc, sc in next sc. Repeat from * around; join.

4th rnd: Sl st in first 2 sts of next ch-4 lp, sc over same lp, * ch 5, sc over next lp. Repeat from * around; join. Break off.

Place oval crocheted mat on center of calico mat and trace oval opening. Cut out. Weave 18″ length ribbon through 1st rnd of crochet and tie in bow (see photograph). Lightly glue crochet to calico. When dry, insert in frame.

Doggy Hot-water-bottle Cover

(Project **9** in group photograph, page **106**)

SIZE About 9″ x 15½″, not including legs, tail and nose.

MATERIALS 45″-wide calico and lightweight terry cloth (1 yard each makes 3); scraps solid-color fabric (¼ yard makes 6 ears and noses); 6-strand embroidery floss for mouth and eyes; ¾″-wide grosgrain ribbon (¾ yard trims 1); small amount cotton batting to stuff legs and nose.

Enlarge dog, nose and ear diagrams (see How to Enlarge Patterns, page 158) and make patterns. Cut out one piece calico for front, adding ¼″ seam allowance to all edges. Back cover has 2 openings. For back pattern, trace again and cut apart across neck and 2½″ from end (see bottle-shape diagram). Cut one piece calico each from patterns A, B and C, adding ½″ to each edge X and 1″ to each edge Y and ¼″ to all other edges. Cut backs and front from terry in same manner. Pin matching terry and calico pieces together, wrong sides facing, and treat as single fabric. From calico, cut eight 2″ x 3″ leg pieces and two 1½″ x 3¾″ tail pieces (¼″ seam allowance is included). From solid-color fabric, cut 2 nose pieces and 2 ear pieces, adding ¼″ seam allowance.

Using all 6 strands floss, embroider mouth in outline stitch and eye in satin stitch on front piece (for stitch diagrams, see page 159). Turn under edges X and Y ½″ and hem with zigzag machine stitch. With wrong sides facing, stitch pairs of legs together, leaving tops open. Stitch nose pieces and tail pieces together, leaving base open.

Clip curves on all pieces and turn; stuff lightly.

Pin sections A, B and C together, lapping edges Y about ½″ over edges X (test-fit by placing back on top of front). With raw edges matching, pin legs in pairs along bottom of right side of front piece, nose on face and tail on back. With right sides facing and legs, tail and nose sandwiched between, pin front and back together; stitch and turn.

Stitch ear pieces together, leaving base open. Clip curves and turn. Fold base under and sew to head. Cut ribbon 1″ longer than front neck. Turn ends in, place ribbon across neck and sew ends to top and bottom neck seams. Make neat bow of remaining ribbon and sew at top neck.

Hot-water bottle is inserted through back opening, filled through neck opening.

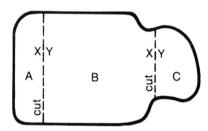

Bottle cover

Each sq. = ½″

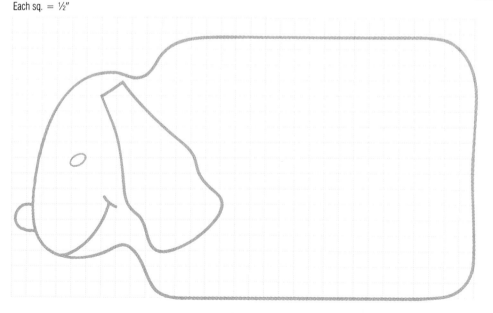

Drawstring Shoebags

SIZE 7″ x 15″.

MATERIALS ½ yard 36″-wide jersey; matching sewing thread; 2 yards 1″-wide striped grosgrain ribbon.

Cut two 15″ x 17″ pieces jersey. Fold in half lengthwise, wrong side out. Stitch sides and one end with ½″ seam allowance; turn. Fold in open end ½″, then another 1″; topstitch to form casing. Cut ribbon trim ½″ longer than side seam from casing stitchline to bottom. Turn in ends ¼″ and topstitch (or hand slipstitch) over side seam. Carefully open side seam on right side of casing. Run 21″ length ribbon through casing and sew ends together. Hide joined ends in casing.

Lips
Cosmetic Bag

SIZE 7″ x 13¾″.

MATERIALS ¼ yard 36″-wide red fabric-lined vinyl; red sewing thread; 7″ white zipper.

Enlarge bag pattern (see How to Enlarge Patterns, page 158), cutting one pattern piece of entire mouth for back of bag and 2 pieces (upper and lower lips) for front. From vinyl cut 1 back (do not add seam allowance); cut upper and lower lips for front, adding ½″ to edge X on each piece.

With right sides facing, stitch upper and lower lips together with ½″ seams, starting at corners and leaving center 7″ open. Insert zipper. Fold seam allowances flat and topstitch on each side of seam. With wrong sides facing, topstitch front and back of lips together ¹⁄₁₆″ from edge, then again ⅛″ from edge.

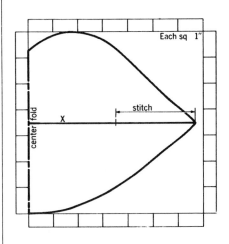

**gems for
desk, den &
sewing area**

Starting at top left: **1.** Folding needleholders, page 126. **2.** Trinket box with puffy pincushion lid (made from a round oatmeal box), page 127. **3.** Decorated four-in-one matchboxes, page 119. **4.** Padded plaid box with ribbon-tied lid, page 119. **5.** and **6.** Plaid-covered notepaper folders and decorated stationery sets, page 120. **7.** Fabric-covered filecases (blue plaid and red calico), page 119. **8.** Hanging calico pad and pencil holder, page 120. **9.** Calico yardstick holder, page 126. **10.** Calico pincushion balls on neck ribbons, page 124. **11.** Picture-gallery wall hanging (using a plastic credit-card packet), page 123. **12.** Flower wrist pincushions, page 125. **13.** and **14.** Calico-covered memo pads with attached pencils (13) and notebooks (14), page 122. **15.** Photo-trimmed pencil holder, page 119. **16.** Clip-on mitten bookmarks in felt, page 122. **17.** Slipcovers for paperback books, page 122. **18.** Cupcake pincushions with crocheted "icing" and yarn scrap decorations (mock cherry pompon, non pareils, chocolate sprinkles), page 125.

Gems for desk, den and sewing area add radiant color to workaday conveniences, plus some brilliant thoughts of their own: a pad that comes with an attached pencil; notepaper folders with stationery inside; a hanging holder to keep a yardstick where you can find it; bookmarks that clip; a handy-for-anything box with a pincushion lid. Down-to-business crispness with a decorator look—quite a combination. It might even make doing taxes a pleasure!

gems for den, desk and sewing area

It's said that good design follows function, but too often, in everyday necessities, it ends up dull. These colorful coordinates put an end to all that. With them to liven things up, no routine activity—writing letters, paying bills, sewing a hem— need ever be humdrum again.

Downspout Desk Set

SIZE About 5½" x 14".

MATERIALS 10' of 2½"-square vinyl downspout (you need only 2', in case you have some on hand; otherwise, it must be purchased in 10' lengths); 2' of ½ x 4 pine; 8" of ¼" aluminum hollow tube; two ⅜" No. 8 panhead self-tapping screws; wood glue; stain and polyurethane for base; hacksaw; offset screwdriver.

Use hacksaw to cut two 5¾" and three 3" pieces from downspout. On side of large pieces, mark angle cut so that low side is 3" and high side is 5½"; cut. Across two opposite sides of small pieces, draw line 1¾" from bottom edge. On other two sides, draw lines diagonally from 1¾" mark to center of top. Following photograph, cut away sides. Drill ¼"-diameter hole ¾" from peak on opposite sides. On one angled side of large pieces (side that will face in when assembled), mark for pilot hole centered 3⅛" from bottom. Drill pilot hole for No. 8 screw.

Cut 14" length of pine for base. Cut five 2⅜"-square floors with rounded corners to fit snugly inside downspout. Sand, stain and finish all pine pieces. Glue floor into bottom of 3 small pieces. Line up all 5 pieces of downspout, centered, on base with 8" tube spacing the 2 large pieces; lightly mark location of ends and glue 2 remaining floors to base at marks. Glue large downspout pieces to floors with pilot holes facing. Thread small pieces on tube. Using offset screwdriver from inside, attach large end pieces with screws into tube.

Photo-trimmed Pencil Holder

(Project **15** in group photograph, page **116**)

MATERIALS Large fruit or tomato can about 5″ tall x 4″ diameter; scraps gift wrap (11″ x 19″ piece covers one can); plastic credit-card holder and pictures to fill pockets; rubber cement.

Clean can and remove label. Cut strip of gift wrap 1″ wider than can height and long enough to fit around inside of can, plus 1″. Make 1″ cuts, about ½″ apart, along one long edge; bend cut lengths to right side. Brush rubber cement around entire inside of can. Insert strip, clipped edge down, into can (top of paper should be about ⅛″ below top edge of can). Press paper against sides and clipped lengths to bottom. Apply rubber cement to over-lapped vertical edge and press smooth. Cut gift-wrap circle to fit inside bottom; cement in place. Cover outside of can with strip of gift-wrap. Test-fit photo holder around can; cut off excess pockets. Fill pockets that will be used with pictures. Cement photo holder around can.

Padded Plaid Box

(Project **4** in group photograph, page **116**)

MATERIALS Cardboard box (box shown is 3″ wide x 8″ long x 2½″ tall, but any size will work); 45″-wide calico, ½ yard covers box size given above; 1 yard 1″-wide ribbon per box; Elmer's® Glue-All and brush; polyester fiberfill for padding.

See General Tips for Bazaar Projects, page 157, for help in covering box and lid.

Cut 2 strips ribbon to cross lid as shown, folding ends to inside. Glue in place. Make flat bow and glue to center of lid.

Fabric-covered Filecases

(Project **7** in group photograph, page **116**)

SIZE 9½″ x 16″.

MATERIALS 45″-wide printed fabric and iron-on interfacing (1½ yards of each make 5 briefcases); 1″-wide bias tape, 1 (3-yard) package trims 2 briefcases; sewing thread to match tape; 2 decorative buttons.

Iron interfacing to wrong side of fabric, then cut 16″ x 24″ rectangle. Round corners at one 16″ edge (cutting a simple cardboard pattern from first and using to cut second so the two will match). Turn in straight 16″ edge ½″ and topstitch. Fold hemmed end 9″ to wrong side (see filecase diagram). Bind shaped edge and sides to form pocket and flap.

Cut two 4″ lengths tape for button loops. Fold in half lengthwise and topstitch. Fold into loops and sew ends to inside of flap at dots. Sew buttons to pocket.

Four-in-one Matchboxes

(Project **3** in group photograph, page **116**)

MATERIALS 4 small (1″ x 1¾″) match-boxes per unit; thin cardboard and gift-wrap (two 24″-square sheets each make 64 units); ⅜″-wide gros-grain ribbon (1 yard makes pulls for about 4 units); white glue or rubber cement.

Glue matchboxes together to form square unit (there will be small square hole in center of unit), making sure all boxes are right side up. Glue gift-wrap to cardboard and cut out 2 squares same size as assembled unit. Glue cardboard side of pieces to top and bottom of unit. Cut ribbon into 2″ lengths. Fold each in half crosswise and glue ends together. Pull out boxes and glue ends of one loop to bottom of each, leaving ⅜″ extended for pull. When dry, fill and replace boxes.

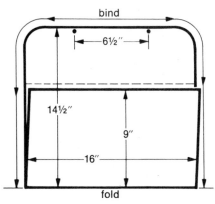

Fabric-Covered Filecase

Plaid-covered Notepaper Folders

(Project **5**, shown in group photograph, page **116**, with decorated stationery, right)

SIZE 10″ x 12″, folded.

MATERIALS 45″-wide printed fabric and interfacing (1½ yards of each make 4); 1″-wide bias tape, 1 (3-yard) package trims 4; sewing thread to match tape.

Iron interfacing to wrong side of fabric, then cut 20″ x 25″ rectangle. Turn in 20″ edges ½″ and topstitch. Fold one hemmed end 4″ to wrong side and other hemmed end 8″ to wrong side so that they touch (see folder diagram). Topstitch vertically along center. Bind open ends so that case forms 4 pockets.

Decorated Stationery

(Project **6** in group photograph, page **116**; shown with No. **5** Plaid Folders)

MATERIALS Purchased notepaper or cards and envelopes; new, clean pencil erasers; ink pads in assorted colors; single-edged razor blade.

Use 1 eraser for each ink pad. Using razor blade, slice sides of erasers to form small rounds or squares. Press on ink pads and stamp paper, following photograph for designs (or make up your own). Wipe erasers clean from time to time to keep imprint sharp.

Stack paper and envelopes; tie with ribbon or tuck into folders, as in photograph.

Hanging Calico Pad and Pencil Holder

(Project **8** in group photograph, page **116**)

SIZE 7½″ x 11″.

MATERIALS 45″-wide calico and non-woven, iron-on interfacing (1 yard of each makes 10); 1¼ yards 1″-wide taffeta ribbon per holder; 3′ of ⅜″-diameter dowel (makes 4); 4″ x 6″ notepad! and 2 pencils; white glue.

Cut calico 8½″ x 13″ and interfacing 7½″ x 12″. Center interfacing on wrong side of calico and iron in place.

From ribbon, cut one 8½″ length and one 10″ length. Pin shorter length across calico 1¼″ from bottom of holder. Arrange 2 pencils vertically on calico (see photograph) and place longer ribbon length across them, as shown, 4″ from top edge of holder. Pin ribbon to both sides of each pencil to form 2 loop holders, then pin across calico. Remove pencils and topstitch vertical lines to make pencil pockets and wide pocket to fit cardboard backing on notepad; then topstitch close to top and bottom edges of ribbon, being careful to leave pockets open. Topstitch close to both long edges of bottom ribbon. Topstitch ⅜″ finished hems on all edges of holder, catching ends of ribbon in hems.

Cut 8½″ length dowel. Fold top of holder over it loosely to form casing; topstitch. Cut 22″ length ribbon. Notch ends of dowel and knot ribbon ends around them as shown, adding dab of glue to hold. Slide pencils and notepad into pockets.

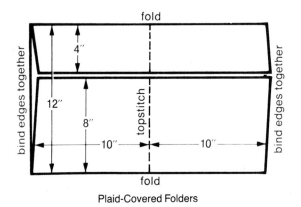

Plaid-Covered Folders

Desk and den money-making multiples

PLASTER PAPERWEIGHTS Fill rubber ball sections with plaster. When it hardens, peel off rubber, seal plaster shape with shellac, and paint. Glue on glitter, sequins, stars, radiant rickrack.

VELVET BOOKMARK String beads on 16-inch length of velvet ribbon; knot ends so beads stay in place.

MINI-PHOTO DISPLAY Mount small photographs on cardboard squares or ovals, cover with clear acetate and frame with bright cloth tape or self-adhesive paper. Tape 24-inch ribbons, looped and crossed, to backs.

COOKIE-CUTTER BOOKMARKS Trace, on heavy plastic, around cookie-cutter shapes. Cut silhouettes out and slit them to slip over page.

Calico-covered Memo Pads and Notebooks

(Projects **13** and **14** in group photograph, page **116**)

MATERIALS Memo pads, school composition books, account books, etc; 45″-wide calico (closely woven so glue won't bleed through) to cover notebooks (½ yard covers twelve 4″ x 6″ memo pads, four 7½″ x 10″ composition books or four 5¼″ x 11½″ account books and 3 memo pads); cardboard to reinforce covers on memo pads (or any pad with flexible cover); Elmer's® Glue-All and brush; single-edged razor blade or X-acto® knife; pencils for memo pads.

See General Tips for Bazaar Projects, page 157, to apply fabric to cardboard.

For any notebook needing reinforced cover, first cut cardboard same size as cover and glue to cover with full-strength glue. For all notebooks, take measurements of closed book across front, around spine and across back, then measure height of book. For memo pad, add 1¾″ to length for pencil holder.

Fabric cover is made in one piece. Cut fabric slightly larger than entire book. First, brush diluted glue on back of book only; then smooth fabric in place, allowing 1¾″ to extend from lower edge of memo pad. Brush glue on spine and front of book, then smooth remainder of fabric over it. Trim fabric, leaving the 1¾″ extension at lower edge of back cover on memo pad. Roll extension around pencil to establish size of holder, remove pencil and glue excess fabric to inside of cover.

Clip-on Mitten Bookmarks

(Project **16** in group photograph, page **116**)

MATERIALS Scraps felt (¼ yard 45″-wide felt makes 30 bookmarks); scraps ⅝″-wide lace (1 yard trims 4 bookmarks); pincurl clips; 6-strand embroidery floss.

Enlarge mitten diagram (see How to Enlarge Patterns, page 158) and make pattern to cut out mittens (4 for each bookmark). Hold 2 together and work blanket stitch with 2 strands floss around edges, leaving top open. Work a flower of 5 lazy daisy stitches in center of mitten. (For stitch diagrams, see page 159). Make another mitten in same manner, making sure flower is on outside when mittens are held together. Slide pincurl clip into mittens with one prong in each mitten. Sew mittens together at top, close to extending end of clip, then take 2 or 3 stitches around loop on clip and through mitten to prevent clip from slipping out. Cut 8″ length lace, gather 1 edge to fit around "wrist" of mitten and sew in place. Pinching end of clip opens mittens.

Each sq. = ½″

Slipcovers for Paperback Books

(Project **17** in group photograph, page **116**)

SIZE Fits average 4¼″ x 7″ paperback with spine up to 1″ wide.

MATERIALS 45″-wide fabric and iron-on woven interfacing (½ yard of each makes 5 covers); 1″-wide bias tape, 1 (3-yard) package binds about 3 covers; sewing thread to match tape.

Iron interfacing to wrong side of fabric. Cut out 7½″ x 16½″ rectangle. Bind long edges with tape. Turn in ends ½″ and topstitch. Fold in ends 3″ and pin to form 2 pockets for covers of book. Topstitch 1⁄16″ from taped edges.

Inlaid Frame

SIZE Fits 5" x 7" picture.

MATERIALS 4' of ½ x 2 clear pine; 2' of ¼" x ⅞" pine lattice; 4 inlay strips each 3' with a combined width of 1" (available from woodworker's supply house); 5" x 7" piece ⅛" glass; 5" x 7" piece light cardboard; ½" wire brads or glazier's tips; 4" of thin chain; ½" x ¾" hinge with four ¼" No. 2 screws; two ¼" screw eyes; white wood glue; white shellac; 1"-wide masking tape. For general woodworking guidance, see page 161.

Rip ¼" from edge of ½ x 2 to give 2 pieces, ½" x 1¹⁄₁₆" and ¼" x ½".

Tape inlay strips together edge to edge in desired arrangement, covering face of strips with masking tape. With white glue, glue and clamp strips to ½" x 1¹⁄₁₆" pine.

When glue is dry, remove tape and trim away excess pine. Sand away excess glue. Cut into 4 pieces, two 5½" long and two 7½" long. Assemble pieces into a frame with butt joints, following placement shown in photograph. Clamp until dry (if you don't have clamps, attach with glue and 2" finishing nails, setting nailheads and filling with putty). Inside dimensions of frame will be 4½" x 6½".

Cut pieces from ¼" x ½" pine to frame back, making an inside dimension of 5" x 7", to hold glass and picture. Attach pieces to back of frame with glue and brads.

To make frame stand, cut 7¾" length of lattice. Hinge to center top of frame back with ¼" screws. Attach a screw eye at center bottom of frame back and another inside center bottom of lattice piece. Connect screw eyes with 4" chain.

Finish frame with several coats of shellac, sanding lightly between coats.

Insert glass, picture and cardboard. Secure with brads or glazier's tips, placed parallel to picture in ¼" edge of back framing pieces.

Picture-gallery Wall Hanging

(Project **11** in group photograph, page **116**)

MATERIALS Plastic credit-card packet; ¼"-diameter dowel (3' of dowel makes 3 holders); ½" yard 1"-wide striped grosgrain ribbon for 5 pockets; D-ring; acrylic paint; assorted pictures; rubber cement.

Cut dowel into two 5" lengths. Paint and let dry. Cut holder to 5 pockets, leaving 1½" excess at each end. Fill pockets with pictures. Cut ribbon the length of pockets plus 3". Roll and cement excess strip at top and bottom around dowels. Insert end of ribbon through D-ring; cement to ring and around top dowel. Hang ribbon down back of holder and cement end around bottom dowel.

Calico Pincushion Balls on Neck Ribbons

(Project **10** in group photograph, page **116**)

MATERIALS 2⅝"-diameter wooden curtain rings; scraps calico (½ yard 45"-wide fabric makes 19 pincushions); bunches of tiny artificial flowers (about 3 flowers per pincushion); small screw eyes; ¼"-wide satin ribbon, 1 yard per pincushion; scrap cardboard; white glue; pinking shears (optional); polyester fiberfill for stuffing; acrylic paint to match ribbon.

Paint curtain rings. When thoroughly dry, insert screw eye in outer edge. Cut 6"-diameter calico circle and 2¼"-diameter cardboard circle. Sew running stitches ¼" from edge of calico circle and draw up slightly to form pouch; stuff. Insert cardboard and draw fabric tightly around it; fasten. Glue to ring. Tack and glue 3 flowers between ring and cushion below screw eye.

It is easier to make bottoms for 4 rings at one time: Cut 5"-squares calico and cardboard. Glue fabric to cardboard; let dry. Draw four 2¼"-diameter circles on cardboard side. Cut out with pinking or regular shears. Glue a circle to bottom of ring.

Fold 1 yard ribbon in half. Slide looped end through screw eye, then draw ends through loop. Pull up to tighten.

Toadstool Pincushion

MATERIALS (for 1) Scraps of cotton or cotton-blend polka-dot fabric, white felt and baby rickrack; small empty wooden thread spool; polyester or cotton stuffing; white paint; glue.

Paint spool. Cut 3"-diameter circles from fabric and felt. With right sides together, taking ¼" seam, sew fabric and felt circles together. Cut a hole slightly smaller than top of spool in center of felt, turn right side out; stuff. Dab glue around underside of spool rim; insert rim into hole in felt, stretching felt to fit. Tack rickrack around pincushion as shown.

Pincushion in a Basket

MATERIALS (for 1) Small basket (top of basket used has 4½" diameter); circle of cardboard to fit into top of basket; ⅜ yard 45" fabric (will decorate about 3 baskets of this size); 1"-wide lace to fit around cardboard circles; scrap ribbon; polyester fiberfill or cotton batting for stuffing; acrylic paint; needle and thread.

Paint basket. Cut one fabric circle to fit cardboard and another 3" larger in diameter. Take running stitches close to edge of larger circle and gather slightly; insert stuffing and cardboard; gather tightly. Turn under edge of smaller circle and sew to back of pincushion. Sew lace along seam, inserting ends of ribbon for a pull tab. Cut 3" x 12" fabric strip. Press long edges under ¾" and tie into bow; tack to top of basket. Place removable cushion in top of basket, use bottom for sewing notions.

Cupcake Pincushions

(Project **18** in group photograph, page **116**)

SIZE About 3½″ tall.

MATERIALS Knitting-worsted-weight yarn (one (4-ounce) skein each color A for icing and B for cake makes 8 cupcakes); scraps yarn in brown and assorted colors for sprinkles and non pareils, and red for cherry; aluminum crochet hook size G (or international size 4:50 mm) **or the size that will give you the correct gauge;** yarn scraps for stuffing; large-eyed tapestry needle.

GAUGE 4 sc = 1″.

NOTE Work tightly.

ICING The side facing you as you work is wrong side of icing. Starting at center with color A, ch 2. **1st rnd:** Work 6 sc in 2nd ch from hook; join with sl st in ch-1. **2nd rnd:** Ch 1, work 2 sc in each sc around; join. **3rd rnd:** Ch 1, sc in each sc, increasing 6 sc evenly spaced around; join. Repeat 3rd rnd 5 times more (48 sc). **9th rnd:** Sc in each sc around; join. Break off. Using yarn, scatter straight-st sprinkles or French-knot non pareils over icing. (Stitch diagrams, page 159.) For cherry, make 1½″-diameter red yarn pompon and sew to icing. (Pompon directions, page 160.)

CAKE Base With color B, work as for icing through 5th rnd. Break off.

    Sides Ch 9. **1st row:** Sc in 2nd ch from hook and in each ch across (8 sc); ch 1, turn. **2nd row:** Working in back lp only of each st, sc in each sc across; ch 1, turn. Repeat 2nd row until sides fit around base. Break off. Sew side seam to form ring, then sew sides around base to form cup. Stuffing as you go, sew icing to cake, drawing in edge of icing.

Flower Wrist Pincushions

(Project **12** in group photograph, page **116**)

MATERIALS Scraps yellow and/or green felt (¼ yard green felt makes leaves for 30 large pincushions or 88 small pincushions; ¼ yard yellow felt makes 54 flowers for small pincushions); scraps calico (¼ yard 45″-wide calico makes 45 small or 18 large pincushions); polyester fiberfill for stuffing; 1 yard ½″-wide elastic (makes 4 pincushions); white glue.

CUTTING Enlarge flower and double leaf shapes (see How to Enlarge Patterns, page 158) and make patterns. Use patterns to cut 3 felt double leaves for large pincushion, 1 double leaf and 1 flower for small pincushion. Cut 5″-diameter circle for large and 3″-diameter circle for small pincushion.

LARGE PINCUSHION

Sew leaf units together at center, spreading leaves out in circle as shown in photograph. Cut 7″ length elastic. Overlap ends and sew securely. Sew fastened ends to underside of leaves. Cut fabric into 5″-diameter circle. Sew running stitches ⅛″ from edge and draw up to form cushion, stuffing as you go. Sew edges together; glue cushion to top of leaves.

SMALL PINCUSHION

Glue flower to center of double leaf. Make and attach elastic wristlet and pincushion as for large pincushion, cutting circle 3″ in diameter and gluing to center of flower.

Each sq. = ½″

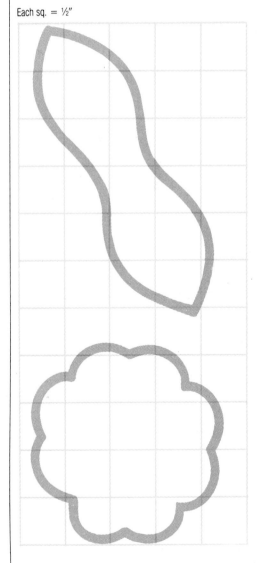

Calico Yardstick Holder

(Project **9** in group photograph, page **116**)

MATERIALS 45″-wide calico, ¼ yard main color (MC) makes 1 holder and pincushion, ¼ yard contrasting color (CC) makes 3 pockets; 36″-wide non-woven, iron-on interfacing, ¼ yard makes 3 holders; scraps green felt; 1 D-ring; sewing thread to match holder; cotton balls; yardstick.

Cut 7″ x 39″ length of MC, 2¾″ x 34″ interfacing and 3″ x 34″ CC. Fold MC in half lengthwise, right sides facing, and stitch with ½″ seam allowance to form tube. Do not turn. Iron flat with seam at center of one side. Stitch ½″ from one end (bottom). Center and iron interfacing to unseamed side, placing end of interfacing at bottom seam line, turn. For yardstick pocket, turn in CC edges ½″ and press; topstitch across one end (will be top). Pin pocket to unseamed side of holder, about ½″ from sides and lower end; topstitch with zigzag stitch along sides and bottom of pocket.

Turn in top of holder ½″ and topstitch. Turn in corners so top end forms tab. Fold tab over D-ring and sew securely.

With MC, make pincushion as for large pincushion under Flower Wrist Pincushions, page 125, and sew to top of pocket. Insert yardstick.

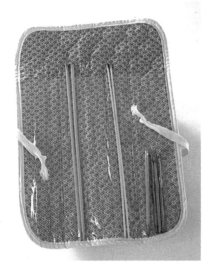

Roll-up Needlework Case

MATERIALS 13″ x 18″ quilted place mat; 13″ square clear plastic; 1 yard double-fold woven tape.

Place plastic on place mat so edges match at one end; round corners of plastic at one end. Stitch plastic and mat together around outer edges, leaving remaining inner edge of plastic free. Marking from open end to stitched end, mark plastic into 6 lengthwise sections as follows: one 3″ wide, four 2″ wide and one 1″ wide. Stitch along markings to form pockets. Then stitch across middle of 3″ pocket and cut plastic just below these stitches to create another pocket. On reverse side of place mat, tack center of tape near center of mat along one stitching line; knot ends.

Insert knitting needles into long pockets and crochet hooks into short ones. Fold and tie tape in bow.

Folding Needleholders

(Project **1** in group photograph, page **116**)

MATERIALS Scraps wallpaper (5¼″ x 6¼″ piece makes one); scraps felt (¼ yard 45″-wide felt makes 60); white glue; stapler; sewing needles for holder.

Cut 4″ x 5⅝″ piece wallpaper. Following needleholder diagram, cut out corners. Fold in and glue 1″ sides. Fold in ⅝″ end and staple ⅛″ from fold (piece should resemble open matchbook). Cut 1¼″ x 4½″ strip each from wallpaper and felt. Matching one end of wallpaper to end X of holder, glue edges of strip along center of holder. Glue felt on top. When dry, insert needles, fold and close holder.

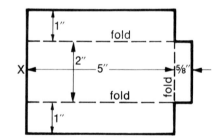

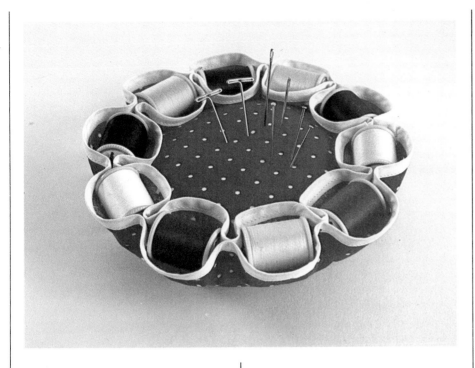

Calico Sewing Caddy

SIZE About 6½″ diameter.

MATERIALS ¼ yard polka-dot fabric; 2 yards double-fold bias tape; 1 yard round elastic; 10 small spools thread; polyester fiberfill for stuffing; large-eyed needle.

Cut two 8″ circles from fabric. Mark 5″ circle in center of each. Encase and topstitch outer edge of each circle with bias tape. With wrong sides together, stitch circles together along marked center-circle line, leaving 2″ opening. Stuff center firmly; stitch opening closed. Divide outer edges into 10 equal sections; tack at each division through both thicknesses, forming pockets for spools. Thread elastic through needle and * string spool on elastic; insert needle under tack separating 2 pockets. Repeat from * around. Pull up elastic so that spools and pockets are as shown; knot to secure.

Trinket Box with Pincushion Lid

(Project **2** in group photograph, page **116**)

SIZE About 4″ tall.

MATERIALS Round cardboard oatmeal box; scraps green felt and red woven fabric (1½ yards 45″-wide green felt trim 38 pincushions, ¾ yard red fabric makes 12 pincushions); scraps shiny gift wrap (8″ x 18″ sheet covers 1 box); scraps ½″-wide grosgrain ribbon; rubber cement; white glue; polyester fiberfill for stuffing.

Cut box down to measure 3″ tall and save box top. Cut strip of gift wrap 4½″ wide and long enough to fit around outside of box, plus ½″. Make ¾″-deep cuts about ½″ apart along both long edges. Apply rubber cement to outside of box. Center and wrap strip around box; overlap and glue ends. Apply rubber cement to outside bottom, bend clipped edges and stick to bottom. Fold in top clipped edges and cement to inside of box. Cut strip to fit inside box; cement in place. Cut 2 circles to fit bottom, inside and out; cement in place.

Cut 1¼″-wide strip green felt to fit around box top. Cut one long edge in series of sawtooth points, as shown. From red fabric, cut one circle 1″ larger and 1 circle 4″ larger than box top. Sew circles together with ½″ seam allowance (smaller one will form flat bottom of pincushion), stuffing as you go. Glue to box top, then glue green strip around edge, sawtooth edge up. Cut 4″ length ribbon, fold in half and glue ends to inside of box top, with looped end extending as a pull tab to lift top.

All-star attraction:
The all-Christmas booth

Starting at top left: **1.** Christmas-stocking and Santa-Claus-cap tree ornaments in felt with cotton trim, page 132. **2.** Santa, mouse and elf ornaments in felt on candy-cane sticks, page 133. **3.** Ribbon star ornaments, page 136. **4.** Soft-sculpture heart, star and tree ornaments, page 136. **5.** Pompon wreath 9″ in diameter, page 132. **6.** Puff-heart felt wreath with bows 15″ in diameter, page 130. **7.** Assorted Christmas stockings to sew, page 131. **8.** Gift-tag decorations, page 138. **9.** Gold-painted walnut ornaments, page 136. **10.** Crocheted red-corkscrew wreath ornaments, page 135. **11.** Angel dolls for Christmas table or tree, page 139. **12.** Crocheted white-corkscrew ornaments with red satin bows, page 135. **13.** Red-and-white crocheted boot ornaments with brown-felt gingerbread men, page 132. **14.** Milk-carton gingerbread-house cookie box and cookies, page 138. **15.** "Strawberry" walnut ornaments, page 135. **16.** Crocheted hang-up boots with candy canes, page 133. **17.** Plastic-foam and real egg ornaments decorated with ribbons, stars and sequins, page 135. **18.** Circular ornaments made from old greeting cards and bordered with rickrack, page 135.

This sentimental favorite needs no introduction, no special sales message, no explanatory signs. Christmas comes with everything built in, from color scheme to motifs, and of course universal appeal. Your part in this pageant is powerfully simple but mighty important: Start your Christmas crafting early so you'll have a plentiful supply on hand when the big day arrives. (The big *bazaar* day, that is!) Our projects are "plentiful" in the ways that matter most to you—designs of many kinds, all easy and economical to make so you can produce huge quantities of each. Here's wishing you a productive pre-holiday season!

A merry collection of ideas for spreading the joy of Christmas to the tree and beyond. Adornments for door, wall and mantel . . . embellishments for small, sentimental gifts . . . even a gingerbread cookie-box house with a recipe for people-shaped gingersnap cookies to put in it!

Puff-heart Felt Wreath

(Project **6** in group photograph, page **128**)

SIZE About 15″ diameter.

MATERIALS 45″-wide red felt (1 yard makes 21 hearts); 1″-wide green grosgrain ribbon (3½ yards trim 8 hearts); red sewing thread and red heavy-duty thread; pinking shears; wire coat hanger; pliers; heavy-duty wire cutters.

Enlarge heart diagram (see How to Enlarge Patterns, page 158) and make full pattern. With pinking shears, cut out 16 heart shapes from felt. Topstitch pairs together ¼″ in from edges, leaving 2″ open. Stuff and topstitch opening closed.

With pliers, untwist hook of coat hanger and form hanger into 12″-diameter ring. Twist ends together and cut off excess with clippers. Arrange hearts around ring as shown and sew to ring at back with heavy-duty thread. Cut ribbon into 14″ lengths. Make bows and glue between hearts at points where their edges touch (see photograph).

Each sq. = ½″

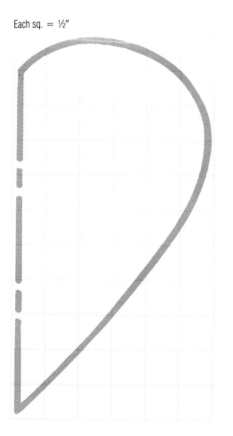

Assorted Christmas Stockings to Sew

(Project **7** in group photograph, page **128**)

SIZES 6″ to 10½″ tall.

MATERIALS 45″-wide cotton-blend print fabrics (a total of ⅜ yard makes 6 small stockings and a total of 1 yard makes 7 large stockings); details such as button for ankle strap, pompon or small bells (3 per stocking); sewing threads to match appliquéd pieces.

Enlarge stockings (see How to Enlarge Patterns, page 158), making one whole pattern or separate patterns for shoes and stockings as directed. When cutting fabric, add ¼″ seam allowance.

BELL STOCKING

Cut 2 fabric stockings (reverse pattern for one). Cut twelve 1¾″ x 3″ x 3″ fabric triangles. With right sides facing, stitch stockings together; turn. Stitch pairs of triangles together on long edges; turn. Pin around top of stocking. Cut 1″ x 12″ strip fabric. Fold long edges in ¼″ and press. Use strip to bind top of stocking, forming excess into hanging loop. Sew bells to 3 triangles.

"MARY JANE" STOCKING

Cut 1 partial stocking and 1 shoe from separate fabrics and 1 whole stocking in reverse. Turn in top edge of shoe and topstitch to partial stocking. Cut 1″ x 4½″ strap, turn in and press long edges and 1 end ¼″; topstitch to stocking. Sew on button. With right sides facing, stitch stockings together; turn. Hem top edge. For hanging loop, cut 1″ x 4″ strip. Fold in long edges ¼″, then fold in half lengthwise; top-stitch. Fold in half and sew ends to top of stocking.

CRISSCROSS STOCKING

Cut 2 fabric stockings (reverse pattern for one). Following photograph, cut 1″-wide strips to crisscross on one piece. Fold in long edges ¼″ and press. Pin in place as shown and topstitch. Trim ends. With right sides facing, stitch stocking halves together; turn. Hem top edge. Make hanging loop as for "Mary Jane" stocking.

BOW-TIED STOCKING

Cut 2 fabric stockings (reverse pattern for one). Cut 1¾″ x 12″ strip. Fold in long edges ¼″ and topstitch vertically to one stocking piece. Cut 1¾″ x 6″ strip, fold in edges and topstitch horizontally to stocking. Cut 1¾″ x 11″ and 1¾″ x 2½″ strips. Fold in long edges as on other strips and topstitch. Fold longer strip into loop, overlap ends and wrap smaller strip around middle to simulate bow. Sew to stocking. With right sides facing, stitch stocking halves together, taking care not to catch bow in stitching; turn. Hem top edge. Cut 1½″ x 6″ strip and make hanging loop as for "Mary Jane."

POMPON STOCKING

Cut and assemble as for "Mary Jane" stocking, omitting strap. Make 1½″-diameter pompon (see pompon instructions, page 160) and sew to shoe.

Each sq. = ½″

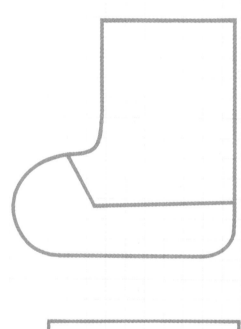

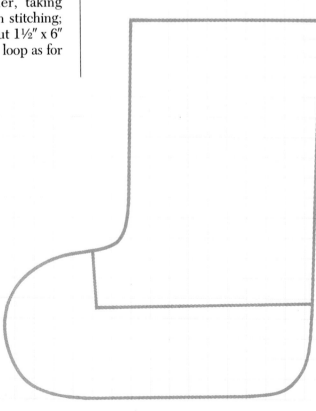

Crocheted Boot Ornaments with Felt Gingerbread Men

(Project **13** in group photograph, page **128**)

SIZE Boot, about 3″ tall.

MATERIALS Thin sport yarn (1 ounce each red and white makes 2 boots); aluminum crochet hook size H (or international size 5:00 mm) **or the size that will give you the correct gauge;** 1 small shank-type bell per boot; scraps brown felt for gingerbread man; scraps fabric for tie; tiny moveable eyes (not recommended for very small child); scrap red embroidery floss; polyester fiberfill for stuffing; white glue.

GAUGE 4 sc = 1″.

BOOT AND CUFF

Make as for Crocheted Hang-up Boot with Candy Canes above, joining seam with red and adding bell.

Each sq. = ½″

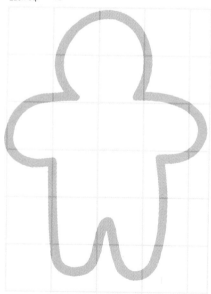

GINGERBREAD MAN

Enlarge gingerbread man diagram (see How to Enlarge Patterns, page 158) and make pattern. Cut out 2 felt pieces. Sew together, overcasting edges and leaving 1″ open. Stuff and sew opening closed. Glue on eyes. Using 2 strands floss, embroider 2 straight sts for mouth (stitch diagram, page 159). Make tiny fabric bow tie and sew in place. Insert gingerbread figure in boot.

Pompon Wreath

(Project **5** in group photograph, page **128**)

SIZE 9″ diameter.

MATERIALS Knitting-worsted-weight yarn (2 ounces each red and white make 1); green yarn for bow (1 ounce makes 1); 9″ square of cardboard.

Make six 2½″-diameter pompons each of red and white, leaving two 4″ ends on each to tie around backing. See page 160 for method of making pompons.

From cardboard, cut 8½″-diameter ring, an even 1½″ wide all around, for backing. Make 12 equidistant holes around center of rim. Insert 1 pompon tie end into each hole, wrap around rim and knot with other end; alternate colors. Cut about twenty-two 32″ lengths green yarn. Hold together and knot group of strands at each end. Tie around rim in bow.

Christmas-stocking and Santa Claus-cap Ornaments

(Project **1** in group photograph, page **128**)

SIZE About 4″ tall.

MATERIALS Scraps of 45″-wide red felt (¼ yard makes about 22); roll of cotton batting; white glue; ¼″-wide satin ribbon (1 yard trims 4); small candy canes.

Enlarge small stocking diagram (see How to Enlarge Patterns, page 158) and make pattern. For cap, cut triangle pattern 2½″ x 3″ x 3″. Cut 2 felt pieces for each ornament, adding ⅛″ seam allowance to all but top edge. Stitch halves together and turn. Cut 1½″-wide cuff from batting and glue around top of ornament. Glue circle of batting to peak of cap. Cut 9″ long ribbon handle and glue ends inside ornament. Insert candy cane.

Each sq. = ½″

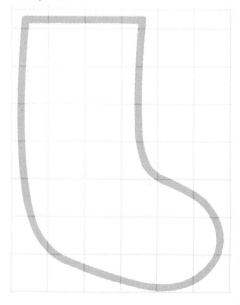

Crocheted Hang-up Boots with Candy Canes

(Project **16** in group photograph, page **128**)

SIZE About 4″ tall.

MATERIALS Knitting-worsted-weight yarn (1 ounce each red and green makes 2); aluminum crochet hook size H (or international size 5:00 mm) **or the size that will give you the correct gauge;** small candy canes.

GAUGE 3 sc = 1″.

BOOT Starting at center with red or green, ch 8. Join with sl st to form ring. **1st rnd:** Ch 3, 2 dc in ring, ch 2, (3 dc in ring, ch 2) 5 times; join with sl st to top of ch-3. **2nd rnd:** Sl st to first ch-2 sp, ch 3, 2 dc in same sp, ch 2, 3 dc in same sp, ch 1, work * (3 dc, ch 2 and 3 dc) in next ch-2 sp, ch 1. Repeat from * 4 times more; join. **3rd rnd:** Sl st between ch-3 and next dc, ch 3, dc in next sp between 2 dc, * 5 dc in next ch-2 sp, (dc in next sp between 2 dc) 5 times. Repeat from * 4 times more; dc in next ch-2 sp, (dc in next sp between 2 dc) 3 times; join. Break off. Fold piece in half (last 11 single dc made form top edge). With contrasting color, join sole and back seam with row of sc. Break off.

CUFF 1st rnd: With same color as seam, work 21 sc around top of boot. Do not join, but mark beg of rnds. **2nd rnd:** Sc in each sc around. Repeat last rnd 4 times more; join. Break off. Fold cuff down. For hanging loop, ch 10 and form ring; sl st in back of boot. Break off. Insert candy cane in boot.

Santa, Mouse and Elf Ornaments

(Project **2** in group photograph, page **128**)

MATERIALS Scraps of felt in assorted colors; contrasting sewing threads; crochet cord for hanging loops; sequins for eyes; white glue; large-eyed needle; clear-wrapped candy canes.

Enlarge head diagrams for Santa, mouse and elf (see How to Enlarge Patterns, page 158) and make pattern for each section of each head. Cut 2 felt pieces from each pattern. Glue pieces together for each half of ornament, as follows: **Santa:** Glue face on beard, then join beard and hat with cuff. Glue circle on top. **Mouse:** Glue inner-ear circle on ear and nose on face. **Elf:** Glue hair on face, hat on hair and circle on hat. **All pieces:** Topstitch halves of ornaments together, leaving opening at bottom. Glue on sequin eyes. Cut 12″ length cord, thread in needle and run through top of ornament; knot ends together. Glue straight end of wrapped candy cane in opening.

Each sq. = ½″

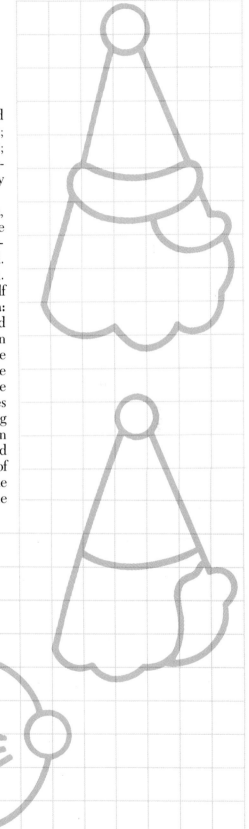

Crocheted Red-corkscrew Wreath Ornaments

(Project **10** in group photograph, page **128**)

MATERIALS Red knitting-worsted-weight yarn (1 ounce makes 1); aluminum crochet hook size G (or international size 4:50 mm); green ¼"-wide satin ribbon (1 yard makes 4 bows).

Ch 52. Work 4 hdc in 2nd ch from hook and in each ch across, spiralling finished work as you go. Sl st in first ch. Break off and tie ends into 2" loop. Cut 8" length ribbon, tie in bow and sew to wreath.

Crocheted White-corkscrew Ornaments

(Project **12** in group photograph, page **128**)

MATERIALS See materials for Red-corkscrew Wreaths, above; use white yarn and red ribbon.

Ch 36. Work 4 hdc in 2nd ch from hook and in each ch across, spiralling finished work as you go. Break off and tie ends into 2" loop. Cut 8" length ribbon, tie into bow and sew to top of ornament.

Gift-wrapped tree trims. Simply stitch and cut out cardboard shapes, glue on paper and ribbon of your choice.

Circular Ornaments

(Project **18** in group photograph, page **128**)

MATERIALS Lid from large juice container (removed by peeling strip); white regular rickrack and red baby rickrack (1 yard of each trims about 2); scrap yarn for hanger; small pictures from Christmas cards, gift wrap or magazines; white glue; heavy paper for mounting.

Cut out 2 pictures to fit lid and glue to heavy paper. When glued unit is dry, cut circles. Glue 1 picture to each side of lid. Glue regular rickrack around each picture, then glue baby rickrack on top. Cut 2" length of yarn and glue ends behind rickrack for hanger.

"Strawberry" Walnut Ornaments

(Project **15** in group photograph, page **128**)

MATERIALS Bag of whole walnuts; red acrylic paint; scrap green felt; scrap red yarn; white seed beads (about 22 per ornament); white glue.

Paint walnuts red. Cut 2"-diameter circle from green felt. Cut edges in sawtooth pattern. Cut small hole in center. Cut 4" length of red yarn. Draw ends of yarn ½" through hole. Glue cap and yarn ends to top of walnut. Glue about 22 beads over walnut as shown in photograph.

Egg Ornaments

(Project **17** in group photograph, page **128**)

MATERIALS Real eggs or 4"-long plastic-foam eggs; ¼"-wide ribbons for each small egg, ¾ yard color A, ½ yard each colors B and C; ¼"- to ⅝"-wide ribbons for each large egg, ¾ yard each color A, B and C; sequin and star decorations; green cord (1 yard trims 3); straight pins.

SMALL EGGS

Carefully pierce small hole in point of raw egg and larger hole (about ¼" diameter) in large end of egg. Hold egg over bowl and blow gently through small hole; yolk and white will fall through other hole. Rinse emptied egg thoroughly.

Cut 1 piece each A, B and C ribbons to fit lengthwise around egg, and one piece A ribbon 14" long. Spacing ribbons equally, glue the 3 short ones around egg, leaving space for 4th ribbon. Cut 10" green cord, draw ends through center of 14" ribbon and knot, forming hanger. With knot at point of egg, glue long ribbon around egg, allowing ends to hang from bottom (see photograph). Glue stars between ribbons.

LARGE EGG

Cut two 22" lengths color A ribbon to fit lengthwise around egg, and one 22" length each B and C. Glue one A ribbon around egg with ends hanging from bottom. Attach cord to other A ribbon as for small egg and glue around egg, forming cross at each end and with cord extending from point of egg. Spacing equally, glue on B and C ribbons. Secure with pins at base. Glue 3 sequins in each section between ribbons. (See photograph for all positioning.)

Soft-sculpture Heart, Star and Tree Ornaments

(Project **4** in group photograph, page **128**)

MATERIALS 45"-wide plain or dotted fabric (⅜ yard makes 7); ⅛"-wide satin ribbon (1 yard trims 4); polyester fiberfill for stuffing.

Enlarge heart, star and tree diagrams (see How to Enlarge Patterns, page 158) and make full patterns. Cut 2 fabric pieces for each ornament (reverse pattern for one star), adding ¼" seam allowance.

With right sides facing, stitch halves together, leaving 2" open. Clip curves and notch inner corners, turn and stuff. Cut 9" length ribbon. Insert ends in opening and sew closed.

Gold-painted Walnut Ornaments

(Project **9** in group photograph, page **128**)

MATERIALS Bag of whole walnuts; gold paint; ⅜"-wide plaid ribbon (2 yards make bows for 5 ornaments); gold cord (1 yard makes hangers for 3 ornaments); 1 small nail per ornament.

Paint walnuts gold. Hammer small nail three-quarters of the way into top of walnut. Cut 10" length gold cord and 14" length ribbon. Tie cord around nail, then knot ends together to form loop. Tie ribbon in bow around nail.

Ribbon Star Ornaments

(Project **3** in group photograph, page **128**)

SIZES 4"-diameter and 5"-diameter stars.

MATERIALS 1"-wide dotted green and plain red grosgrain ribbon (1¾ yards of each make 3 large stars or 3 yards of each make 6 small); scraps regular rickrack, ½ yard trims 2 large stars; white glue; red or green cord.

LARGE STAR

Cut four 5" strips each from green and red ribbons. Glue together in matched pairs, back to back, to form 2 red and 2 green lengths. Notch ends. Cross and glue as shown in photograph. Cut two 4" strips rickrack; glue to centers of red ribbons. Cut 1" square of green ribbon and glue to center of star. Cut 8" length cord; glue ends to back for hanger.

SMALL STAR

Work as for large star, cutting ribbons 4" long and omitting rickrack.

Speedy suggestions in
a festive mood

GIFT BAGS Sew together, on 3 sides, rectangles of Christmas-color fabric (these are 6″ x 7″); hem the tops. Fill with tea bags or coffee beans; tie and tag in the same holiday spirit.

CHRISTMAS TRAY AND NAPKIN RING With a festive print and Elmer's Glue-All®, convert a metal tray and slices of cardboard tubing to seasonal snack sets. Spray with clear acrylic; tidy the napkin ring edges with tape.

PINE TREE SACHETS Cut pairs of tree shapes from felt. Stitch satin ribbon down one piece, leaving an end long enough to loop. Stitch the two pieces together, except for an opening at the top for pine-needle stuffing and loop. Stuff with pine needles. Loop ribbon end into opening and stitch opening closed.

GIFT BASKET Using pinking shears, cut a fabric square or rectangle to line and overflow basket, a circle to decorate a jam-jar lid. Add ribbon bows and cinnamon sticks; tuck in a few tiny flowers.

Gingerbread-house Cookie Box and Cookies

(Project **14** in group photograph, page **128**)

SIZE Box is 4″ x 4″ x 7″ tall.

MATERIALS 2-quart cardboard milk container; brown paper (grocery bags can be used); glossy, solid-color gift wrap, printed gift wrap and white paper; rubber cement; yarn for handle; paper punch.

BOX

Cut milk container to 7½″ tall; discard top section. Following dimensions on cookie box diagram, cut roof flaps as shown, slightly bending back top edge of flaps ½″ on broken lines. Cut brown paper

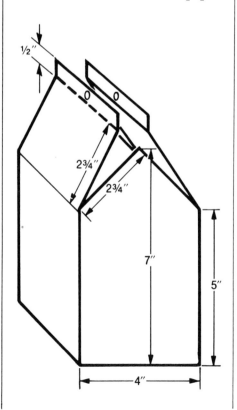

pieces to fit outside of box and both sides of flaps (fold paper over top edges of flaps); cement in place. Following photograph, decorate box with cutout white paper and gift wrap: outside dimensions of door are 2″ x 3″, heart window is 1″ x 2¼″, window on other side is 1¾″ x 2½″. Wavy border varies from ¼″ to ½″ wide. Roof stripes are ½″ wide.

Punch hole in each flap. Cut 18″ length of yarn, draw through holes and knot ends to hold in place. Fill box with cookies (recipe follows):

GINGERSNAP PEOPLE

- ½ cup butter or margarine, softened
- ¾ cup sugar
- ⅓ cup water
- 1 tablespoon dark corn syrup
- 1½ teaspoons each cinnamon, cloves and ginger
- 1 teaspoon ground cardamom (optional)
- 2½ cups flour mixed with ¾ teaspoon baking soda
  Icing (recipe follows)
  Food coloring
  Cookie cutters for gingerbread figures.

Place butter and sugar in bowl. In small saucepan bring water, corn syrup and spices to boil. Pour over butter and sugar; beat until well blended. Gradually stir in flour mixture until well blended and smooth. Wrap dough airtight; chill overnight.

To bake, preheat oven to 375°. On lightly floured surface roll out half of dough ⅛″ thick. (Pastry cloth and stockinette-covered rolling pin are helpful.) Cut in desired shapes. Place ¼″ apart on ungreased cookie sheets. Reroll scraps; repeat with remaining dough. Bake in preheated oven 8 to 10 minutes, or until well browned. Let cool on cookie sheets. Decorate as desired with icing (recipe below) spooned into small cone made of parchment or double layers of waxed paper

and squeezed onto cookies. Dry on racks or cookie sheets until icing is firm. Store loosely covered in cool, dry place. Makes about 25 large cookies.

Icing Beat 2 cups confectioners' sugar, 1 egg white and 1 teaspoon lemon juice until well blended. Add drop of food coloring, if desired, and mix. Divide into separate bowls if you wish to use more than one tint.

Gift-tag Decorations

(Project **8** in group photograph, page **128**)

MATERIALS Heavy illustration board; glossy gift wrap; paper punch; cord or ⅛″-wide ribbon (1 yard trims 3); scraps green felt; scraps of 45″-wide calico (½ yard makes 27 candy-cane pouches); rubber cement and white glue; pinking shears; 3″ candy canes; ruler and triangle; mat knife.

Cement sheet of glossy paper to one side of illustration board. Following photograph for shape and using ruler and triangle, mark off 2¾″ x 5¾″ tags on uncovered side of board. Mark point at one end. Cut out with mat knife. Punch hole at point.

Using pinking shears, cut 4¾″ calico circle. From felt, cut 2 free-form holly leaves about 1″ x 1½″. Cut 12″ cord. Wrap circle around candy cane and tie tightly with cord. Glue felt leaves over cord to hold in place. Slide 1 end of cord through hole in tag and tie.

Bell and Tree Felt Photo Frames

SIZES Tree measures about 5½" square; bell measures about 4" x 4¼".

MATERIALS For both Scraps red and green felt; 12" piece ½"-wide woven decorative ribbon and scrap white string for each; white glue; photo; pinking shears. **For tree** Scrap black felt; **For bell** Small jingle bell.

PATTERNS Enlarge tree and bell diagrams (see How to Enlarge Patterns, page 158) and make patterns (be sure to mark broken lines for smaller piece and oval opening). On solid line, cut larger piece for each ornament with pinking shears. Using regular scissors and following broken lines, cut smaller pieces and oval opening.

ASSEMBLING Center smaller bell or tree on larger shape; glue at top and bottom, sandwiching loop of string between layers at top for hanging. Glue black trunk on tree. Sew jingle bell on felt bell. Make bow and tack on as shown. Insert photo.

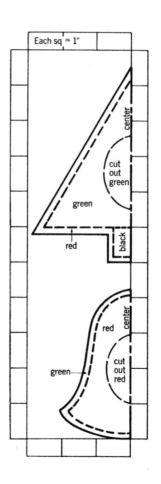

Each sq = 1"

center

cut out green

green

red

black

red center

green

cut out red

Angel Dolls

(Project **11** in group photograph, page **128**)

SIZE About 6" tall.

MATERIALS 45"-wide dotted fabric (1⅛ yards make 12 dresses); ⅜"-wide lace (1 yard trims 1 dress); 4"-diameter white paper doilies (3 per doll); 1½"-diameter plastic-foam ball; scraps yarn; cardboard tube from bathroom tissue; ⅛"-wide satin ribbon (1 yard trims 3); 3 small beads for eyes and mouth; pink crayon; ⅜"-wide gold looped trim (1 yard makes 7 halos); white glue; pinking shears; T pin.

With pinking shears, cut out 11"-diameter circle and 3"-diameter circle from fabric. Lap edge of larger circle ⅛" over lace and glue. Center end of cardboard tube on wrong side of larger circle and glue. Fold circle around tube and tie with 12" length ribbon about 1" from top.

Cut oval center from one doily and glue to center of small circle. Center and glue circle on doily rim to form dress bodice. Glue bodice over top of dress as shown in photograph. Cut about twenty-five 4" lengths of yarn for hair. Tie together in center, spread over plastic-foam ball and glue. Push and glue beads into ball for features. Color cheeks with crayon. Insert T pin down through center top of bodice into tube, allowing head of pin to extend about ½". Push and glue pin head into doll's head, then push and glue doll's head down onto bodice.

Fold 2 doilies in half and glue. Glue to back of doll as shown, for wings. Cut 5" gold-trim halo, lap ends and glue, then glue halo to head.

Guaranteed to collect a crowd

There are certain bazaar features that, though they take some extra thought and planning, pay off handsomely enough to warrant it. What follows describes three that are well worth considering, and how to go about instituting each of them at your bazaar.

How to give your raffle powerful pull: That's a question you should be asking yourself, and soon, because a well-run raffle can attract both profits and publicity. The center of interest and drawing card, of course, is the raffle prize. Since only one has to be made, you can—and should—go all out on a spectacular piece of needlework, and get started on it right away so it is available for promotional purposes. For your convenience, a collection of just such treasures, called *Gallery of Prize Needlework*, directly follows the introduction to raffles.

While-You-Wait Personalizing is a service designed to make cash customers of casual browsers. The attraction here: Instant ways to add the names, initials and monograms that everyone loves to many kinds of purchases. Personalizing is perfect, of course, for gifts, but it might well inspire people to make some "impulse buys" strictly for themselves.

Made to order, sure to please recognizes a fact crucial to success with the handsome handcrafts people are most drawn to: the baby sets, sweaters, afghans and such too time-consuming to produce in quantity. Usually, too, they require better-than-average skill and, to complicate matters even further, often involve sizing. The answer is: Take advance orders. If you do, you will never have to turn away an eager buyer; also, you can continue to offer any designs that sell out quickly. Right after the suggestions about setting up your "made to order" service, you will find an illustrated list of candidates for it—including, at the end, an inventory of likely quick sell-outs that you might well want to add.

how to give your raffle powerful pull

If you're diligent about promoting the prize drawing, a raffle can bring in lots of customers. The key is a prize so spectacular no one can resist.

Planning a raffle. For a raffle, go all out on a handcrafted prize in the heirloom class—an afghan, a full-size quilt or a baby blanket, for example—that can honestly be billed as a needlework treasure. In the collectors' market, handmade quilts and afghans currently command hundreds of dollars, and they can only increase in value. But non-experts know, too, that such needlework is one of the best investments you can make, so most people will gladly risk a dollar on the chance of such a reward.

A raffle is one of the first parts of the bazaar to plan for, particularly when the prize will be a major piece of handwork. If you want to tap the time and talents of your volunteers, choose a design such as a sectioned or paneled afghan or patched quilt that can be worked and assembled by several people. Set deadlines and schedule working sessions well in advance, and stick to them.

Promoting a raffle. The faster you can complete the prize, the sooner you can use it to promote the raffle. Nothing sells tickets so effectively as the prize piece itself, on display at the local shopping center, school or post office. Then, too, a raffle can spark publicity for the bazaar as a whole. The local paper might work up a feature about the piece as a work-in-progress, particularly when several crafters are involved. Your publicist should prepare a release describing the design, materials and techniques, and listing the participants. A good release can serve many promotional purposes. Be sure, when the piece is completed, that it is photographed with the people who made it—a surefire "human interest" angle.

Pricing and selling tickets. Naturally you will want your ticket price high enough to get back the money spent on materials—and much more. It helps to set a goal: how many tickets must be sold to reach your profit objective. Enlist as many ticket-sellers as you can, and get them off and running at least six weeks before the bazaar. How much money you make depends almost entirely on how aggressively your agents push sales. It shouldn't be hard to convince people that the price isn't much when they might win an heirloom, but it's bound to help if your salespeople can offer a bit of background about the technique and design—and of course the good cause the money is going to.

Sell tickets right up to drawing time, and be sure to publicize the drawing when it is over. See that the local media get, without delay, a photograph and a statement about bazaar profits. A bazaar raffle, done with energy and enthusiasm, is a guaranteed success. Let people know how well it worked, and it might well become an annual money-making tradition.

Some suitable raffle prizes. Many of the pieces in the Needlework Gallery that follows would make handsome raffle prizes. For projects that can be worked in parts, see the Patchwork Pillow design (page 144), which would adapt easily to a quilt; the Textured Afghan (page 146); the Triangle Afghan and Pillow Set (page 148); and the Bold Baby Blanket (page 149). The shawls on pages 42 to 45 are also elegant raffle-prize candidates.

*Gallery of
Prize Needlework*

Moon and Sun Pillows

Slightly padded appliqué designs are quick and easy—everything is machine-sewn, including the zigzag-stitch outlines.

SIZE 14″ square.

MATERIALS Assorted color-coordinated small-print fabrics (use mostly cool blues for moon pillow and warm browns and yellows for sun): for each pillow, ½ yard for outer border and back (color A), ½ yard for middle border, sun, moon and stars (B), 10½″ square for background (C); matching sewing threads; 14″-square muslin-covered pillow form.

BASIC PILLOW For each pillow, cut 2 color A pieces 15″ square. Cut B 11½″ square and C 10½″ square. Turn in edges of B and C ½″; press.

PILLOW DESIGNS Enlarge pattern (same diagram works for both). See How to Enlarge Patterns, page 158. **For moon pillow,** cut moon circle (omit rays) and 4 stars from B. Using darker shade of sewing thread, machine-appliqué to C square with ¹⁄₁₆″-wide close zigzag stitch. Add details, using same stitch. **For sun pillow,** cut sun circle. Machine-appliqué to C square and add details, both with zigzag stitch. Topstitch C square to B square and B square to an A square. Stitch pillow front and back together on 3 sides; turn, insert pillow form and slipstitch open edge closed.

Each sq 1″

Striped Knitted Pillow

Fringed standout knits up fast in several sizzling colors.

SIZE 15″ square, not including fringe.

MATERIALS Knitting-worsted-weight yarn, 4 ounces each burnt orange (color A) and dark rose (B), 2 ounces light rose (C), 1 ounce each red (D) and lilac (E); 1 pair No. 9 knitting needles (or English needles No. 4) **or the size that will give you the correct gauge;** aluminum crochet hook size G (or international size 4:50 mm); 15″-square pillow form.

GAUGE 4 st = 1″; 6 rows = 1″.

PILLOW BACK With A, cast on 60 sts. Work even in stockinette st for 15″. Bind off.

PATTERN STITCH 1st row: K 4, * p 4, k 4. Repeat from * across. **2nd row:** P 4, * k 4, p 4. Repeat from * across. **3rd and 4th rows:** Repeat 1st and 2nd rows. **5th through 8th rows:** Repeat 2nd and 1st rows twice. **9th row:** K across. **10th row:** P across. Repeat 1st through 10th rows for pattern stitch.

PILLOW FRONT With C, cast on 60 st. Work even in pattern st in color sequence of 8 rows C, 2 A, 8 C, 2 B, 8 D, 2 E, 8 B, 2 A, 8 B, 2 E; work 1st through 4th rows with A, 9th and 10th rows with B; starting with 1st row of pattern st, work 8 rows E, 2 D, 8 C, 2 B, 8 D. Bind off.

FINISHING Pin edges of back and front around pillow form. **Edging: 1st rnd:** With B, crochet 1 rnd sc through both thicknesses, working 3 sc at each corner. **2nd rnd:** Sc in each sc around, working 3 sc at each corner; join. Break off. **Fringe:** Follow General Directions, page 160, to work fringe in each sc, using two 4″ strands B for each tassel.

Patchwork Pillow

Classic quilt square makes a stunning but most economical pillow.

SIZE 17″ square.

MATERIALS ½ yard 45″-wide yellow calico, ¼ yard each red and blue calico; ½ yard muslin for lining; 17″-square foam pillow form or polyester-fiberfill stuffing; cardboard for patterns; graph paper.

PATTERNS On graph paper mark off 7″ square, 5″ square and 5″ x 3½″ x 3½″ triangle. Cut out and trace on cardboard. Cut out the cardboard patterns.

CUTTING For front pattern, on wrong side of fabric trace one 7″ yellow square, four 5″ red squares, 4 red triangles and 8 blue triangles (leave at least ½″ between pieces). Cut out pieces, adding ¼″ seam allowance to all edges. Also from yellow calico, cut four 1¾″ x 18″ strips for border and an 18″ square for pillow back.

STITCHING Following photograph for arrangement, stitch 2 blue triangles to adjacent sides of each red square. Stitch a free edge on each blue triangle to yellow center square. Stitch 4 red triangles to remaining free edges of blue triangles to complete large square. Press seams to one side at each joining (do not press seams open). Stitch a border strip to each side of large square, mitering corners. With right sides facing, stitch patchwork front and back together with ½″ seams, leaving 15″ open on one side. Turn.

LINING From muslin, cut two 18″ squares. Stitch together with ½″ seams, leaving 15″ open on one side. Turn and insert pillow form or stuffing. Close opening. Slip pillow in patchwork case and slipstitch opening closed.

Cottage Cushions

SIZE About 14″ tall.

MATERIALS ½ yard 45″-wide red or yellow felt for basic cottage; felt scraps for details (see photograph for colors); 3″-thick foam cushion about 14″ square for each pillow; fabric glue; pinking shears; long, sharp kitchen knife; ruler or yardstick.

PATTERNS Enlarge patterns (see How to Enlarge Patterns, page 158), and cut out patterns for basic cottage and details, adding ¼″ for seam allowance to all sides of cot-

tage but not to details. Where one piece appears on top of another, cut the full background piece (for example, 1 rectangular window frame on which 4 windowpanes are glued). From felt, cut out front and back cottage and detail pieces, using pinking shears for cottage.

PILLOW SHAPE Cut seam allowance from cottage pattern. Lay pattern on foam cushion and, using ruler and long, sharp kitchen knife, cut out cottage shape. (If knife is long and sharp enough, you should need only 1 or 2 cuts for each foam edge.)

ASSEMBLING Using pinking shears, cut 3½″-wide felt boxing strip 1″ longer than measurement around pillow. Making ¼″ seam, stitch strip around 1 cottage piece; stitch ends of strip together. Stitch other edge of strip to other cottage piece, leaving bottom open. Turn, insert pillow in case and stitch opening closed.

Following photograph and pattern for placement, glue details to both sides of pillow. If desired, add bush shapes to boxing strip.

Each sq = 1″

basic cottage outline

basic cottage (cut 2)

center fold

basic cottage outline

basic cottage (cut 2)

center fold

Confetti Afghan

Crocheted like one huge granny square, as much fun to make as to win.

SIZE About 66″ square (crocheted like one huge granny square).

MATERIALS Bucilla Win-Knit (acrylic knitting-worsted-weight yarn), 15 (4-ounce) skeins winter white No. 430 (color W), 1 skein each orange No. 444 (O), turquoise No. 412 (T), red No. 433 (R), blue No. 422 (B), yellow No. 477 (Y), green No. 481 (G) and pink No. 425 (P); aluminum crochet hook size F (or international hook size 4:00 mm) **or the size that will give you the correct gauge.**

GAUGE (3-dc shell, ch 1) 3 times = 2″; 6 rnds = 2″.

AFGHAN Starting at center with W, ch 6. Join with sl st to form ring. **1st rnd:** Ch 3, work 2 dc in ring, (ch 2, 3 dc in ring) 3 times, ch 2; join with sl st in ch-3. **2nd rnd:** Sl st in next 2 dc, (work sc, ch 2 and sc in next sp, ch 3) 4 times, ch 3; join with sl st in 1st sc. **3rd rnd:** Sl st in next sp, ch 3, work 2 dc, ch 2 and 3 dc in same sp (1st corner made); (ch 1, shell of

3 dc in next ch-3 sp, ch 1, work corner of 3 dc, ch 2 and 3 dc in next corner sp) 3 times; ch 1, shell in next ch-3 cp, ch 1; join. **4th (ch-3 lp) rnd:** Sl st in next 2 dc, * work sc, ch 2 and sc in corner sp, (ch 3, sc in next ch-1 sp) twice, ch 3. Repeat from * 3 times more (3 ch-3 lp on each side); join. **5th (shell) rnd:** Sl st in corner sp, work 1st corner as for 3rd rnd in same sp, * (ch 1, shell in next ch-3 sp) 3 times; ch 1, work corner in next corner sp. Repeat from * twice more; complete rnd (3 shells on each side); join.

Repeat 4th (lp) rnd and 5th (shell) rnd for pattern throughout, adding 2 more lp to each side on lp rnds and 2 more shells to each side on shell rnds. Work in following colors: 2 more rnds W (ending with shell rnd), * 1 rnd each O, W, T, W, R, W, B, W, Y, W, G, W and P; 7 rnds W. Repeat from * 4 times more. Break off.

Textured Afghan

SIZE About 45″ x 63″.

MATERIALS Bucilla Softex Win-Knit Spectrum (acrylic knitting-worsted-weight yarn), 17 (3-ounce) balls light blue No. 1402; aluminum crochet hook size J (or international size 6:00 mm) **or the size that will give you the correct gauge.**

GAUGE 8 hdc = 3″; 5 rows hdc = 2″.

GENERAL DIRECTIONS

Front Post Dc (f p dc) Follow diagram immediately below. (**NOTE** Diagrams are drawn in simplified manner in order to clarify procedure.) Yo, insert hook from front to back to front again around post (upright part) of next st, yo and draw yarn through, (yo and draw through 2 lps on hook) twice.

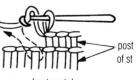

front post dc

Back Post Dc (b p dc) Following diagram immediately below, yo, then, folding top edge of work forward a bit, insert hook from back to front to back again around post of next st, yo and draw yarn through, (yo and draw through 2 lps on hook) twice.

back post dc

Puff Stitch Puff st is worked on wrong side of work but appears on right side. (Yo, draw up lp in same st) 5 times, yo and draw through all 11 lps on hook; ch 1 tightly to form "eye" of st.

NOTE Afghan is worked in 7 separate panels.

PANEL 1 (side border and cable) Ch 21. **1st row:** Work hdc in 3rd ch from hook and in each ch across (20 sts, counting turning ch as 1 st); ch 2, turn. **2nd row (right side):** Skip first st (directly below ch-2), hdc in next 3 sts, work f p dc around next st, hdc in next 2 sts, f p dc around next st, b p dc around next 2 sts, f p dc around next 6 sts, b p dc around next 2 sts, f p dc around next st, hdc in next 2 sts, b p dc around next st, hdc in last st; ch 2, turn. **3rd row:** Skip first st (**NOTE** Always skip first st on each row for all panels), b p dc around next st, f p dc around next 2 sts, b p dc around next 6 sts, f p dc around next 2 sts, b p dc around next st, hdc in next 2 sts, b p dc around next st, hdc in last 4 sts; ch 2, turn. **4th row (cable twist) (NOTE** Cable twists in one direction for right-handed crocheters and in opposite direction for left-handed crocheters): Work 3 hdc, 1 f p dc, 2 hdc, 1 f p dc, 2 b p dc, twist cable as follows: Skip next 3 p dc, then work 1 f p dc in next 3 sts; working in front of last 3 sts worked, work f p dc in 3 skipped sts, starting with first one as shown in diagram; work 2 b p dc, 1 f p dc, 1 hdc; ch 2,

turn. Panel should measure about 5″ wide. **5th row:** Repeat 3rd row. **6th row:** Repeat 2nd row. **7th row:** Repeat 3rd row. Repeat 4th through 7th rows until strip measures about 59″. Break off.

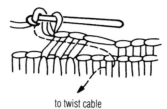

to twist cable

PANEL 2 (puff-st diamonds) Ch 22. **1st row:** Repeat 1st row of Panel 1 (21 sts), turn. **2nd row (right side):** Work 1 f p dc, 17 hdc, 1 f p dc, 1 hdc; ch 2, turn. **3rd row:** Repeat 2nd row, working b p dc instead of f p dc. **4th row:** Repeat 2nd row. Piece should measure about 7¼″ wide. **5th row:** Work 1 b p dc, 8 hdc, puff st in next st, 8 hdc, 1 b p dc, 1 hdc; ch 2, turn. **6th row:** Repeat 2nd row, being careful not to work in eye of puff st. **7th row:** Work 1 b p dc, 7 hdc, 1 puff st, 1 hdc, 1 puff st, 7 hdc, 1 b p dc, 1 hdc; ch 2, turn. **8th row:** Repeat 6th row. **9th row:** Work 1 b p dc, 6 hdc, (1 puff st, 1 hdc) twice; 1 puff st, 6 hdc, 1 b p dc, 1 hdc; ch 2, turn. **10th row:** Repeat 6th row. **11th row:** Repeat 7th row. **12th row:** Repeat 6th row. **13th row:** Repeat 5th row. Repeat 2nd through 13th rows until piece is same length as Panel 1. Break off. Make another panel.

PANEL 3 (basket weave) Ch 28. **1st row:** Repeat 1st row of Panel 1 (27 sts). **2nd row (right side):** Work 1 f p dc, 1 hdc, (3 f p dc, 3 b p dc) 3 times; 3 f p dc, 1 hdc, 1 f p dc, 1 hdc; ch 2, turn. **3rd row:** Work 1 b p dc, 1 hdc, (3 b p dc, 3 f p dc) 3 times; 3 b p dc, 1 hdc, 1 b p dc, 1 hdc; ch 2, turn. **4th row:** Work 1 f p dc, 1 hdc, (3 b p dc, 3 f p dc) 3 times; 3 b p dc, 1 hdc, 1 f p dc, 1 hdc; ch 2, turn. **5th row:** Work 1 b p dc, 1 hdc, (3 f p dc, 3 b p dc) 3 times; 3 f p dc, 1 hdc, 1 b p dc, 1

hdc; ch 2, turn. Piece should measure about 8½″ wide. Repeat 2nd through 5th rows until panel is same length as other panels. Break off. Make another panel.

PANEL 4 (cable) Ch 15. **1st row:** Repeat 1st row of Panel 1 (14 sts). **2nd row (right side):** Work 1 f p dc, 2 b p dc, 6 f p dc, 2 b p dc, 1 f p dc, 1 hdc; ch 2, turn. **3rd row:** Work 1 b p dc, 2 f p dc, 6 b p dc, 2 f p dc, 1 b p dc, 1 hdc; ch 2, turn. **4th row (cable twist):** Work 1 f p dc, 2 b p dc, twist cable as for 4th row of Panel 1; work 2 b p dc, 1 f p dc, 1 hdc; ch 2, turn. Panel should measure about 3½″ wide. **5th row:** Repeat 3rd row. **6th row:** Repeat 2nd row. **7th row:** Repeat 3rd row. Repeat 4th through 7th rows until panel measures same as other panels. Break off.

PANEL 5 (cable and side border) This is the reverse of Panel 1. Work as for Panel 1 through 1st row. **2nd row (right side):** Work 1 f p dc, 2 b p dc, 6 f p dc, 2 b p dc, 1 f p dc, 2 hdc, 1 f p dc, 4 hdc; ch 2, turn. **3rd row:** Work 3 hdc, 1 b p dc, 2 hdc, 1 b p dc, 2 f p dc, 6 b p dc, 2 f p dc, 1 b p dc, 1 hdc; ch 2, turn. Keeping pattern in established sequence, twist cable on next row, then every 4th row as for Panel 1. Work until strip is same length as other strips. Break off.

FINISHING Working on wrong side, whipstitch strips tog in the following numerical order: Panels 1, 2, 3, 4, 3, 2, 5. **End borders: 1st row (wrong side):** Make lp on hook and work hdc in each st across one end of afghan; ch 1, turn. **2nd row:** Sc in each st across. Break off. Work in same manner across other end of afghan.

Multi-striped Afghan

SIZE About 61″ square.

MATERIALS Knitting-worsted-weight yarn, 40 ounces assorted colors, including 8 ounces cream for border and tassels; aluminum crochet hook size K (or international hook size 7:00 mm) **or the size that will give you the correct gauge.**

GAUGE 3 sts = 1″.

AFGHAN Crocheted on the bias. Work in stripes of 1 to 5 rows in colors of your choice as follows: Starting at corner, ch 2. **1st row:** Work (hdc, sc and hdc) in 2nd ch from hook; ch 1, turn. **2nd row:** Work (hdc and sc) in 1st st (1st inc made); hdc in next st, (sc and hdc) in last st (2nd inc made); ch 1, turn. **3rd row:** 1st inc in 1st st; work 1 hdc, 1 sc, 1 hdc; work 2nd inc in last st (last st worked is lower edge; mark lower edge with pin); ch 1, turn. **4th row:** 1st inc in 1st st; 1 hdc, * 1 sc, 1 hdc. Repeat from * to last st, 2nd inc in last st; ch 1, turn.

Repeating 4th row for pattern stitch, work until lower edge (marked with pin) measures about 60″ from beginning, or 2″ less than desired finished size to allow for border.

Dec as follows: **Next row:** Draw up lp in each of 1st 2 sts, yo and draw through all 3 lps on hook (dec made); 1 sc, * 1 hdc, 1 sc. Repeat from * to last 2 sts; dec as before; ch 1, turn. Repeat last row until 3 sts remain. **Last row:** Draw up lp in each of 3 remaining sts, yo and draw through all 4 lps on hook. Break off.

BORDER With cream, sc evenly around entire outer edge of afghan, working 3 sc in each corner; at end of rnd, join with sl st to 1st sc. Repeat this rnd 4 times more. Break off.

Triangle Afghan and Pillow Set

SIZE Afghan 54″ square when blocked. **Pillow** 12″ square.

MATERIALS Unger Roly-Poly (3½-ounce ball acrylic knitting-worsted-weight yarn), 7 balls cream No. 9578 (color A), 1 each heather green No. 9585 (B), skipper blue No. 4556 (C), slate No. 6674 (D), moss No. 6673 (E) and light turquoise No. 1015 (F); crochet hook size G (or international size 4:50 mm) **or the size that will give you the correct gauge;** 12″-pillow form.

GAUGE 3 dc = ¾″.

NOTE To change colors, work off last 2 lps of last dc with next color; fasten off former color.

AFGHAN

TRIANGLE (make 4) Starting at point (center of afghan), with color A, ch 6. **1st row:** Dc in 4th ch from hook and each of next 2 ch (1 bl made); mark side facing you for right side of work; ch 6, turn. **2nd row:** Dc in 4th ch from hook and each of next 2 ch (bl made); sk 3 dc, work (sc, ch 2, 3 dc) around ch-3 at end of bl (bl made); ch 6, turn. **3rd row:** Dc in 4th ch from hook and each of next 2 ch, * sk 3 dc, (sc, ch 2, 3 dc) around next ch; repeat from * across (3 bl). Join D, fasten off A. Ch 6, turn. Repeating 3rd row for pattern (there will be 1 bl inc on each row), * work 1 row D, 3 rows A, 1 B, 3 A, 1 C, 3 A, 1 E, 3 A, 1 F and 3 A; repeat from * once, then work 1 row D, 3 rows A (47 bl); do not fasten off.

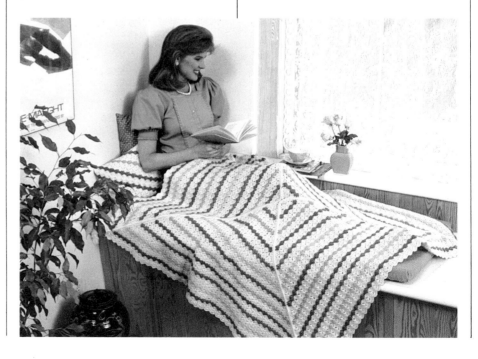

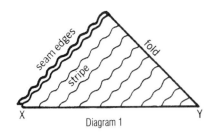

Diagram 1

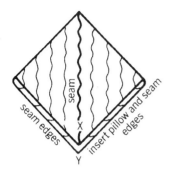

Diagram 2

Edging: Work about 134 sc evenly spaced on each of the 2 shaped side edges of triangle. Fasten off. (**NOTE** There should be the same number of sc on sides of all triangles.)

FINISHING Arrange triangles right side up to form a square with each 1st row at center; from right side, with A, work row of sl st through back lps of matching sts to join triangles.

PILLOW

TRIANGLE (make 1) Work same as afghan triangle for 33 rows; do not fasten off. **Edging:** Sc evenly along the 2 shaped side edges; working in back lp of sts along last row of bl, sc in 3 dc, * sc in sc, sc in 1 ch, sk 1 ch, sc in 3 dc; repeat from * across; join. Fasten off.

FINISHING Fold last row in half, right side out; with A, working in back lps, sl st these edges together (see Diagram 1). Open triangle; refold by bringing corner X to opposite corner Y (Diagram 2) to form square with seam running diagonally across one side; sl st one edge closed; insert pillow; sl st last edge closed.

Bold Baby Blanket

Or lap throw, if you like. Bright squares are crocheted in continuous strips, then sewn together. Ideal for scrap yarn.

SIZE Approximately 41″ x 44″, not including fringe.

MATERIALS 32 ounces assorted colors knitting-worsted-weight yarn; aluminum crochet hook size J (or international size 6:00 mm) **or the size that will give you the correct gauge.**

GAUGE Each 8-dc block measures 2¼″ wide x 2″ deep.

NOTE Afghan is made in 1-block-wide vertical strips that are sewn together later.

STRIP (make 18) Starting at one end with first color, ch 10. **1st row:** Dc in 4th ch from hook and in each ch across (8 dc, counting turning ch as 1 dc); ch 3, turn. **2nd row:** Sk first dc (directly below ch-3), dc in each dc across, dc in top of turning ch; ch 3, turn. Repeat 2nd row twice more, changing colors at end of last row as follows: Work last dc until 2 lps remain on hook; break off color in use, join new color and draw through lps on hook; ch 3, turn.

Continue in this manner, working 4 rows of each color at random, until 22 blocks have been made. Fasten off.

FINISHING Sew strips together with matching yarn. **Fringe:** Mixing colors at random, cut four 6″ strands. Holding strands tog, fold in half and, with crochet hook, draw fold through a stitch, then draw ends through loop formed and pull up tight. Repeat ½″ apart around afghan.

while-you-wait personalizing

Here's a clever way to cash in on the ever-popular names, initials and monograms that people love to see on just about anything: Set up a special table, just off the main traffic area, where, for a small fee, you'll personalize anything people buy.

CHEF'S HAT AND APRONS The big fuzzy letters simply iron on to any sturdy cotton.

MERRY MUGS Eye-catching initials are ever so easy—just peel away the backing and stick them on.

HANKIES AND TOWELS The elegant embroidered look is deceiving—these letters are just ironed on.

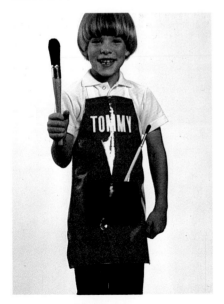

VINYL APRON Plastic peel-off letters come on a sheet, and stick to any vinyl or painted surface.

YOU-NAME-IT T-SHIRT Kids love having their names on things, so these iron-on cartoon-like letters are sure to appeal.

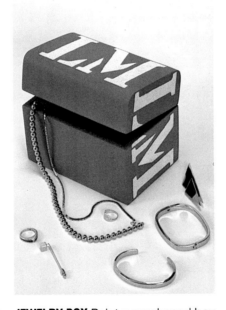

JEWELRY BOX Paint a purchased box with acrylic paint, then initial it, using 3-inch stencils and contrasting paint you pat on with a sponge.

INITIALED STATIONERY Letter-embossed foil stickers make plain notepaper so impressive. Buy both paper and peel-off stickers, and put them together on the spot.

BIG-NAME BASKET Plastic peel-off letters, placed at an angle for fun, jazz up any container.

made to order, sure to please

Have you wondered how you could possibly profit from those handsome but time-consuming pieces eveyone so much admires? Simple: Take orders for them on the day of the fair, for deferred delivery. This is particularly sensible with good-sized articles where, without a guaranteed sale, valuable time and energy might be better spent on group than on individual activities. Such a custom service also opens the way to further sales of the slippers, mittens, scarves and so on that are usually snapped up as soon as the bazaar gets underway.

How profitable—or practical—an advance-order service would be at your bazaar depends on two considerations:

Whether community residents have a strong enough interest in custom-make articles to make such a service worth promoting.

Whether enthusiasm in your working group is high enough that crafters will willingly commit their time to filling orders that are taken.

If there are several retail outlets in your area for handmade goods, residents are more likely to appreciate their value, and to feel that it is worth their while to place orders knowing they must wait for them to be filled. It should be added incentive that they will be getting custom-made goods without the customary retail mark-up.

As for available order-fillers, unless you have at least several people, and preferably a dozen, willing and able to knit, crochet, sew, whittle or whatever else may be called for, the whole business of advance orders becomes a dubious proposition. You cannot create a custom service—or justify selling it to a crowd—on the basis on one knitter, however capable.

When and how to start. The time to begin thinking about advance orders is at the first planning meeting, when booth ideas are being discussed. If the group thinks the idea worth exploring, it should be turned over to the crafters for further discussion of practical details and feasibility. Using this book for reference, you can make tentative judgments about what items might go over big at the bazaar and how many people you could count on to make them to order. As a group, look over the projects suggested as candidates for order-taking and pin down *exactly* how many of each piece each volunteer could, and would be willing, to do. Be sure that each individual is realistic about the time he or she can commit. There may be pieces elsewhere in the book that people could work on more comfortably and faster—because techniques are familiar or for some other reason. Take these into consideration now, too. It's crucial to establish how many of what pieces could *realistically* be made; this sets a limit on the orders per piece that can safely be taken. Ideally you should have several people available to produce the same item. That way seven orders for, let's say, the same sweater, could be farmed out and all seven delivered at roughly the same time. If one person is burdened with making several of the same time-consuming piece, the waiting time would probably be too long for customers to tolerate. Six to eight weeks should be the maximum.

Preparing the booth. Assuming enough volunteers to make the goods and enough suitable projects for them to produce, samples of each piece should be made up for display at the bazaar, in precisely the same materials as will be used to fill the orders. (These samples can also, if you wish, be tagged for on-the-spot sale. If they are, however, they should be kept on display until the end of the bazaar to attract as many orders as possible. Buyers will be good-natured about this when you explain the reason.) If sample-making seems likely to take too much time from volunteer work on other crafts, it might make sense to enlist, and possibly pay, other people to prepare them.

Fasten a small fact sheet to each item (in some way that won't damage it), listing available colors and alternate sizes. If you can attach color swatches or yarns, so much the better. The information must be accurate; it is best supplied by whoever made up the sample, that person having checked availability of the materials with their supplier.

Before the bazaar, prepare a central order book—a looseleaf binder is best—to be used at the booth. Caution everyone to keep a careful record, in triplicate, of each order as it is taken. Section the book by projects, each with an opening page describing the price of the item, the deposit required (enough to cover material costs), the style, size and color variations available, and the names of the needleworkers or crafters who have agreed to fill the orders. After this opening sheet, insert blank pages for orders (setting aside a supply of extras).

Taking orders. Devote a separate page to each order, with pencil carbons between sheets so that copies are made as the order is written up. Print the name, address and telephone number of the customer. Specify, on the order form, the deadline for delivery. Confirm price, size, materials (including color), and anything else that is pertinent—all in writing.

Take (and record) a non-returnable deposit from the customer; confirm in writing the amount of the balance, and that it is to be paid on delivery. Sign each order on behalf of the bazaar committee, and have the customer countersign it.

Give a signed copy of the order to the customer, keep one copy in the binder, and pass the third along to the crafter who will fill the order. This way everyone has exactly the same information—the best way to avoid awkward misunderstandings.

SOME SUITABLE PROJECTS FOR ADVANCE ORDERS

WEARABLES FOR ADULTS

FOR BABIES AND CHILDREN

FOR THE FAMILY DOG

FOR THE KITCHEN

SHAWLS AND STOLE (all crocheted)

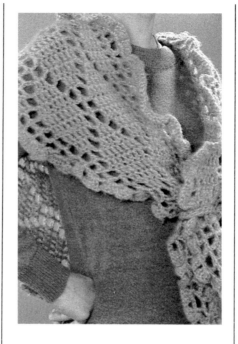

AFGHANS

**Take orders for the following if
sold out at booth**

FAMILY MITTENS

SLIPPERS

DECORATOR PILLOWS

SPECIAL SITUATIONS

CHRISTMAS DECORATIONS

Depending on the bazaar date, customers may *prefer* ordering these in advance to taking them right home. This is not intended to replace but to supplement a sizeable reserve supply, which you should have in any case.

KITCHEN AND DINING ACCESSORIES

If you have a ready source of fabrics in many colors, you may want to offer color choices in potholders, place mats and napkins beyond those on display. This will accommodate those who like the design but feel another color would better suit their decorating scheme.

General tips for bazaar projects

MAKING MULTIPLE ITEMS It is best to make one complete item first, cutting fabric, paper, trims or whatever is required for just one piece. That way you can make adjustments, if necessary, without wasting materials. Then speed things up by cutting multiple fabric pieces and trims at one time.

Depending on the project, an assembly line might be helpful, with one person cutting, another sewing or gluing, a third applying trims, etc.

PATTERNS When making multiple items, we suggest that you make cardboard patterns because they are sturdier and will last longer. They eliminate pinning too. To make, first place tracing paper over enlarged pattern (see page 158 and trace. When only half a pattern is given, draw a full pattern. Using typing carbon paper, transfer traced pattern to lightweight cardboard. Cut out cardboard and reinforce edges with masking tape. Place pattern on wrong side of fabric and draw around it. Being careful to add seam allowance *if called for*, cut out fabric. When tracing multiple items on fabric, arrange pattern repeats so that two sides always have a common cutting line; be sure to allow for seam allowance between them. Do your stitching on the traced line.

It can save time to cut through several layers of fabric, but pin them together carefully and be sure the grain lines are running in the same direction.

ROUNDING CORNERS To be sure rounded corners match, on wrong side of fabric, round one corner with pencil and cut. Cut cardboard pattern of the rounded corner and use to shape other corners.

STITCHING FABRIC PIECES TOGETHER Pin pieces together, right sides facing. Stitch seams, leaving opening large enough so that piece can be turned right side out (and stuffed, if that will be done). Clip any curved edges. Turn and press seam. Stuff, if stuffing is called for, then turn in open edges and slipstitch closed.

BINDING EDGES Purchased bias tape Fold in half to encase edge and topstitch about $\frac{1}{16}$" from folded edge of tape, catching opposite edge of tape on other side. Finish ends by turning in one, lapping over other and topstitching, or by turning in ends separately and topstitching.

Self-made tape Fabric is cut in bias strips and pieced to desired length. Cut strips to specified width, turn in edges $\frac{1}{4}$" and press. Use in same way as purchased tape, above.

APPLYING FABRIC TO CARDBOARD Fabric should be one that is tightly woven so that glue will not penetrate to right side and stain. Cut a little larger than surface to be covered. We suggest test-gluing a scrap of fabric to cardboard. Pour a little glue in a disposable dish. Add a tiny bit of water and mix to brushable consistency. Brush very thin layer on cardboard and smooth fabric quickly over it. Do not press or "work" fabric too much or glue may show through. When piece is thoroughly dry, place it, fabric-side down, on work surface. Slowly, carefully and with even pressure, trim away excess fabric with single-edged razor blade.

TO COVER CARDBOARD BOX Following diagram, cut out one piece of fabric to fit entire box except inside bottom and lid, as follows: First, meas-

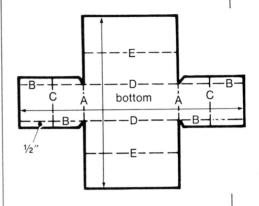

ure, in direction of horizontal arrow, up the inside of box, down the outside, across bottom, up the outside and down the inside; to this measurement add 1". Next, take same measurement in direction of vertical arrow and add 1". Draw rectangle or square (determined from measurements) on fabric and cut out. Cut out corners to shape of box, leaving $\frac{1}{2}$" flaps. Prepare glue as for Applying Fabric to Cardboard, above. Brushing glue on box as you go, place box on exact center of fabric, then fold ends up at A and fold flaps against sides at B. Fold extension of ends to inside at C. Fold up sides at D, then extensions to inside at E. Cut a piece to fit inside bottom and glue that in place.

Lid Measure and cut fabric as for box, but add 1" to center section (top) to allow for padding if it is included. Place fabric, wrong side up, on work surface. Spread even layer of padding on top section (not sides). Brushing glue as you go, place lid, top side down, on padding. Fold and glue to lid as for box. Cut piece for inside and glue in place.

HOW TO ENLARGE PATTERNS

You will need brown wrapping paper (pieced if necessary to make a sheet large enough for pattern), a felt-tipped marker, pencil and ruler. (If pattern you are enlarging has a grid around it, you must first connect lines across pattern, preferably with colored pencil, to form a grid over the picture.) Mark paper with grid as follows: First cut paper into a true square or rectangle. Then mark dots around edges, 1″ or 2″ apart or whatever is specified, making same number of spaces as there are squares around edge of diagram. Form a grid by joining dots across opposite sides of paper. Check to make sure you have the same number of squares as diagram. With marker, draw in each square the same pattern lines you see in corresponding squares on diagram.

EMBROIDERY STITCHES

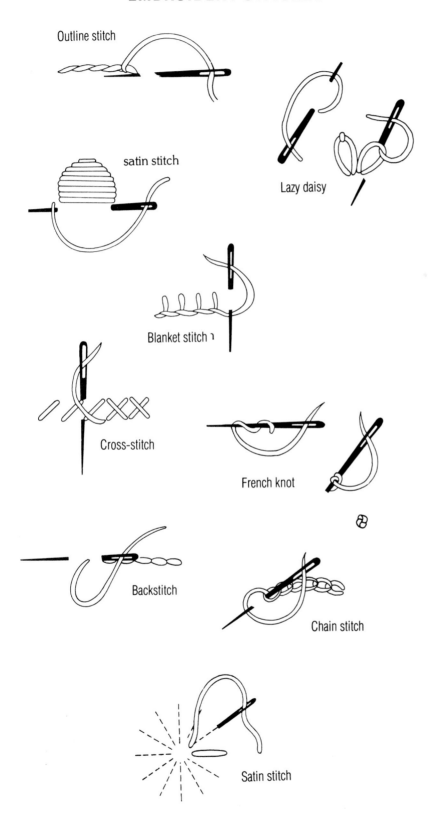

Outline stitch

satin stitch

Lazy daisy

Blanket stitch

Cross-stitch

French knot

Backstitch

Chain stitch

Satin stitch

ABBREVIATIONS AND TERMS
(knitting and crochet)

B — bobble

beg — beginning

bl — block

CC — contrasting color

ch — chain

cl — cluster

dc — double crochet

dec — decrease

dp — double-pointed

dtr — double triple crochet

hdc — half double crochet

inc — increase

k — knit

lp — loop

MC — main color

p — purl

pc — popcorn

psso — pass slipped stitch over

rnd — round

sc — single crochet

sk — skip

sl — slip

sl st — slip stitch

sp — space

ssk — slip, slip, knit

st — stitch

tog — together

tr — triple crochet

yo — yarn over hook or needle

*Asterisk — means repeat instructions following asterisk as many times as specified in addition to the first time

[ ]**Brackets** — indicate change in size

( )**Parentheses** — means repeat instructions in parentheses as many times as specified or in place specified

MAKING POMPONS Cut 2 circles of cardboard the desired diameter of pompon. Cut hole in center of each from ¼" to ½" in diameter. Cut slit from outer edge to center. Place circles together, matching slits. Wrap yarn around and around cardboard rims, sliding it through slit for each wrap. When hole is filled and rim almost covered, slip scissor point between circles, clip yarn around edges, separate circles slightly and tie piece of yarn tightly around center of strands. Remove circles and strands will puff out to form pompon. Trim if necessary to even the ends.

For a tiny pompon, such as a nose on toy, cut a number of 1" yarn strands, tie together tightly at center and trim to desired size.

MAKING FRINGE AND TASSELS To make either, cut strands as specified. **To make fringe tassel:** Hold strands together and fold in half. With crochet hook, draw fold through stitch or space, draw ends through loop and pull to tighten. **To make simple tassel:** Hold strands and fold as above. Tie at center with a strand of yarn; wind several times around the top near the fold. Tassel may be finished off by threading yarn end, passing needle *up* through tassel, and securing yarn at top. Or needle can be taken *down* through tassel so that winding yarn becomes one of the ends.

BASIC GRANNY SQUARE

Work all rnds from right side. Starting at center with color for Rnd 1, ch 5; join with sl st in first ch to form ring.

Rnd 1: Ch 3 (counts as 1 dc), work 2 dc in ring, ch 3, (3 dc in ring, ch 3) 3 times; join with sl st in top of ch-3. **NOTE** If using same color on next rnd, sl st in next 2 dc, sl st in next ch-3 sp. If changing colors on next rnd, fasten off after sl st in top of ch-3, join next color in next ch-3 sp. Work in same manner at end of each rnd. Do not turn.

Rnd 2: (Ch 3, 2 dc, ch 3, 3 dc) in ch-3 sp (first corner made), ch 1, * (3 dc, ch 3, 3 dc) in next ch-3 sp (another corner made), ch 1; repeat from * twice more; join.

Rnd 3: (Ch 3, 2 dc, ch 3, 3 dc) in ch-3 corner sp, * ch 1, 3 dc in next ch-1 sp, ch 1, (3 dc, ch 3, 3 dc) in next corner sp; repeat from * twice more, ch 1, 3 dc in next ch-1 sp, ch 1; join.

Rnd 4: (Ch 3, 2 dc, ch 3, 3 dc) in corner sp, * (ch 1, 3 dc in next ch-1 sp) to next corner, ch 1, (3 dc, ch 3, 3 dc) in corner sp; repeat from * twice more, (ch 1, 3 dc in next ch-1 sp) to end of rnd, ch 1; join. Repeat Rnd 4 to desired size.

WORKING WITH WOOD

MATERIALS AND TOOLS (SOME OR ALL OF THE FOLLOWING) Table saw; saber saw; jigsaw (or coping saw); drill with assorted bits; awl; carpenter's try square; screwdrivers; C clamps; utility knife; nail set; white wood glue; several grades of sandpaper (medium through very fine); clear polyurethane or white shellac; screws or nails as listed. (Wood type and special tools, if any, are listed under specific projects.)

MAKING PATTERNS Enlarge pattern (see How to Enlarge Patterns, page 158). To make one item, mark grid and pattern directly on wood itself. If you are making several of the same item, make a paper pattern. Place sheet of carbon paper face down on wood with pattern on top. Go over outlines with pencil; carbon will mark them on wood. For dark woods, buy special light carbon paper at an art-supply store.

CUTTING WOOD Cut curves with jigsaw or coping saw. For matching parts, clamp together and cut as one when using jigsaw. It is difficult to cut multiple thicknesses of wood, a total of 1½" thick or more, with a coping saw. For broad curves and straight cuts, use a table or saber saw.

DRILLING Use an awl to mark and start holes for drilling. Clamp wood to scrap to prevent splintering as bit comes through bottom. Clamp and drill matching parts at one time. Drill lead, or pilot, holes and countersink for flathead screws. Drill holes in scrap to test-fit dowels.

ASSEMBLY Test-assemble; with carpenter's try square check parts that should be square. Assemble when parts fit, gluing, then screwing or nailing. Clamp with scrap between clamp and wood and wipe away excess glue immediately and completely with damp, clean cloth.

NAILING For thin wood use brads; for thick wood use finishing nails of a length at least ⅛" shorter than combined thickness of parts to be joined. For added strength, first glue joints to be nailed. After nailing, drive nails slightly below surface with a nail set.

SANDING AND FILLING Sand smooth before finishing. Fill nail holes and countersunk screws with putty and sand smooth. Fill any plywood voids or wood defects in same manner.

FINISHING Apply 2 to 3 coats of polyurethane, sanding and wiping down between coats.

index